WITH MORE THAN 180 simple, gratifying recipes, this collection invites you to indulge in more than 50 of the most popular fresh olive oils and balsamic vinegars available in tasting rooms and shops across the continent. Amplify the flavor in dishes such as:

‡ Pear Breakfast Coffee Cake
‡ Lemongrass Mint Pork Bahn Mi
‡ Red Apple Beef Bourguignon
‡ Arugula Salad with Grapefruit Vinaigrette
‡ Cranberry Apple Onion Balsamic Jam
‡ Blood Orange Pot de Crème

and many more.

By experimenting with the variations and special sections on marinades, salad dressings, brines, and even cocktails, you'll never run out of ways to reinvent *l'huile*.

Written by a level two olive oil sommelier, the revised and updated *Olive Oil & Vinegar Lover's Cookbook* offers you endless, delightful, and surprising possibilities.

THE

OLIVE OIL &
VINEGAR LOVER'S

COOKBOOK

THE
Olive Oil
&
Vinegar
Lover's
COOKBOOK

EMILY LYCOPOLUS

PHOTOGRAPHY BY DL ACKEN

TOUCHWOOD

*To Aunt Maria, who inspired us to
start this journey.*

CONTENTS

INTRODUCTION

When my husband, Stephen, and I were first married, we stuffed two suitcases to capacity and jumped on a plane to the lovely city of Mainz, Germany. We had been invited there by some close friends to help them launch a café. While we were in the middle of learning a new language, starting a new business, making new friends, and getting acquainted with our new home, we often visited some very close family friends who lived in Italy: Aunt Maria and her daughter, Aunt Graziella (who is one of Stephen's mother's closest friends from childhood). The pair of them lived in their ancestral family home, a small, thriving olive grove just outside of Fano, Italy.

Fano is a quaint, old city in the region of Marche. This little-known and often-forgotten region has since become very close to our hearts. It's set right along the coast of the Adriatic Sea, bordered by Emilia-Romagna on the north and Arbruzzo to the south, and shares inland borders with both Tuscany and Umbria. It epitomizes the pastoral landscape we all think of when we picture Italy—rolling hills dotted with little yellow houses (these are made from local clay soil and are characteristic of the region) divided by rows of oak trees. The town of Fano itself is incredibly charming. Its bustling markets offer such a wonderful variety of amazing food: fresh local produce, cured meats like prosciutto (which is sliced right there by the lovely local butcher), and bread and cheese to die for (and the cheese sits on carts with wheels the same size as me!). While Germany was becoming our new home, Fano was becoming our new home away from home.

Harvest time at the aunties' olive grove was always a big event! All of their friends and family would come and help pick olives, and then everyone would head over to the *frantoio* (a local olive oil press) to celebrate with a huge party, complete with food, wine, and music—all the hallmarks of a lively Italian-style get-together. Aunt Maria passed away in 2015, but Aunt Graziella still harvests the olives every year and her friends still turn up to help her.

And how delicious their olive oil is! We ate it on absolutely everything: We drizzled it over toast for breakfast, we ate it with charcuterie and cheese, we tossed pasta in it, and we bathed potatoes and roasts in it. To be honest, we would even drink it straight. But where had this elixir been all my life? It was absolutely nothing like the extra virgin olive oil I was able to buy at the grocery store back home in North America.

When we moved back home, we were disappointed and frustrated by the greasy, flat, and mostly plastic-tasting olive oils that were available to us. And we tried a lot of them. Why did the fifty-dollar bottle and the eight-dollar bottle taste basically the same? And, more importantly, why did neither of them taste anything like the olive oil we enjoyed back in Marche, Italy?

We eventually found out that olive oil (as it's meant to be enjoyed) is an evolving, changing, fresh juice that should be consumed quickly. There really isn't much difference between squeezing juice from an orange and extracting oil from an olive, yet in North America, olive oil is viewed as more of a shelf-stable condiment that will last forever. As a result, the olive oil we're used to consuming is actually considered to be old and rancid. Food science is a fast-paced world and it can be difficult to keep up, but I'm increasingly convinced we'd be safer avoiding consuming older oils, especially if they're sold in plastic bottles.

The Mediterranean diet is so healthy primarily because of all the antioxidants and healthful properties found in fresh extra virgin olive oil. There have been countless reliable studies done on the positive effects of fresh olive oil, and I never tire of looking for fresh research on the subject. Diets and eating habits seem to come and go, but olive oil is a constant. It's been the popular choice for over 2,000 years, and I don't see it going anywhere soon.

Stephen and I decided we'd have to act on our newfound knowledge, and we soon put our hearts into educating people about real, fresh olive oil by opening up a small retail store in our hometown of Victoria, BC, Canada. Our aim was to teach people how to taste it, how to enjoy it, and how to integrate it into everyday life, and we worked with olive groves and suppliers who deal with the absolute best-quality, fresh olive oils and balsamic vinegars.

I loved talking to customers about all the fun things they could do with their new ingredients, and it was not uncommon for many of those customers to come back to the store to tell me they'd forgotten my suggestions. At first, I typed up my own recipes and printed them out to give away in the retail store, but I simply couldn't keep up with the demand. People wanted more ideas and more ways to use more types of olive oil and vinegar. Customers eventually asked us to start offering cooking classes, which we did. Everything I do builds on my personal mission statement: change the way people think and feel about olive oil and how they use it on a daily basis. Writing a cookbook therefore seemed like the next logical step.

As much as we loved retail sales and interacting with customers on a daily basis, though, I felt it was time to broaden the horizon of my mission, so I invested some time in becoming an olive oil sommelier. As I combined my love and passion for feeding people, tasting olive oil, and learning as much as I can about this ingredient, I realized it was time to reach out to more than our lovely loyal customers every day. I wanted to introduce a broader range of people to the world of olive oils and how to use them. Revising this cookbook is part of that expanded purpose, as I continue to share my knowledge and explain how to integrate olive oil into every meal, simply, healthfully, and deliciously.

The table is traditionally where loved ones meet. And the dinner table is where we found *olio nuovo*, "new oil" or "fresh oil," at Aunt Maria and Aunt Graziella's home in Fano. It is the center of the home, of the family. It is where connections are established and conversations begin, where ideas form and life happens, all over delicious meals. Ensuring the food is delicious, so everyone wants to sit and chat to make the most of it, but simple enough that it doesn't take hours to make, is vital to me, and I've tried my best to incorporate that approach into these recipes, so you can spend even more time with family and friends around the table.

I hope that you'll join me in discovering how good-quality olive oil is the everyday ingredient that can transform every meal into something truly special. Delicious food doesn't need to be to be complicated; and using olive oil means that quality, simple ingredients will shine brightly, no matter the dish. If you ask me, olive oil is the silent hero of the cooking world. I don't know anyone who picks out their olive oil to determine what they will cook that evening (well, aside from myself); usually the protein or starch is the hero, and all the other ingredients fall into place. Maybe it's time to change that approach. For example, you can cook two versions of the one prawn recipe in exactly the same way, using good olive oil in one and old olive oil in the other; people will think they're different dishes, when it's actually all down to the olive oil.

I hope that within these pages you'll find straightforward, uncomplicated staples that will heighten every day dishes, elevate old staples, and make every day simply delicious.

HOW TO USE THIS BOOK

A PALETTE OF FLAVORS

To get a fuller idea of the versatility of fresh extra virgin olive oils and balsamic vinegar, think of them as paint. The contents of each bottle are the different colors on your palette. Your kitchen is your studio, these recipes (and even your own standby recipes) are your canvas, and this book is your painting workshop. I aim to show you how a little bit of skill and a lot of creativity can come together to make delectable works of art.

The aim of this book is not to teach you all about how olive oils and vinegars are made, or even about all of their health properties (although these are both worthwhile subjects to pursue, so I've provided a list of some resources on pages 344–345 in case you'd like to investigate them in more detail). Instead, its aim is to help you get the maximum joy and satisfaction out of baking and cooking with fresh olive oil and vinegar by teaching you how to use them and inspiring you to use them in more recipes and more ways than you might otherwise have considered.

HOW THIS BOOK IS ORGANIZED

Figuring out how to organize this book was a bit tricky. I wanted to show you how to use specific types of fresh olive oils and balsamic vinegars for the best results, but I also wanted to encourage you to have fun. So to accomplish the first goal and to make sure that you can easily find recipes that work with the exact product you purchase from your local olive oil tasting room, I've divided this book up by product (see pages 8–9 for the full list). When you go to that specific olive oil's page (say, **Blood Orange** fused olive oil), you'll find a full list of recipes in this book that call for that specific olive oil, either in the main recipe or in a variation thereof.

I also wanted to give you as many variations as I could possibly think of in an attempt to show you just how creative you can get with olive oil and balsamic vinegar (but note that not every recipe has a variation). I wanted to show you how when you throw in a bit of this and a dash of that, you can stand back and see what comes alive. Having fun in the kitchen can lead to happy accidents. If a recipe calls for **Pomegranate** dark balsamic vinegar and you only have **Wild Blueberry** in your cupboard, don't be afraid to make the substitution—and enjoy the result. Remember, the possibilities are endless.

If you're looking for a recipe according to any other ingredients you've got on hand (beef, spinach, noodles), go to the index. And, of course, if you're looking for a certain type of dish (appetizers, cakes, soups), the index is the best way to find that too.

SPECIAL SECTIONS

Remember the paint palette I mentioned? I've included four special sections to inspire your creativity even further. This is where you can create dishes and pairings that suit your personal tastes. These sections offer great ways to put a new spin on things you're familiar with. Most of us know how to make a salad dressing or a marinade, for example—they're both well within our comfort zone—but the special sections encourage you to leave your comfort zone by making them with a new or unfamiliar ingredient.

In the Salad Dressings section (pages 40–43), I've not only provided two basic salad dressing recipes, I've also included pointers on how you can riff on them in dozens of different ways. (And be sure to use the index to find more dressing recipes in various other sections.)

In the Marinades section (pages 152–154), I've given you a basic marinade recipe that you can adapt according to the type of food you're preparing (poultry, beef, fish, etc.), as well as a timing guideline. And don't forget to refer to the flavor-pairing chart in the Perfect Pairings section on page 343 for even more ideas.

In the Vinegar Brines section (pages 248–251), I introduce you to the underappreciated world of brining with vinegar. This method of brining keeps meats extra-moist and is a great alternative to salt brining. It's another great place to experiment.

Keep an eye open for the cocktail recipes throughout the book to discover a whole host of ways you can use balsamic vinegars at your next party. We're talking way beyond appetizers.

FINAL NOTES

A lot of these recipes use more than one olive oil or balsamic vinegar. That's part of the magic. You can combine different oils and vinegars in fabulous and often unexpected ways to great effect in a single recipe (e.g., dill and pomegranate on page 168). I've listed alternative oils or vinegars in almost every recipe, but just make sure to read over the recipe carefully to make sure you've got everything you need before you begin.

Note too that I haven't included every single kind of olive oil or infusion you can buy. I've tried to stick with the more popular and versatile olive oils and balsamics while providing a good cross section of what's available. Aji Verde, Butter, Black Currant, Lavender, Mexican Spice, Passionfruit, Pepperoncino, and Rosé are all olive oils and balsamics that I refer to in this book, but I haven't included lists of recipes that use them. They are fantastic, though, and I encourage you to visit your local tasting room to try them. You might be inspired!

BUILDING YOUR PANTRY

If you're new to the world of specialty olive oils and balsamic vinegars, it can seem overwhelming. So many choices, flavors, and recipes to try. How do you even begin to choose? My advice is to start with the basics and expand your collection as you explore flavor combinations and discover your own preferences. The type of food you cook will affect your choices; just as you likely rely on a few old favorites from your spice cupboard, you will probably find yourself using certain olive oils as staples on a daily basis. If you typically cook Italian food at home, for example, **Tuscan Herb**, **Basil**, or **Rosemary** olive oils might be more easily integrated into your daily diet than, say, **Harissa**. If Middle Eastern food is your go-to cuisine, however, **Harissa** might be a great place to start.

This book is intended to be quite comprehensive. If you're just starting to use olive oils and vinegars on a daily basis, or you're curious about how they can make specific meals extremely tasty, I've also written a series of smaller cookbooks that each contain fifty recipes and focus on a specific country's cuisine (Greece, Italy, Spain, and Syria). The recipes in those books only use two olive oils and two balsamic vinegars to make every single recipe. They are a great introduction to the world of olive oils and balsamics—and they make a great gift for a foodie, especially if you bundle up a book with its products.

The recipes in this book list my favorite olive oil and balsamic options in the ingredients for each particular dish, and all the recipes are tested as written, but play with them and adapt them to your own taste repertoire. (The white space on the pages is there for you to take notes! All my well-loved cookbooks are sticky-noted and written in.) Please don't feel you need to purchase the entire inventory in a tasting room to make this book useful—that is not the idea. Try new things, discover new favorites, and you'll be surprised by all the tasty dishes you can create.

THE BEGINNER'S PANTRY

You can make the majority of the recipes in this book with the following list of oils and vinegars, so this is a good selection to start with. Any oil-vinegar combination from this pantry list will be amazing. For example, a salad dressing made from **Blood Orange** (or **Lemon** or **Lime**) fused olive oil and a fruity dark balsamic is fantastic. **Tuscan Herb** infused olive oil and **Traditional** dark balsamic or an **extra virgin** olive oil with **Sicilian Lemon** white balsamic are supreme combinations for bread-dipping. (This combination also makes a great gift as well! It's like a six-pack for foodies.)

- **Extra virgin** olive oil
- Citrus fused olive oil (for example, **Blood Orange**, **Lemon**, **Lime**—your choice!)
- **Tuscan Herb** infused olive oil
- **Traditional** dark balsamic
- Fruit infused dark balsamic (your choice!)
- **Sicilian Lemon** white balsamic

THE ADVANCED PANTRY

When you're ready for more adventurous culinary exploring, add these to your collection:

- **Rosemary**, **Basil**, or **Garlic** fused olive oil
- **Chipotle** infused olive oil
- **Espresso** dark balsamic
- **Pomegranate** dark balsamic
- **Cranberry Pear** white balsamic

THE GOURMAND'S PANTRY

If you're already comfortable using olive oils and balsamic vinegars in your cooking, indulge in the following additions for maximum experimentation potential:

- **Extra virgin** olive oil: mild
- **Extra virgin** olive oil: robust
- **Harissa** fused olive oil
- **Basil** infused olive oil
- **Wild Mushroom & Sage** infused olive oil
- **Blackberry Ginger** dark balsamic
- **Strawberry** dark balsamic
- **Coconut** white balsamic
- **Lemongrass Mint** white balsamic
- **Peach** white balsamic

Single Varietal Extra Virgin Olive Oils

Fused & Infused Olive Oils

Dark Balsamic Vinegars

White Balsamic Vinegars

Extra Virgin Olive Oils

Fresh **extra virgin olive oil** can be used in almost any recipe you can think of with great results, and it works well with any recipe in this book. From roasting vegetables in it and slathering it onto a chicken, to baking it into sweets and whipping it into homemade ice cream, the possibilities are endless.

But before you add any variety of olive oil into a recipe, get to know it a bit. Know the difference between a mild and a robust oil, and a fruity and an herbaceous oil. This will make all the difference when you're choosing which varietal to use in which recipe. Adding an herbaceous, robust **Picual**, with its green tomato notes and peppery intensity, to your grandma's homemade cinnamon bun recipe won't win you a blue ribbon at the county fair. (I tried that already.)

A lovely **Arbosana** filled with notes of creamy avocado, artichoke, and pink peppercorn would be great for making hollandaise or savory scones, or for frying a mild white fish. An extra-fruity **Hojiblanca** with a beautifully grassy nose and notes of nectarine, apricot, and banana probably wouldn't shine in savory biscuits, but it would be great massaged into kale and then tossed into a red quinoa salad with dried blueberries and feta (see page 96). Although I recommend a few specific varieties for each recipe in this section, olive oils vary from harvest to harvest, as you'll find out below.

WHERE TO BUY YOUR OLIVE OILS

Although it's not impossible to find high-quality olive oil in the supermarket, it's unlikely. Your best bet is to visit your local olive oil tasting room or specialty store, keeping in mind that it's not a guaranteed source of good-quality olive oil either, although typically in these establishments, you can taste the olive oil before purchasing it, which ensures you're taking home exactly what you want. The olive oil industry is rife with quality-control issues, so you can never be sure that what you're getting is top quality unless you do your research and find a reputable olive oil dealer. Tom Mueller's book, *Extra Virginity*, and his blog, truthinoliveoil.com will prove useful for this. For more information on the chemical analysis of and current standards for extra virgin olive oil, visit the International Olive Oil Council website at internationaloliveoil.com or the Extra Virgin Alliance at extravirginalliance.org. For information related to the California olive oil industry, visit the UC Davis Olive Center site at olivecenter.ucdavis.edu, or the California Olive Oil Council (COOC) site at cooc.com. Any bottle of olive oil from California that displays the

COOC seal has been tasted by a certified tasting panel and passed their sensory analysis testing process to be designated extra virgin.

Always taste the oil first to test its quality. Ask where the oil is from, and don't be afraid to ask lots of questions. The proprietor should have quick answers for the following and will probably be delighted that you're asking!

- **What's the date of harvest?** Remember that olive oil is good up to a year after harvest.

- **Does it come in a dark-colored glass bottle?** Light, heat, and oxygen are the enemies of olive oil. Also, do not buy olive oil that comes in a plastic bottle chemistry 101: like dissolves like.

- **Is there a chemical analysis available for the oil?** If you can find any chemistry listed on a bottle of olive oil, it's a good sign, but a full analysis is always best. Be careful: Sometimes you'll find standards listed on the bottle rather than an analysis of the actual contents of the bottle.

- **What is the polyphenol count?** This antioxidant value not only shows the health benefits the higher the better in the oil, it also determines the pungency or intensity of the oil. Less than 200 is a mild oil, 200–350 is a medium to robust oil, and more than 350 is a robust oil.

- **What is its free fatty acid level FFA?** You are looking for something that is less than 0.8%, but ideally you should be able to find something that is at or below 0.3%. The lower the FFA, the more stable the oil will be for high-heat cooking.

If you're looking for a healthy oil, make sure you ask for the oleic acid level, also known as omega-9 (the monounsaturated fat in olive oil that makes it so healthy). It should be more than 55, but more than 65 is ideal.

If you want to know long your oil will last, the diacylglycerol level (DAG) is a good indication of the overall quality of olive oil and how long it will last. An olive oil with a DAG of over 90 at the time of harvest, for example, will keep under ideal conditions (away from light, heat, and oxygen) for up to 18 months.

We've all heard of "cold-pressed" olive oil, although it is more a North American marketing term than anything these days as the majority of olive oil is no longer pressed. It's extracted through modern mechanical means, instead of traditional stone mills and hemp mat presses. The pyropheophytin (PPP) of an olive oil is the measure of damaged chlorophyll found inside the oil. Since this is one of the most fragile compounds in the olive oil, it is a very good indicator to ensure that the olive oil was created under cold circumstances and was not refined or damaged in anyway during harvest, milling, or storage.

These last two standards are only now becoming part of the norm in olive oil testing standards. Australia was the first to adopt them and use them not only to determine an olive oil's grade, but also to protect against adulteration. DAG and PPP are now part of the Extra Virgin Alliance and COOC standards, as consumers are more aware of quality issues in olive oil and want traceable practices to be the norm.

TASTING OLIVE OIL

There are hundreds of varieties of olives—1,551 to be exact, not including the different common names that some varieties are known by—and much like wine grapes, each variety has its own particular characteristics. But the taste of the olive oil isn't determined by the variety alone. Again, like wine grapes, the specific conditions in which the olives are grown also affect the taste and pungency of the oil: the soil, the weather, the ripeness of the olives, and the way the olives are handled or stored are all factors that will affect the final product. For example, a **Picual** from Spain will taste different from a **Picual** from Australia. They may have some similar notes or characteristics because they are the same varietal, but not necessarily. And keep in mind that a **Picual** from Spain one year can taste very different from a **Picual** grown the following year in the very same place.

INTENSITY

Another factor in your olive oil tasting experience is intensity (or pungency), which is determined by the polyphenol count of the oil. A big, peppery, full-bodied robust oil is best with a robust-tasting ingredient, like beef, or stronger flavors. A mild oil is best with more delicate flavors.

The polyphenol count for any one varietal can vary across different countries or regions. Take, for example, three **Koroneikis**: one from California has a polyphenol count of 174 ppm (mild), one from Australia has a polyphenol count of 241 ppm (medium), and one from Chile has a polyphenol count of 321 ppm (medium-robust). Three varietals, all with similar tasting notes but very different intensities. **Koroneiki**, the most common olive variety grown for oil in Greece shares the widest variation in flavor profiles of any other variety due to the different landscapes and weather patterns found across Greece.

Some people favor one variety and stick with it regardless of its intensity; others prefer, for example, robust olive oils regardless of variety. There is no right or wrong; this is about personal preference and taste. The key is remembering that every harvest yields different results. Your local olive oil tasting room can let you know what's new and exciting, and you'll eventually discover what suits your own personal tastes and what goes best with your favorite recipes. Consider spending some time at your local olive oil tasting room. Chances are the staff will be happy to share their knowledge with you.

On the following pages are a few tasting notes and details on a few popular varietals. This is far from an exhaustive list! I've chosen a few that are more readily available, and I've tried to give a fair cross-section of the different olive-producing regions while giving you an overview of their different flavor profiles. Remember, there are so many varieties of olive oil, and many olive groves in the southern hemisphere produce incredible oil. Don't hesitate to try them too!

ARBEQUINA

COUNTRY OF ORIGIN — SPAIN

This olive is extremely tiny with a large pit, which keeps the taste very rich and creamy. With notes of fresh artichoke, green almond, and butter, this is an amazing all-purpose oil. This olive varietal, grown in both Catalonia and Andalucía, is a very common all-purpose variety. Used mostly for olive oil, it can also be brined and enjoyed as a table olive as well.

ARBOSANA

COUNTRY OF ORIGIN — SPAIN

This rich, creamy varietal tends to be as fruity and floral as it is herbaceous. Notes of ripe green olives, fresh cut grass, and a uniquely floral finish are typical for this varietal. It thrives in super high-density growing conditions and is one of the most common varieties grown in California.

CORATINA

COUNTRY OF ORIGIN — ITALY

Most often this is a big, delicious, robust **extra virgin**, although depending on harvest it can be creamy and light. The **Coratina** will display notes of fresh green apple peel and herbaceous arugula and is lovely on fresh green salads.

HOJIBLANCA

COUNTRY OF ORIGIN — SPAIN

Full of stone fruit and ripe fruit notes, this olive variety is like olive oil fruit punch. Usually quite grassy with notes of nectarine, unripe peach, and apricot, it's perfect for baking, salads, and for drizzling over roasted root vegetables.

KORONEIKI

COUNTRY OF ORIGIN — GREECE

Deliciously creamy whether mild or robust, this oil is hardly bitter, and has notes of green banana, apple peel, and fresh cut grass. This olive variety has one of the widest varieties of tasting profiles, as it is the most common olive oil variety grown in Greece. Due to the wide variety of weather and landscape conditions across the Greek landscape olive oil from this olive can be incredibly diverse.

FRANTOIO

COUNTRY OF ORIGIN — ITALY

An Italian classic, most commonly grown in Tuscany. Bright, pungent, and bitter this olive oil is almost tannic in how it puckers your cheeks when you taste it. Notes of arugula and radicchio are common as well as a round herbaceous quality, finishing with an almost capsicum-like pungent finish.

MANZANILLO

COUNTRY OF ORIGIN — SPAIN

This olive is one of the few varieties that can be used for both oil and table olives. It is a large olive with a thin long pit. It creates an olive oil robust, bitter, and herbaceous. Lovely for bitter green salads, roasting vegetables, and meats.

PICUAL

COUNTRY OF ORIGIN — SPAIN

The most commonly grown olive in Spain, this well-loved cultivar typically has notes of green tomato, fresh-cut grass, and even green tomato leaf. This is a favorite for pairing with creamy fresh mozzarella and tossing with pasta due to its clean, crisp, and fresh flavor profile.

Aioli is simple to make, and there are endless variations to keep it interesting. Try a dollop on roasted potatoes, serve as a dip with fries, spread some on a sandwich, or serve it alongside roast beef. Aioli is traditionally prepared with olive oil (unlike mayonnaise, which is usually made with a more neutral-tasting oil like canola). The olive oil adds fruitiness and tempers the garlic's intensity. **MAKES 1 CUP**

Simple Aioli

1 garlic clove
1 egg yolk
1 Tbsp **Sicilian Lemon** white balsamic vinegar
Pinch dry mustard
¾ cup **extra virgin** olive oil
Flaky sea salt

RECOMMENDED VARIETALS
Arbequina or **Hojiblanca**

Basil Aioli Perfect on a chicken sandwich. Substitute half the olive oil with **Basil** infused olive oil, and gently mix in 1 Tbsp of freshly torn basil leaves.

Chipotle Aioli Great as a burger or sandwich sauce, and a must-have as a dip for your sweet potato fries. Substitute half the olive oil with **Chipotle** infused olive oil.

Roasted Garlic Aioli You can't go wrong with this classic—it's delicious on everything! Preheat the oven to 350°F. Peel 3 cloves of garlic, place them in a small ramekin, and drizzle with 1 Tbsp of a mild **extra virgin** olive oil. Cover with aluminum foil, or a small ovenproof lid, and roast for 25 minutes. Let the cloves cool for a few minutes, then mash with a fork; use in place of the 1 clove of garlic in the recipe above.

Truffle Aioli Serve with fancy twice-baked potatoes, eggs Benedict, gourmet burgers, or roasted asparagus wrapped in prosciutto. Slowly drizzle in 1 Tbsp **Black** or **White Truffle extra virgin olive oil** when all the single varietal **extra virgin** olive oil has been emulsified and absorbed.

MORTAR AND PESTLE METHOD Mash the garlic clove to a paste in a mortar with a pestle. In a small bowl, whisk in the yolk, balsamic vinegar, and mustard by hand and beat until frothy. Very slowly add 1 Tbsp of the olive oil, just ¼ tsp at a time, whisking well after each addition. Then slowly begin to drizzle in the remaining oil in a fine stream, continuing to whisk until the aioli is thick and creamy. Finish with a sprinkle of sea salt to taste.

FOOD PROCESSOR METHOD In the bowl of a food processor or blender, combine the garlic, egg yolk, balsamic, and mustard. Pulse until the mixture is fully combined. With the machine running on low, slowly begin to add the olive oil, starting with just a few drops. Once the first few drops are emulsified, begin to drizzle in the remaining oil. Continue to pulse as the oil emulsifies with the yolk mixture and forms a white creamy mixture. Season to taste with sea salt and enjoy!

Since there is raw egg in the aioli, be sure to keep in an airtight non-reactive container (a Mason jar works great) in the fridge for up to 3 days.

Tapenade is so easy and so tasty. This version is a perfect base recipe. To make it traditional, add two washed anchovy fillets. To spice it up, add some pickled chilies. Or to make a Greek version, switch out the parsley for oregano. Spread tapenade on toast or crackers (with or without cheese), toss with some pasta in place of pesto, or use as a non-dairy veggie dip. I like to use green, black, pimento, or jalapeño-stuffed olives for a bit of a kick. **MAKES 1 CUP**

Tapenade

³/₄ cup pitted mixed olives

1 small garlic clove

2 Tbsp capers

2 tsp finely chopped fresh flat-leaf parsley

1 Tbsp **Sicilian Lemon** white balsamic
  vinegar

3 Tbsp robust **extra virgin** olive oil

RECOMMENDED VARIETALS
Arbosana, Frantoio, Manzanillo

For a more herbacous version, use the **Neopolitan Herb** dark balsamic or the **Oregano** white balsamic in place of the **Sicilian Lemon**.

Place the olives, garlic, capers, parsley, and balsamic in a food processor. Pulse until coarsely chopped and well blended. As you continue to pulse, slowly drizzle in the olive oil.

This can be stored in an airtight container in the fridge for up to 1 week.

This bread is best used as a vehicle to get something delicious into one's mouth—hummus, dip, curry, for example. I tend to throw this together in a stand mixer with the dough hook attached and let it knead while I do the dishes or finish prepping something. Once it reaches the sticky point you need to switch to using your hands. When I make it by hand, I start with 2 cups of flour in the bowl and knead in the final cup after I've turned it onto the counter. **SERVES 4–6**

Easy Flatbread

3 cups all-purpose flour, plus more for
    dusting.
2 tsp coarse sea salt
1 tsp quick-rising yeast
1 tsp baking power
1 cup warm water (110°F–115°F)
5 Tbsp robust **extra virgin** olive oil, divided
Coarse sea salt or seasoning of choice for
    sprinkling

RECOMMENDED VARIETALS
Arbosana, Coratina, Frantoio, Manzanillo

Garlic Flatbread Smear with roasted garlic and some Garlic infused olive oil before baking.

Greek Flatbread Season with Basil infused olive oil and fresh oregano and a sprinkle of sliced Kalamata olives and feta cheese before baking.

Lebanese Flatbread Sprinkle with za'atar (see page 266) before baking.

Middle Eastern Flatbread Season with sumac and freshly roasted cumin before baking.

Pizza Flatbread Roll the dough out a bit thinner than 1/2 inch thick, drizzle with Tuscan Herb infused or Garlic infused olive oil, spread with tomato sauce, and sprinkle with cheese before baking.

Rosemary Flatbread Drizzle bread dough with Rosemary infused olive oil and a few sprigs of chopped fresh rosemary before baking.

In a large bowl, place the flour, salt, yeast, and baking powder. Mix well to combine.

Make a well in the flour mixture and pour in the warm water and 3 Tbsp of the olive oil. Mix with a wooden spoon until everything is well combined and the dough is sticky. Turn onto a well-floured surface and knead for 8–10 minutes, until smooth and elastic (continue to add flour as needed to keep the dough from sticking).

Transfer to a greased bowl, cover with a tea towel, and let rest in a warm, draft-free place for 10–12 minutes. Alternatively, preheat your oven to 200°F, then turn it off and let the dough rise in the warm oven.

Punch down the dough, kneading it slightly, and divide it into six equal pieces. Using your hands, shape each piece into an oval, about 1/2 inch thick, and place on a well-floured cookie sheet. Drizzle the flatbreads with the remaining olive oil and sprinkle with coarse ground salt (or your seasoning of choice; see sidebar) and let sit in the warm oven for another 20 minutes, then remove from oven.

Preheat the oven to 425°F. Bake the bread for 6–8 minutes.

These potatoes are the perfect addition to any meal: for breakfast, served with fried eggs and more bacon; for lunch, on their own tossed with a simple vinaigrette; or alongside chicken or roast beef for dinner. To make them vegetarian-friendly, omit the bacon and increase the olive oil by 1 Tbsp. **SERVES 4 AS A SIDE**

Pan-Fried Potatoes

1 lb fingerling potatoes
½ lb bacon
1 medium red onion
Sea salt and ground black pepper
¼ cup robust **extra virgin** olive oil
Chopped green onions or curly-leaf parsley

RECOMMENDED VARIETALS
Arbosana, Frantoio, Manzanillo

Rosemary Pan-Fried Potatoes Use Rosemary infused olive oil in place of **extra virgin**.

Pan-Fried Potatoes with Gremolata Use Milanese Gremolata infused olive oil in place of the **extra virgin**.

Wash, scrub, and slice the fingerling potatoes into dollar rounds. Set aside. Dice the bacon and roughly chop the onion.

In a large frying pan, fry the bacon over medium heat. When it has just started to crisp, add the onion and salt and pepper to taste.

When the onion just begins to soften, drain off all but 1 Tbsp of the bacon grease. Add the potatoes and olive oil. Continue to stir and turn the potatoes until they are soft and crispy on the outside. Garnish with green onions or parsley.

Portobellos make great vegetarian burgers but can also be eaten with salad and no bread for a light, tasty lunch. The olive oil and balsamic vinegar in this recipe soften the mushrooms and give them an extra-juicy feel as well as bringing out their exceptional flavor. **SERVES 2**

Marinated Portobello Mushrooms

2 Portobello mushrooms
$\frac{1}{2}$ cup robust **extra virgin** olive oil
$\frac{1}{4}$ cup **Traditional** dark balsamic vinegar
1 garlic clove, minced
1 shallot, thinly sliced
1 sprig fresh rosemary, chopped, or 1 tsp
    dried rosemary
$\frac{1}{4}$ tsp smoked paprika
$\frac{1}{4}$ tsp sea salt
$\frac{1}{4}$ tsp cracked black pepper

RECOMMENDED VARIETALS
Coratina, Frantoio, Picual

Substitute **Tuscan Herb** or **Basil** infused olive oil in place of the **extra virgin** for a more herbaceous marinade, or use **Neapolitan Herb** dark balsamic vinegar instead of **Traditional** for an even bigger pop of flavor.

Whip some cream cheese or goat cheese with **Oregano** white balsamic vinegar and **Garlic** infused olive oil for a delicious stuffing; sprinkle fresh rosemary over top before cooking.

Discard the mushroom stalks and scrape out the gills. Wipe the mushroom caps with a damp kitchen towel to remove any dirt and place them in a baking dish just large enough to hold them without crowding. Combine remaining ingredients in a bowl and pour them over the mushrooms. Flip the mushrooms to ensure they are fully and evenly coated with marinade, cover with plastic wrap, and marinate in the fridge for at least 2 hours, or overnight.

Preheat the oven to 375°F. Line a baking pan with parchment paper and place mushrooms on it, gill side up. Bake the mushrooms for 20 minutes. Alternatively, grill over medium-high heat on a barbecue.

Risotto is comfort food with a touch of elegance. This version is packed with warm mozzarella and tomato goodness, making it a perfect dinner on a cold winter's day or a classy appetizer for a dinner party. To increase the sophistication factor, try a beet and red wine or mushroom and truffle version. **SERVES 4 AS A MAIN DISH, 6 AS A SIDE**

Italian Caprese–Style Risotto

3 cups tomato juice

2 cups chicken or vegetable stock

2 shallots, minced

¼ cup robust **extra virgin** olive oil

1½ cups Arborio rice

½ cup **Sicilian Lemon** white balsamic vinegar

1 cup crushed tomatoes (canned or fresh)

½ cup cherry-sized fresh mozzarella balls, plus more for garnish

½ cup torn basil leaves, plus a few whole leaves for garnish

Sea salt

RECOMMENDED VARIETALS

Arbequina, Frantoio, Picual (for a creamier option)

Wild Mushroom Risotto with Roasted Butternut Squash Substitute the tomato juice with chicken or vegetable stock (for a total of 5 cups of stock), the single varietal **extra virgin** olive oil with **Wild Mushroom & Sage** infused olive oil, the **Sicilian Lemon** white balsamic with **Honey Ginger** white balsamic, basil with diced wild mushrooms (porcini, chanterelle, lobster, etc.), the crushed tomatoes with 1 cup diced acorn roasted squash, and the mozzarella with ½ cup grated Parmesan cheese.

For an even more herbaceous version, substitute **Sicilian Lemon** white balsamic vinegar for the **Neapolitan Herb** dark balsamic and use **Garlic** or **Basil** infused olive oil instead of the **extra virgin**.

In a large saucepan, bring the tomato juice and stock to a simmer over medium heat, cover, and continue to simmer without reaching a boil.

In a large frying pan over medium heat, sauté the shallots in the olive oil until soft but not golden, about 3 minutes. Add the rice and mix to coat it evenly with olive oil, ensuring the rice is shiny and translucent.

Add the balsamic to deglaze the pan and scrape up any bits of shallot that may have stuck, stirring constantly. Keep the heat on medium.

Keep stirring until the balsamic has evaporated, about 2 minutes. Slowly add the stock, ½ cup at a time, stirring between each addition to ensure that the rice is absorbing the stock slowly and consistently. Only add the next addition of stock when the pan is almost dry.

Once three-quarters of the stock has been added and the rice is starting to look plump, check the texture of the rice. If it's creamy and smooth, it's time to add the tomatoes. If it still has a bit of a crunch to it, add another splash of stock, stir until it has been fully absorbed, then add the tomatoes and test again. Stir in the mozzarella and basil.

Place the risotto in a serving bowl or on individual plates, sprinkle with a touch of sea salt, drizzle generously with more olive oil, and top with a few pieces of mozzarella and a couple of basil leaves. Serve immediately.

Baking fish in parchment (en papillote sounds so much fancier!) seals in all the goodness so it stays tender and juicy—and makes for incredibly easy cleanup. Ask the fish vendor to clean and scale your fish to make life easier. (See page 327 for another fish en papillote recipe.) **SERVES 4**

Whole Fish en Papillote

4 garlic cloves

4–5 lb cleaned trout (or whole fish of your choice)

4 Tbsp creamy, mild **extra virgin** olive oil, divided

Sea salt and ground black or white pepper

2 Tbsp **Honey Ginger** white balsamic vinegar

1 lemon, sliced into rounds

RECOMMENDED VARIETALS
Arbequina, Hojiblanca, Koroneiki, Manzanillo

Use 2 Tbsp of **Sicilian Lemon** white balsamic instead of the **Honey Ginger** to make a classic lemon–garlic combo and put some fresh dill on top.

If you're making this recipe with salmon, drizzle over some **Maple** dark balsamic vinegar or maple syrup instead of, or in addition to, using lemon slices.

Preheat the oven to 400°F.

Take a baking pan large enough to hold the fish without crowding and line it with enough parchment to let you pull the ends up to fold them over and seal the fish in.

Place the flat of a chef's knife over the garlic cloves and bring your hand down hard to smash the garlic.

Open the fish and scatter the garlic evenly throughout the cavity, drizzle the cavity with 2 Tbsp of the olive oil, and season to taste with salt and pepper. Place the fish in the center of the parchment. Pour the balsamic over and around the fish and drizzle the remaining olive oil over top. Place the rounds of lemon evenly over top to cover the fish.

Seal the packet by bringing the long ends of the paper together over the fish and folding them downwards and into themselves. Twist the ends of the paper and tuck under the fish, making a little roasting packet.

Bake for 30 minutes, open the packet (be careful of steam!), and let the fish rest for 15 minutes. Remove the lemon from the fish before serving if desired.

This is perfect alongside Pan-Fried Potatoes (page 23) and a fresh green salad.

I love making quick, simple recipes that look like they took hours to prepare. Use an herbaceous, robust **extra virgin** olive oil here. It won't get lost among all the other flavors but will instead increase their depth as they all work together. Serve with Roasted Beet Salad with Cinnamon Pear Balsamic & Goat Cheese Crumble (page 232) or haricots verts. **SERVES 4**

Crusted Rack of Pork

1 (3–4 lb) pork loin with ribs in
Sea salt and ground black pepper
2 Tbsp Dijon mustard
1 large Spanish onion
4 garlic cloves, crushed
4 Tbsp robust **extra virgin** olive oil, divided
¼ cup brown sugar, packed
1 cup dried bread crumbs or Panko
2 tsp grated lemon zest
2 tsp fresh thyme or ¾ tsp dried thyme
½ tsp ground allspice

RECOMMENDED VARIETALS
Coratina, Frantoio, Manzanillo, Picual

For a slightly lighter dish, use **Blood Orange** fused olive oil in place of the **extra virgin**; for something more herbaceous, try **Rosemary, Tuscan Herb, Milanese Gremolata**, or **Herbes de Provence** infused olive oil. For a spicy version, use **Harissa** infused olive oil, or try **Chipotle** for a welcome smoky addition.

Wash the pork and pat it dry. Lightly season with salt and pepper and coat with the Dijon.

Preheat the oven to 400°F.

In a nonstick frying pan, sauté the onion and garlic in 2 Tbsp of the olive oil until almost tender, about 5 minutes. Sprinkle with the sugar and let it caramelize, about 2 additional minutes, stirring constantly. Toss in the bread crumbs, lemon zest, thyme, and allspice, and lightly toast, stirring to combine. Mix in the remaining 2 Tbsp olive oil so that everything is evenly coated and moist.

Press the bread crumb mixture into all sides of the pork, place it in a roasting pan, cover with aluminum foil, and bake for 25 minutes. Turn down the heat to 350°F, uncover the pork, and bake for an additional 20 minutes until its internal temperature is 140°F. Remove from the oven, cover loosely with foil again, and let stand for 10 minutes before carving.

I find that olive oil really changes the texture in baking—for the better! These scones are light and fluffy, rather than dense and heavy, and they stay moist for so much longer than scones made with traditional shortening or butter. Adding the pepper and green onions gives a tasty, savory twist on a traditional breakfast scone, but these would be equally good with cranberries or frozen blueberries instead if you're looking for something sweeter. (And they make a great base for eggs Benedict!) **MAKES 6–8 SCONES**

Savory Ricotta Scones

2 cups all-purpose flour
1 Tbsp baking powder
¼ tsp sea salt
⅓ cup robust **extra virgin** olive oil
1 cup diced bell pepper, variety of colors
1 Tbsp finely chopped green onions
¾ cup ricotta cheese
½ cup table (18%) cream

RECOMMENDED VARIETALS
Arbequina, **Coratina**, **Picual**

For an even more savory and herbaceous version, use **Basil**, **Wild Dill**, or **Rosemary** infused olive oil instead of the **extra virgin**.

Blood Orange Blueberry Scones Use **Blood Orange** fused olive oil in place of the **extra virgin**, substitute 1 cup of fresh blueberries for the peppers, and omit the onions.

Cranberry Lemon Scones Substitute the **extra virgin** olive oil with **Lemon** fused olive oil, use 1 cup of dried cranberries instead of the peppers, and omit the onions.

In a mixing bowl, place the flour, baking powder, and salt. Using a butter knife, swirl the flour to mix everything together well. Pour in the olive oil. Use two butter knives or a pastry blender to mix it in until the mixture resembles coarse oatmeal.

Add the bell pepper and green onions, mixing gently to combine, then add the ricotta and cream.

Mix gently to form a gooey mixture. It's supposed to be wet, so don't panic. On a well-floured counter, turn the batter onto the flour, turning once to coat. Knead gently and form into a disk, about 1 inch thick. It will firm up slightly as it absorbs the flour from the counter while you knead it, but should still be nice and soft.

Preheat the oven to 450°F. Line a baking tray with parchment paper.

Choose a glass or cookie cutter in the size you would like the scones to be and get cutting. For mini scones, a champagne flute is perfect. Otherwise, a standard water glass is good. Sometimes I take the round of dough and score it into triangles. If you're using a glass, dip it in some flour to coat the inside rim and then cut out the scones.

Place the dough rounds on the prepared baking tray and bake for 10 minutes for 1- to 2-inch scones, 13 minutes for 3-inch scones, and 25 minutes if you're keeping it whole (10-inch scone).

Remove from the oven and let stand for 1 minute before transferring to a wire rack to cool completely before serving.

This juicy flank steak is perfect for a last-minute dinner on the grill. Flank steak isn't known as one of best cuts of meat, but marinating makes it so tender and so delicious. The cut is usually easy to find and inexpensive, so this can easily be doubled to feed a crowd, or just make extra and use for leftovers in steak sandwiches or stir-fries. The **Chocolate** dark balsamic vinegar adds a delicious sweetness to the meat, and the **extra virgin** olive oil keeps the meat extra moist. Serve with a Caesar salad and Tuscan Herb Olive Oil Croutons (page 83). **SERVES 4**

Tender Flank Steak with Herb Olive Oil Chimichurri

STEAK
2–3 lb flank steak
¼ cup robust **extra virgin** olive oil
⅓ cup **Chocolate** dark balsamic vinegar
2 Tbsp grainy Dijon mustard
1 Tbsp brown sugar
2 tsp Worcestershire sauce
2 tsp minced garlic
1 tsp freshly cracked black pepper
½ tsp ground thyme
½ tsp dried rosemary
½ tsp dried parsley

CHIMICHURRI
1 small red chili pepper
½ cup finely chopped curly-leaf parsley
1 Tbsp finely chopped fresh oregano
1 Tbsp finely chopped fresh rosemary
2 tsp chopped fresh thyme leaves
1 tsp sea salt
½ cup robust **extra virgin** olive oil
2 Tbsp **Honey Ginger** white balsamic vinegar

RECOMMENDED VARIETALS
Coratina, Manzanillo, Picual

For a French twist, use **Herbes de Provence** infused olive oil instead of the single varietal and **Plum** white balsamic instead of the **Chocolate** dark balsamic.

For a smoky spice flavor, **Chipotle** infused olive oil works well with the **Chocolate** dark balsamic vinegar. It also makes a light and refreshing dish when partnered with **Lemongrass Mint** white balsamic.

Rinse the steak in hot water and pat dry. If the cuts of meat are really large, slice into desired serving sized pieces. Place in a rimmed baking dish or a plate with a lip and set aside.

In a small mixing bowl or liquid measuring cup, add the remaining ingredients and whisk to completely combine. Pour over the steak and turn to coat evenly. Cover with plastic wrap and allow to marinate for at least 1 hour, or overnight, in the fridge.

Preheat the grill to high heat. Place the meat on the grill, drizzling the remaining marinade over top. Sear the meat on each side for 3–4 minutes for medium rare. Add 1 minute more for medium, 2 minutes more for well done. Remove from the grill when desired doneness is reached, and place on a cutting board. Allow the meat to rest for at least 3 minutes so the juices redistribute back into the meat.

To make the chimichurri, slice the chili pepper in half, discard the seeds, and finely dice the chili. In a small bowl, whisk the chili with the herbs, salt, olive oil, and balsamic to create a very loose sauce.

Slice the steak into thin strips across the grain of the meat and drizzle with the chimichurri. Serve and enjoy!

Near my home, there is a little staple of a restaurant called John's Place that's a great spot to go for breakfast. But you have to arrive just late enough for them to have baked the bread for lunch, as you can't leave without a loaf: crusty on the outside, soft and pillow-like inside, and scented with fresh rosemary. This recipe is a nod to John's Place bread. We call it our housewarming loaf because the scent of the rosemary while baking is, well, divine, and makes your home smell utterly inviting. **MAKES TWO (8- × 4-INCH) LOAVES OR 1 LARGE ROUND LOAF**

Homemade Housewarming Loaf

1 cup 2% milk

5 cups all-purpose flour, divided

2 Tbsp granulated sugar

1 Tbsp quick-rising yeast

⅓ cup chopped fresh rosemary leaves

2 tsp coarse sea salt

¼ cup + 1 Tbsp herbaceous **extra virgin** olive oil

RECOMMENDED VARIETALS

Frantoio, Manzanillo, Picual

For an even more herbaceous and rosemary-forward loaf, try using **Rosemary** infused olive oil in place of the **extra virgin**.

Italian-Style Olive Bread Another delicious variation on this tasty loaf is to add ⅔ cup of sliced black olives in addition to the fresh rosemary and to use **Tuscan Herb** infused olive oil in place of the **extra virgin**.

In a small pot, heat the milk with 1 cup water to 115°F.

STAND MIXER METHOD In the bowl of a stand mixer fitted with a dough hook, combine 2½ cups of the flour with the sugar, yeast, rosemary, and salt.

Start the mixer on low speed, and slowly pour in the water/milk mixture and the ¼ cup olive oil. When the dough begins to come together and pulls away from the bowl, sprinkle in the remaining flour and continue to mix on low until all the flour is combined and the dough is soft and elastic to the touch.

HAND MIXING METHOD In a large bowl, combine 2½ cups of the flour with the sugar, yeast, rosemary, and salt. Make a well in the flour, add the water/milk mixture and ¼ cup olive oil, and mix with a wooden spoon until the flour is well combined. It should be pulling away from the bowl but still be sticky. Place 1 cup of the remaining flour on a clean work surface, turn out the dough, and knead until all the flour is absorbed. Dust with the remaining flour and continue to knead until it is smooth and elastic, about 10 minutes, dusting with more flour as you knead.

To make the bread, shape the dough into a ball, rub all over with the remaining 1 Tbsp of olive oil, and place in a large, lightly oiled bowl. Roll it around a bit to pick up the oil then cover with a clean damp kitchen towel or plastic wrap and set in a warm, draft-free spot until doubled in size, 10–15 minutes.

CONTINUED →

Once the dough has risen, cut it in half and shape each half into an oval loaf. Dust the tops with a little flour and cover with a damp towel. Let rise until doubled again, about 40 minutes.

Preheat the oven to 400°F with a baking stone or 2 stacked sheet pans set upside down in oven (doubling the sheet pans will help prevent the loaves from burning on the bottom).

Once the dough has doubled again, spritz the loaves with water and score the tops with a sharp knife in a crisscross fashion. Carefully place the loaves on the hot stone/sheet pans, spritz one more time with water, and bake for 20 minutes. Spritz the loaves again with water, turn down the oven to 350°F, and bake for an additional 20 minutes until the bread sounds hollow when tapped. Let cool on a wire rack before cutting—or slather with **extra virgin** olive oil while it's warm if you can't wait.

Olive oil in ice cream, you say? You're in for a treat. If you make this recipe with a single varietal, I highly recommend using a fruity one. Talk to someone at your local olive oil bar for an in-season recommendation. Sprinkle with some flaked sea salt, fleur de sel, or Himalayan pink salt for a salty-sweet delicacy. This recipe was inspired by one created by a close friend and chef, Lesley. **MAKES ABOUT 4 CUPS (8- X 4-INCH LOAF PAN)**

Olive Oil Ice Cream

2 ½ cups half-and-half (10–12%) cream
1 tsp sea salt
4 large egg yolks
¾ cup granulated sugar
½ cup fruity **extra virgin** olive oil
½ tsp pure vanilla extract

RECOMMENDED VARIETALS
Arbequina, Hojiblanca, Koroneiki

This recipe is perfect for experimenting with fused and infused olive oils, and variations totally depend on your own taste preferences. **Blood Orange**, **Lemon**, and **Lime** fused olive oils are definitely favorites for their classic but subtle and extra-creamy flavors. **Basil** infused olive oil makes a delicious savory ice cream. Serve it with a prosciutto crisp and a drizzle of **Wild Blueberry** balsamic crème (see page 159). Actually, you can serve it with any kind of balsamic crème (see page 255 for another version).

Prepare an ice bath.

In a heavy saucepan set over medium heat, warm the half-and-half and sea salt to 180°F.

While the half-and-half is heating, beat the egg yolks with the sugar until pale yellow and fluffy.

Remove the saucepan from the heat. Whisking constantly, add ½ cup of the hot half-and-half to the egg yolks, then place the egg yolk mixture in the saucepan, still whisking constantly.

Place the saucepan back on medium heat and whisk constantly until the mixture thickens enough to coat the back of a spoon, about 3 minutes.

Strain the mixture into a bowl set in the ice bath. Stir every now and then until cooled to room temperature.

Whisk in the olive oil and vanilla. Pour the custard into an 8- × 4-inch loaf pan and refrigerate, uncovered, until chilled, but preferably overnight, before transferring to the freezer.

This is the sweet version of the flatbread "vehicle" on page 22. Just add fresh or frozen fruit, nuts, chocolate chips . . . you name it. These are adapted from Giada De Laurentiis's recipe. Arrivederci, mundane mornings! **MAKES 12 MUFFINS**

Olive the Morning Muffins

2 cups all-purpose flour
2 tsp baking powder
½ tsp baking soda
½ tsp sea salt
1 cup granulated sugar
4 eggs
1 tsp pure vanilla extract
3 Tbsp any fruity white balsamic vinegar
   (see variations below)
2 Tbsp 2% milk
¾ cup fruity **extra virgin** olive oil

RECOMMENDED VARIETALS
Arbequina, Hojiblanca, Koroneiki

Preheat the oven to 350°F. Line a muffin tin with paper liners.

In a large bowl, combine the flour, baking powder, baking soda, and salt. Set aside.

Using a handheld mixer, beat the sugar, eggs, and vanilla on high speed until frothy, pale, and creamy, 2–3 minutes. Add the balsamic and milk and continue to beat for 1 minute. Switch off the mixer and slowly drizzle in the olive oil. Use a wooden spoon or a spatula to gently fold it into the flour mixture until just combined. Fill the muffin cups three-quarters full. Bake for 20 minutes, or until a toothpick inserted in the center of a muffin comes out clean.

Cinnamon Pear and Walnut Use **Cinnamon Pear** dark balsamic for the vinegar and a fruity single varietal **extra virgin** olive oil for the olive oil. Add 1 peeled and diced pear, ½ cup chopped walnuts, and 1 tsp ground cinnamon.

Lemon Blueberry Use **Lemon** fused olive oil for the olive oil and **Sicilian Lemon** white balsamic for the vinegar. Add 1½ cups frozen blueberries and 3 tsp grated lemon zest.

Mango Lime Use ¾ cup **Lime** fused olive oil for the olive oil and **Mango** white balsamic for the vinegar. Add 1 cup chopped fresh mango.

Peach and White Chocolate Use **Arbequina** for the olive oil and **Peach** white balsamic for the vinegar. Add 1½ cups sliced frozen peach chunks, ½ cup white chocolate chunks, and 3 tsp orange zest.

Raspberry Chocolate Chunk Use **Lime** fused olive oil and **Apricot** white balsamic for the vinegar. Add 1½ cups frozen raspberries, ½ cup dark chocolate chunks, and 3 tsp grated lime zest.

When I was growing up, we had an annual fall cleanup party at our cottage, and Mom always made this amazing pumpkin cake that you could smell for miles. This take on her recipe is made in a sheet pan, as it's easier to slice for a crowd. You can also bake it into cupcakes if you prefer. Buttercream or cream cheese frosting would work here, but I prefer the glaze; it lets the pumpkin flavor shine through. **MAKES ONE (9-× 13-INCH) SHEET CAKE OR 36 CUPCAKES**

Pumpkin Spice Sheet Cake with Honey Ginger Glaze

CAKE
3 cups all-purpose flour
2 tsp baking soda
2 tsp baking powder
2 tsp ground cinnamon
1 tsp ground ginger
½ tsp ground nutmeg
½ tsp ground allspice
½ tsp salt
2 cups canned pumpkin (about one 28 oz can)
1 cup brown sugar, packed
½ cup honey
1 cup **extra virgin** olive oil
2 eggs
½ cup roughly chopped candied ginger

RECOMMENDED VARIETALS
Arbequina, Coratina, Hojiblanca

GLAZE
1 Tbsp **Honey Ginger** white balsamic vinegar
1 Tbsp orange juice
½ cup icing sugar

You can use **Blood Orange** fused olive oil in the cake instead of a single varietal **extra virgin** olive oil to brighten the flavor even more.

Preheat the oven to 350°F. Oil and flour a 9-× 13-inch baking pan (or line 3 cupcake pans with paper liners).

In a large bowl, sift together the flour, baking soda, baking powder, cinnamon, ginger, nutmeg, allspice, and salt.

In a separate bowl, combine the pumpkin with the sugar and honey.

Make a well in the flour and add the pumpkin mixture. With a wooden spoon, gently stir everything together, then drizzle in the olive oil and add the eggs. Fold flour mixture around the outside of the bowl into the wet ingredients, combining everything and mixing well until the batter is smooth and creamy. Finally, fold in the candied ginger.

Spoon the batter into the prepared pan and bake for 40 minutes (18–20 minutes for cupcakes), or until a toothpick inserted in the center of the cake comes out clean, with only a few crumbs attached.

Remove the pan from the oven and gently run a knife around the edges of the cake. Place a serving plate upside down on top of pan, and quickly invert and tap the cake pan to release the cake onto the plate.

In a small bowl, whisk together the balsamic, orange juice, and sugar until no lumps remain. Drizzle over the cooled cake and let set before serving—if you can wait that long.

SALAD DRESSINGS

Salad dressing is usually the first thing people think of when they think about olive oil and balsamic vinegar. And who can blame them? When you know the building blocks for a great dressing, you can really start experimenting. I've included some of my tastiest oil and vinegar dressing combinations here, plus some recipes to build your salads from the bottom up, just to get you started.

CHOOSING YOUR OIL

First, use a very flavorful **extra virgin** olive oil, but remember that you want your dressing to complement the ingredients in your salad. For a green salad with lots of vegetables, stick to the herbaceous single varietals. If you're using an infused or fused olive oil, choose something like **Wild Dill**, **Rosemary**, **Herbes de Provence**, **Tuscan Herb**, or **Milanese Gremolata**. But if your salad is full of fresh fruit, including avocado, or sweeter vegetables like red peppers or carrots, use a mild but fruity olive oil like **Hojiblanca**. Infused olive oils that are a touch on the sweet side are also amazing with this type of salad; any of the fused citrus oils are incredible, but **Blood Orange**, **Lemon**, and **Lime** stand out. For suggestions on pairing oils with vinegars, please see Perfect Pairings on pages 342–343.

CHOOSING YOUR VINEGAR

You can choose from many kinds of vinegar, but be aware of the acid content. If you use a really acidic vinegar (6% or higher), such as sherry vinegar, champagne vinegar, red or white wine vinegar, or apple cider vinegar, the acid will react with the lipid molecules in the oil, which makes combining (or emulsifying) them much harder. Some balsamics have only 4% acidity, making them sweeter and less acidic than wine vinegars, but the balsamic you're most likely to find at your local grocery store will have 6% acidity. This causes the dressing to separate on the leaves and creates puddles in the bottom of your bowl. So, what do you do if you love the flavor of super-bright vinegars? You could take a sharper vinegar than the one listed in the recipe, add half the volume specified, and double the mustard. Yum!

A pet peeve of mine is brown dressing. If I have fresh butter lettuce from the garden and am filling my salad bowl with yellow tomatoes, mango, and avocado, I really don't want a dark brown dressing. A red wine vinegar or dark balsamic in a creamy dressing just looks awful, in my opinion. So a white balsamic vinegar is a wonderful alternative. It has many of the flavor characteristics that dark balsamic does but is light in color.

EMULSIFYING

If the oil and vinegar keep separating as you make a dressing, add a touch of mustard (any kind—Dijon, whole grain, or even dry mustard) and whisk to bring it all together. Mustard is a great emulsifier. Don't like mustard? Use a mild honey mustard or a grainy Dijon. Their flavors are much milder than most prepared or hot mustards. Honey can actually work on its own as an emulsifier, but most people find it a bit sweet to use this way. If you like to add a bit of nuttiness to your dressing, try tahini. Whisk a few tablespoons into your dressing, especially a citrus-based one, and you'll have a perfect dressing that won't need to be shaken every few minutes.

SHALLOTS

Another secret weapon in the dressing armory is the shallot. While garlic is delicious, it can be a bit overpowering; shallots offer a lovely balance between the sweetness of onion and the tang of garlic.

Finely mincing your shallot helps distribute the flavor through the dressing and creates a perfect bite every time. If you find mincing a challenge, take a small chunk and put it in your garlic press.

This basic balsamic can be adapted to suit any taste, any dish, and any occasion by choosing from the oil and vinegar combos from the Perfect Pairings chart on page 343. **MAKES 1 CUP**

Basic Balsamic Vinaigrette

¼ cup dark or white balsamic vinegar
1 Tbsp Dijon mustard
1 Tbsp honey
1 small shallot, minced
¼ tsp sea salt
¼ tsp ground black pepper
½ cup **extra virgin** olive oil

Whisk together the balsamic, Dijon, honey, shallot, salt, and pepper until blended. Gradually whisk in the olive oil, blending well. Use immediately, or store in an airtight container in the fridge for up to 24 hours, and allow to come to room temperature before serving as the oil will have solidified.

This basic buttermilk dressing is easy to make and is a great base for variations. If you don't have buttermilk on hand, you can make your own version by adding 1 Tbsp lemon juice to whole or 2% milk to make ½ cup total; let it sit for about 5 minutes before using. Use it to make a creamy coleslaw, dress some bitter greens, or make a creamy kale or a potato salad. See below for some flavor combination ideas. **MAKES 1 CUP**

Basic Buttermilk Dressing

½ cup buttermilk
2 Tbsp **extra virgin** olive oil
¼ cup mayonnaise
2 Tbsp white balsamic vinegar (see Variations)
1 tsp Worcestershire sauce
1 tsp honey
1 small shallot, minced
¼ tsp sea salt
¼ tsp cracked pepper

Whisk together all the ingredients in a small bowl, or place them all in a Mason jar and shake very well.

This will keep in an airtight container in the fridge for up to 3 days.

Blue Cheese Dressing Use sherry vinegar for your balsamic and add ¼ cup of crumbled blue cheese.

Citrus Dressing Use Grapefruit white balsamic for the vinegar and substitute ¼ cup tahini for the mayo if desired.

Creamy Ranch-Style Dressing Use Oregano white balsamic for the vinegar and Wild Dill infused olive oil in place of the **extra virgin**, omit the shallot, add 2 tsp each of minced garlic, fresh chives, fresh dill, and fresh parsley (curly or flat-leaf), and then add a pinch of cayenne.

Honey Ginger Coleslaw Dressing Use Honey Ginger white balsamic for the vinegar.

QUICK & EASY SALADS

Here are some ideas for salad ingredients to combine with olive oils and vinegars. Use the basic balsamic vinaigrette recipe on page 42 as the base for the dressings; the olive oil and vinegar combinations suggested here will give it a twist.

ASIAN CHARM

Take mixed greens, sliced green and red bell peppers, carrots, baby corn, water chestnuts, and grape tomatoes and top them with a dressing that uses **Honey Ginger** white balsamic vinegar and **Blood Orange** fused olive oil. Top with toasted sesame seeds and mandarin oranges slices before serving.

CLASSIC STRAWBERRY AND SPINACH SALAD

Prepare a bed of baby spinach leaves, and add fresh sliced strawberries, whole green grapes, and pears cut into bite-sized pieces. Make the dressing with **Strawberry** dark balsamic vinegar and **Blood Orange** fused olive oil and toss with the salad. Top with crumbled goat cheese and chopped, toasted walnuts.

FALL CREATIONS

Tear some red and green leaf lettuce leaves and toss with sliced apples, candied walnuts or pecans, and dried cranberries. Make the dressing with **Cinnamon Pear** dark balsamic and a fruity single varietal **extra virgin** olive oil. Add the dressing and top with chunks of Brie.

GERMAN POTATO SALAD

Quarter then boil 1 lb of fingerling potatoes. Use **Sicilian Lemon** white balsamic for your vinegar, **Wild Dill** infused olive oil for your oil, and grainy Dijon for your mustard. Add 1 crushed garlic clove and ¼–½ cup of diced red onion, and dress the hot potatoes.

INSALATA CAPRESE

Mix together pieces of fresh mozzarella cheese, sliced fresh tomatoes, and fresh basil leaves. Make the dressing with **Neapolitan Herb** or **Traditional** dark balsamic vinegar and **Basil** infused olive oil or a creamy single varietal **extra virgin** olive oil (see pages 16–17).

ITALIAN CAESAR

Use Romaine lettuce for this one. Make the dressing with **Tuscan Herb** infused olive oil and **Sicilian Lemon** white balsamic vinegar, and add 1 egg yolk, ¼–½ tsp Worcestershire sauce, and 1 crushed garlic clove. Toss croutons and bacon bits with the lettuce, toss with the dressing, and garnish with freshly grated Parmesan cheese.

SUPER SALAD

Toss together spinach leaves, arugula, and kale, then add slices of red onion and red bell peppers, and matchsticks of carrots. Make the dressing with **Fig** dark balsamic vinegar and a robust single varietal **extra virgin** olive oil, add to the salad, and toss to combine. Garnish with kiwi slices, fresh blueberries, and pomegranate seeds.

TROPICAL SALAD

Toss Boston lettuce with sliced mango, mandarin oranges, red bell peppers, and red onion. Make the dressing with **Coconut** white balsamic vinegar and **Lime** fused olive oil. Add to the salad, toss to combine, and garnish with pomegranate seeds and a mild cheese of your choice.

Fused & Infused Olive Oils

Someone made a wonderful discovery! You can add real, natural flavors to fresh extra virgin olive oil, and the results are commonly referred to as fused or infused olive oils. The process of making fused and infused olive oil is an art. And I'm not referring to "arts and crafts." Remember when it was trendy to make your own decorative bottles of "infused" olive oil by dropping some herbs into a pretty bottle, filling it with oil, and sealing the top with red wax? If you do this, please do not use this oil. Ingesting oil made in this way is actually the number one cause of botulism poisoning in North America.

Leave it to the experts; they can safely produce the most intense and surprisingly authentic flavored oils because the method they use preserves the integrity of the fruit or vegetable and they do it in a way that balances perfectly with the oil. Making fused and infused olive oil is not about taking leftover oil and masking it with an ingredient in an attempt to use it up. It's about matching the right olive oil or blend of oils with the right amount of the right ingredient using the correct process.

When oil is "fused," it means that the olives have been simultaneously crushed alongside a fresh fruit or spicy chili pepper, and it's referred to as the agrumato method. Only specific ingredients can be used to make fused oil, and these are determined based on their citric acid and capsicum levels (these act as their own defense mechanisms to prevent bacteria growth).

When an olive is "infused," it means that the essential oil of the herb or spices have been added to an extra virgin olive oil that was specifically chosen to complement that flavor.

When done right, these oils are an incredible addition to your pantry.

Blood Orange Fused Olive Oil

This fused olive oil really delivers with its beautiful, warm, sweet citrus notes. Best on fish, seafood, chicken, or salads, it is delightful when paired with a fruity white balsamic, especially the **Cranberry Pear**. It's a must for your pantry, and you'll find it in a lot of recipes in this book! You'll find **Blood Orange** fused olive oil in the following recipes (and in several recipe variations throughout the book):

The key to jar salads is simple: it's all about how you pack the jar. If you make the dressing your first layer and put crisp veggies, nuts, and seeds directly on top of it, you create a natural barrier between the lettuce and the dressing, so the lettuce doesn't come in contact with the dressing until you shake the jar when you're ready to eat. You can easily put a few of these together and store them in the fridge to grab and go in the morning, or for a healthy snack after work. See pages 40–45 for a ton of salad and salad dressing ideas.

The Blood Orange poppy seed dressing is perfect for this salad, but it's also great drizzled over grilled peaches or even served with a gingersnap. **SERVES ONE AND MAKES ONE JAR (1 CUP OF DRESSING)**

Lunchtime Jar Salad

DRESSING

½ cup Greek yogurt
¼ cup **Blood Orange** fused olive oil
2 Tbsp **Mango** white balsamic vinegar
2 Tbsp honey
2 tsp grainy Dijon mustard
1 tsp minced shallot
¼ tsp sea salt

SALAD

1 cup baby spinach
¼ cup chopped walnuts
2 Tbsp dried cranberries
1 Tbsp sunflower seeds
¼ cup chopped carrots
¼ cup chopped red bell pepper
1 Tbsp poppy seeds

To make the dressing, whisk together all the ingredients in a small bowl, or place them all in a small jar and shake very well. This dressing will keep well in an airtight jar (minus the poppy seeds) in the fridge for up to 3 days. This makes plenty of dressing for multiple salads.

Wash and pat dry the spinach and tear it gently into bite-size pieces.

Pour 2–3 Tbsp of the dressing into a 2-cup Mason jar. Place the walnuts, then the cranberries and sunflower seeds, then the carrots, and the bell pepper in the jar. Top with the spinach and the poppy seeds. Put the lid on tight.

When you're ready to eat, shake the jar really well so the dressing coats the leaves. Open and enjoy.

Eating a piece of this cake is a great way to start the day. The wheat germ here adds its unique texture and makes the cake feel even more breakfast-like. This can also be baked as muffins, if you prefer. The **Blood Orange** olive oil infuses through the batter so well that it's present in every bite, although you'll notice a softer flavor than orange juice would give. **MAKES ONE (9-INCH) CAKE OR 12 MUFFINS**

Pear Breakfast Coffee Cake

CAKE

3 ripe pears, skin on (about 2 cups diced)
1 ½ cups all-purpose flour
1 tsp baking powder
¼ tsp baking soda
½ tsp sea salt
¾ cup wheat germ
1 egg
¼ cup 2% milk
⅓ cup honey
¼ cup **Blood Orange** fused olive oil

STREUSEL TOPPING

¼ cup all-purpose flour
¼ cup brown sugar, packed
2 Tbsp **Blood Orange** fused olive oil
2 tsp **Cinnamon Pear** dark balsamic vinegar

Apple Cranberry Breakfast Coffee Cake
Substitute 2 apples plus 1 cup fresh or frozen cranberries for the 3 pears—just increase the cooking time by a few minutes if using frozen cranberries as they will make the cake even moister. **Lemon** fused olive oil can be substituted in place of the **Blood Orange** if desired as well.

Preheat the oven to 400°F. Grease a 9-inch round cake pan or insert paper liners in a muffin tin.

To make the cake, core and finely dice the pears without peeling them. Sift together the flour, baking powder, baking soda, and salt. Stir in the wheat germ. Beat the egg slightly and blend with the milk, honey, and olive oil in a liquid measuring cup. Slowly mix this into the dry ingredients (by hand or using a mixer). When fully incorporated, mix in the pears. Fold gently until the pears are fully incorporated as well.

To make the streusel topping, combine all the topping ingredients in a small bowl and mix with a fork until crumbly.

Pour the batter into the prepared cake pan or muffin tin and sprinkle with the streusel topping. Garnish with some pear slices, if desired. Bake the cake for 25–30 minutes, or the muffins for 17–20 minutes, until the streusel topping is golden brown. Let it cool in the pan on a wire rack. For the cake, run a knife around the edge of the pan when it comes out the oven to loosen it a bit.

This cake never lasts longer than a day, but it will keep in an airtight container for up to a week.

This is one of those quick and easy dinners you can throw into the oven when you walk in the door from work and enjoy in no time at all. Pair this with Arugula Salad with Grapefruit Vinaigrette (page 269) or Couscous Tabbouleh Salad (page 143) and Wild Mushroom & Sage Roasted Acorn Squash (page 112). **SERVES 4**

Honey-Glazed Chicken

¹/₄ cup honey
2 Tbsp **Blood Orange** fused olive oil
2 tsp curry powder
1 tsp ground cardamom
¹/₂ tsp ground ginger
4 chicken breasts (bone-in or boneless)
¹/₂ tsp sea salt

> Although the **Blood Orange** oil is delicious here, feel free to try this recipe with **Lemon** or **Lime** fused olive oil; if those aren't in the cupboard, **Herbes de Provence** or just a mild **extra virgin** olive oil are all really delicious.

Preheat the oven to 375°F.

To make the glaze, in a small bowl whisk together the honey, olive oil, curry powder, ground cardamom, and ground ginger until you have a smooth paste-like mixture.

Wash the chicken breasts in hot water, remove the skin, and pat dry.

Place the chicken breasts in a small roasting pan. The chicken should be tightly packed with the edges touching and little space left around the outside of the pan.

Drizzle the chicken with the glaze and spread it evenly with the back of a spoon or pastry brush.

Bake for 20 minutes for boneless breasts, 30–35 minutes for bone-in. A meat thermometer is the most reliable way to test if they're ready, ideally 165°F.

Remove the pan from the oven, spoon the cooking juices over the breasts, and let rest for 3 minutes before serving.

If you're using bone-in breasts, the bones create added flavor and juices. You can use the juice for a great pan sauce or gravy to drizzle over roasted sweet potatoes or squash to tie dinner all together.

These muffins are a take on my grandmother's oatmeal muffin recipe. Don't like oats? Don't worry. They almost disappear because they are so soft from soaking up the milk. The streusel topping isn't necessary, but it is a nice treat. **MAKES 12 MUFFINS**

Blood Orange Oatmeal Muffins

1 ½ cups 2% milk
1 cup quick-cooking oats
2 cups all-purpose flour
½ cup granulated sugar
3 tsp baking powder
1 tsp baking soda
1 tsp sea salt
½ cup **Blood Orange** fused olive oil
2 eggs, lightly beaten

STREUSEL
½ cup all-purpose flour
¼ cup brown sugar
½ cup blood orange fused olive oil
1 tsp cinnamon
½ tsp nutmeg

For a change of taste, try using **Lemon** or **Lime** fused olive oil instead of the **Blood Orange**. You can also add ½ cup of dried cranberries, raisins, or chopped dried apricots if desired.

Preheat the oven to 375°F. Grease the cups of a muffin tin or line the cups with paper liners.

In a small bowl, combine the milk and oats and let them sit for 10 minutes (or even overnight) to soften the oats.

In a large bowl, mix the flour with the sugar, baking powder, baking soda, and salt. Create a well in the center, and add the olive oil, beaten eggs, and milk/oat mixture. Fold in gently until just combined.

Prepare the streusel by mixing all ingredients in a small bowl until well combined and crumbly in texture. Sprinkle evenly over muffins before putting in the oven.

Fill the muffin cups three-quarters full with the batter. Top each muffin with streusel, dividing it evenly between the muffins. Bake for 13 minutes, until a toothpick inserted in the center of a muffin comes out clean. These are delicious straight from the oven.

This jam is dangerously delicious, so consider yourself warned. The **Honey Ginger** white balsamic adds a warm spiciness, but the peaches and the **Blood Orange** fused olive oil keep it bright and summery. It's perfect with cream cheese on a bagel for breakfast along with a hot cup of tea or served on Olive Oil Ice Cream (page 35) for a summer treat. Make a sweet variation of the Savory Ricotta Scones (page 29), and put some of this jam on top, or make the Gingersnap Crinkle Cookies (page 56) into ice cream sandwiches with a dollop of this. **MAKES 3 PINTS**

Southern Peach Jam

10–12 small peaches, roughly chopped
1 cup brown sugar, packed
1 cup granulated sugar
2 Tbsp bourbon (optional)
¼ cup **Honey Ginger** white balsamic vinegar
2 Tbsp **Blood Orange** fused olive oil
1 tsp ground cardamom
½ tsp ground nutmeg
1 cinnamon stick
2 packages (each 6 oz) of liquid pectin

Prepare an ice-water bath.

Bring a medium saucepan of water to a boil. Score the bottom of the peaches with a crisscross and submerge the peaches in boiling water for about 30–40 seconds. Remove and place in the ice-water bath to cool.

Slip the skins off the peaches (if they don't give, peeling with a paring knife works well) and then chop them and place them in a medium saucepan with all the remaining ingredients, except the pectin, over medium-high heat. Bring to a boil, turn down heat, and simmer, uncovered, for about 20 minutes. The fruit should be softened and reduced in volume.

Carefully, and in batches, purée the jam in a blender. Or you can purée only half of the mixture if you'd prefer a slightly chunky jam.

Return to the saucepan and bring to a rolling boil. Boil hard for 1 minute, add the liquid pectin, and stir in well. Remove from the heat.

Ladle the jam into hot, sterilized jars and seal with lids and rings. Process the jars in a water bath for 10 minutes, then place the jars on a clean tea towel to cool completely and seal. Ensure all the jars are sealed; it could take up to 4–6 hours for the lids to pop (such a satisfying sound!). If a jar doesn't seal, use it first and store in the fridge.

These cookies were a staple after-school treat when I was young. The **Blood Orange** fused olive oil really complements the ginger and makes them way more addictive than your standard gingersnap. If you want a crunchy cookie for dunking in your tea, bake them for 2 minutes longer or make them smaller; for a softer cookie, reduce the baking time by 1 minute. **MAKES 24 (3-INCH) COOKIES OR 36 (2-INCH) COOKIES**

Gingersnap Crinkle Cookies

2 ¼ cups all-purpose flour
1 ½ tsp baking soda
¼ tsp sea salt
2 tsp ground ginger
1 tsp ground cinnamon
½ tsp ground cloves
⅛ tsp ground nutmeg
1 egg
1 ¼ cups granulated sugar, divided
2 tsp grated orange zest
⅔ cup **Blood Orange** fused olive oil
¼ cup molasses

Preheat the oven to 350°F. Line a cookie sheet with parchment paper.

Sift the flour, baking soda, salt, and spices onto a large piece of parchment paper.

In the bowl of a stand mixer, whisk the egg with 1 cup of the sugar and the orange zest until creamy and fluffy, then drizzle in the olive oil, continuing to whisk until fully combined. Whisk in the molasses until the mixture is all creamy and golden. Lift up the parchment paper and gently pour the flour mixture into the wet ingredients. Stir with a wooden spoon until everything is fully combined. The dough does get stiff, so be sure to scrape everything from the bottom of the bowl to mix well.

Scoop the dough into small balls, about 2 Tbsp each, and then dip each one in the ¼ cup sugar. Place the cookie dough balls 2 inches apart on the prepared cookie sheet and press down lightly, slightly flattening the dough. Bake for 7–9 minutes for a soft chewy cookie with a lightly browned bottom, or 9–10 minutes for a firmer, crisp, perfect-for-dunking cookie. Cool the cookies on the cookie sheet for 5 minutes before transferring them to a cooling rack.

Store these in an airtight container for up to 1 week to keep them soft and chewy. The crisp version can be stored on a plate, covered with a tea towel, on the counter for a couple of days.

These bars whip up in a flash, and because they are easily made ahead and totally transportable, they are perfect to take to a potluck. Using the **Blood Orange** fused olive oil and brown sugar makes them not too sweet. You can also make them with a creamy mild **extra virgin** oil, but I think the **Blood Orange** shows them at their best. MAKES ONE (9- × 13-INCH) PAN

Chocolate Orange Oat Bars

²/₃ cup **Blood Orange** fused olive oil

1¹/₂ cups brown sugar, packed

2 eggs

1³/₄ cups all-purpose flour

³/₄ tsp baking soda

1 cup rolled oats

1¹/₂ cups semisweet chocolate chips, divided

³/₄ tsp sea salt

Preheat the oven to 350°F. Line a 9- × 13-inch baking pan with parchment paper.

In a large bowl, combine the olive oil with the brown sugar and beat until fluffy. Add the eggs one at a time, beating after each addition and continuing to beat until the mixture is frothy and creamy.

Sift in the flour and baking soda. Mixing gently with a wooden spoon, stir in the oats, ¾ cup of the chocolate chips, and the salt.

Turn the mixture into the prepared pan and use your hands to press the oat mixture down firmly.

Bake for 20–25 minutes, until the top is golden brown and the edges are crisp. Remove from the oven and use a spatula to spread the remaining ¾ cup of chocolate chips evenly over the bars to create a chocolate glaze. Let cool completely in the pan and then cut into bars.

These will keep in an airtight container for up to 1 week.

These are decadent, so beware. Transform them into sundaes by serving them with Olive Oil Ice Cream (page 35) and a balsamic crème (pages 159 and 255). Use a mini muffin tin to make a two-bite brownie that's perfect for adding to packed lunches.

You can add ½ cup walnuts or pecans if you like, but these really are perfect as is. **MAKES ONE (8- × 8-INCH) PAN**

Olive Oil Brownies

½ cup **Blood Orange** fused olive oil
1 cup granulated sugar
2 large eggs
2 tsp **Espresso** dark balsamic vinegar
¾ cup Dutch process cocoa powder
½ cup all-purpose flour
½ tsp baking powder
¼ tsp fine sea salt

Feel free to drizzle these brownies with any aged dark balsamic vinegar to enhance your experience. Try **Black Cherry** dark balsamic instead of the **Espresso**—delicious!

You can also substitute strong espresso coffee for the balsamic.

Preheat the oven to 350°F. Line an 8- × 8-inch baking pan with parchment paper.

In a large mixing bowl, use a wooden spoon to combine the olive oil with the sugar. Add the eggs and balsamic and stir just until blended. Sift the cocoa, flour, baking powder, and salt into the oil/sugar mixture. Be careful not to overmix and beat in too much air—otherwise they'll turn out too dense and be more like cake than brownie.

Pour the mixture into the prepared pan and bake for 20 minutes, or until the brownie just starts to pull away from the sides of the pan. Cool completely in the pan before cutting.

The first time I ever tried to make pot de crème it ended up more like chocolate soup! I promise this recipe produces much better results. The creamy texture of the custard complements the intensity of the chocolate. (I use Askinosie chocolate, and it is remarkable!) If you don't have any whipping (35%) cream for the custard, you can use the same volume of table (18%) cream plus an additional egg yolk and increase the cooking time by 2 minutes. This recipe is easily doubled, or tripled, or even halved. **MAKES 2 MUGS OR FOUR (4-OUNCE) RAMEKINS**

Blood Orange Pot de Crème

1 cup whipping (35%) cream, divided
¼ cup chopped dark (at least 70%) chocolate
¼ cup granulated sugar
2 egg yolks
¼ cup **Blood Orange** fused olive oil
1 Tbsp **Espresso** dark balsamic vinegar

In a small saucepan, bring ¾ cup of the cream to a simmer over medium heat, being careful not to let it boil. Remove from the heat and add the chocolate and sugar, but don't stir them in. Let stand for 5 minutes.

Preheat the oven to 325°F.

In a mixing bowl, whisk the egg yolks until light and fluffy and slowly drizzle in the olive oil. (If you're using a mixer, keep it running while you drizzle in the oil.)

Now stir the cream mixture to encourage the chocolate to melt and continue to stir until completely combined and smooth.

Whisk the egg mixture as you slowly pour in the chocolate cream, whisking to fully combine.

Divide between four ramekins, or two small ovenproof mugs, and place them in an 8- × 8-inch baking dish. Add hot water until it reaches halfway up the ramekins or mugs.

Bake for 35 minutes, or until the center is almost set. The custard will firm as it cools. This can be made ahead and kept in the fridge, covered or uncovered, for a maximum of 2 days. If you're planning to eat it straight away, just let it cool on a wire rack.

Whip the remaining ¼ cup of cream. When serving, place a dollop of whipped cream over each pot de crème and drizzle with the balsamic! Yum!

Lemon Fused Olive Oil

This refreshing and bright fused olive oil is as versatile as the fruit it's made from. In the agrumato method, the whole lemon is used in the process instead of just the oil from the zest, creating a round full flavor. It's perfect for sautéing scallops or drizzling over chicken or fish. It's also easily whipped into pancakes for a bit of breakfast charm. You'll find **Lemon** fused olive oil in the following recipes (and in several recipe variations throughout the book):

Making pesto at home is a necessity for me because we have nut allergies in our home, and 99% of pestos contain nuts. But pesto's too tasty—and versatile!—to give up completely. Frozen artichoke hearts are easiest here, as preparing fresh is time-consuming. Pickled artichoke hearts are also delicious, but rinse them well and omit the lemon juice from the recipe, as they will already be quite acidic. If you're using hearts packed in oil, rinse them well and pat them dry before using. **MAKES 1 1/2 CUPS**

Creamy Artichoke Pesto

4 garlic cloves, peeled
1 tsp sea salt
1/4 cup finely chopped fresh parsley (any type)
1 cup artichoke hearts
1/2 cup **Lemon** fused olive oil
1/4 cup lemon juice (about 2 lemons)
2/3 cup grated Parmesan cheese
Pinch chili flakes

For a more herbaceous version, the **Milanese Gremolata** is a delicious substitution for the lemon olive oil here.

MORTAR AND PESTLE METHOD Using the back of a knife, squish the garlic cloves. Place them in a mortar, add the salt and then the parsley, and mash it all together. Roughly chop the artichoke hearts and mash them in to mix everything together. Pour in the olive oil, lemon juice, Parmesan, and chili flakes. Use a spatula to fold everything in and incorporate.

FOOD PROCESSOR METHOD Put the garlic in the bowl of a food processor and roughly chop. Add the salt and parsley, pulse to combine, and then add the artichoke hearts. With the machine running, drizzle in the olive oil and lemon juice. Add the cheese and chili flakes and pulse until fully combined.

This will keep in an airtight container in the fridge for 1 week.

The white beans make this hummus creamier and lighter than traditional chickpea hummus, and the **Lemon** fused olive oil gives it a lovely, subtle lemony hit, rather than adding a sharpness. If you only have chickpeas in the cupboard, and no white kidney or cannellini beans, they'll be just fine here. The key to perfect chickpea hummus is shelling your chickpeas (yes, shelling canned chickpeas!). It takes a few minutes but is actually quite relaxing and definitely worth the effort. Chickpeas are generally a bit drier than white beans, so you might want to increase the water by 2 Tbsp if you're using them. **MAKES 2 CUPS**

Lemon White Bean Hummus

1 (19 oz) can white kidney beans or cannellini beans, drained and rinsed
¼ cup tahini
¼ cup **Lemon** fused olive oil, plus an extra drizzle
1 small garlic clove
Pinch chili flakes
Sea salt

Purée the beans, tahini, olive oil, and garlic in a food processor until smooth. With the machine running, drizzle in up to ¼ cup water to thin the hummus and attain the desired consistency.

Dollop the hummus into a serving bowl and sprinkle with an additional drizzle of olive oil, plus some chili flakes and sea salt.

For a spicy version, substitute half the **Lemon** fused olive oil for **Harissa** or **Chipotle** infused olive oil. For an herbaceous dip, substitute half the **Lemon** fused olive oil with 2 Tbsp of **Herbes de Provence** or **Milanese Gremolata** infused olive oil.

Spring might be salad season, but it's also asparagus season, and most of us can't get enough of it. It's best simply prepared so its natural flavor is predominant. Always make sure your oven or grill is fully preheated when you're cooking asparagus. When these are roasted for 15 minutes at the right temperature they will be perfectly done. **SERVES 4**

Lemon Roasted Asparagus

1 large bunch of asparagus
2 Tbsp **Lemon** fused olive oil
Sea salt and ground black pepper

For a fresh and herbaceous option, replace all the **Lemon** fused olive oil with **Tuscan Herb** or **Herbes de Provence** infused olive oil and add a splash of **Sicilian Lemon** white balsamic if desired to add a bit of zip to the finished product.

For an herbaceous yet still lemony variation, substitute half the **Lemon** fused olive oil with **Milanese Gremolata**.

Looking for something delicious and sweet? Drizzle the asparagus on the serving plate with 1–2 Tbsp of **Traditional**, **Fig**, **Neapolitan Herb**, or **Pomegranate** dark balsamic right before serving.

Preheat the oven or grill to 400°F.

Wash the asparagus and snap off the woody ends. Arrange in a single layer on a rimmed baking sheet covered with parchment paper. Drizzle with the olive oil, salt, and pepper. Roll around on the sheet to evenly coat the spears of asparagus.

Place in the oven, or on the grill, and roast for 15 minutes. Remove and serve immediately.

Rubbing the chicken with the **Lemon** fused olive oil imparts moisture as well as a subtle lemon flavor into the skin and meat, and the salt helps to dry out the excess water from the skin. I like to wash my chicken in steaming hot water and then pat it dry because it results in a crispier skin when the oil, salt, and pepper are all rubbed in. Serve this with Pan-Fried Potatoes (page 23). **SERVES 4–6**

Quick Whole Roast Chicken

2 large onions
½ cup **Lemon** fused olive oil, divided
1 (4–5 lb) chicken
2 tsp sea salt, divided
2 tsp ground black pepper, divided
4 garlic cloves

Any extra drippings can also be made into a tasty onion gravy. Simply whisk 2 Tbsp of cornstarch with ¼ cup water. Carefully pour the drippings from the pan into a small pot and place over medium heat. Add in the cornstarch mixture and stir constantly until it bubbles and turns translucent.

If you're an herbaceous chicken lover, substituting the **Lemon** fused olive oil with **Tuscan Herb**, **Herbes de Provence**, **Basil**, **Cilantro & Onion**, or **Rosemary** infused olive oil will yield delicious results. If I'm using one of these, I'll often splash on a few teaspoons of **Sicilian Lemon** or **Apricot** white balsamic as soon as the chicken comes out of the oven. The smell of the steam created by the balsamic is intoxicating and utterly delicious, and the acid in it seals the skin and keeps it crispy.

Preheat the oven to 425°F.

Slice the onions into rounds and place them in a roasting pan. Drizzle with 1 Tbsp of the olive oil.

Pat dry the chicken.

Sprinkle the cavity with 1 tsp each of the sea salt and pepper. Peel the garlic and place the whole cloves in the cavity. Place the chicken breast side up on top of the onions in the roasting pan. Drizzle the remaining olive oil over the chicken, rub it in thoroughly, then sprinkle with the remaining salt and pepper.

Roast for 50–65 minutes, until the internal temperature reaches 170°F. Remove from the oven and let sit for 5 minutes before diving in.

There is nothing quite like cake for breakfast, especially if it contains the flavors of refreshingly tart rhubarb. I use a 9-inch springform pan, but you can use a 9-× 5-inch loaf pan if you prefer. Just increase the cooking time by 5 minutes. **MAKES ONE (9-INCH) ROUND CAKE**

Easy Rhubarb Coffee Cake

CAKE

½ cup brown sugar, packed
¾ cup **Lemon** fused olive oil
2 eggs
1½ cups all-purpose flour
1 tsp baking powder
1 tsp baking soda
½ tsp sea salt
¼ cup 2% milk
1 cup chopped rhubarb

STREUSEL TOPPING

½ cup all-purpose flour
¼ cup steel-cut oats
3 Tbsp brown sugar
2 tsp grated lemon zest
3 Tbsp **Lemon** fused olive oil

I much prefer to use **Lemon** fused olive oil in this recipe, but it is almost as good with **Blood Orange** fused olive oil or **Arbequina** olive oil, especially if you use 1 cup fresh blueberries in place of the rhubarb and orange zest instead of lemon zest in the streusel topping. (If you use frozen blueberries, increase the cooking time by 3–5 minutes.)

Preheat the oven to 350°F. Grease a 9-inch springform pan.

To make the cake, in a large mixing bowl, whisk the brown sugar with the olive oil and eggs until frothy.

Sift the flour, baking powder, baking soda, and salt over top, and fold in with a wooden spoon or spatula to form a soft batter. Add the milk and stir to combine, then fold in the rhubarb.

Pour the batter into the prepared cake pan. Tap the pan on the counter several times to ensure the batter is level and to remove any air bubbles.

To make the streusel topping, in a small bowl, combine the flour, oats, sugar, and zest. Drizzle in the olive oil and stir to combine into a coarse crumb mixture. Sprinkle this evenly over the cake batter.

Bake the cake for 35–40 minutes, or until a toothpick inserted in the center comes out clean. Remove from the oven, run a knife around the outside, and remove the sides of the pan. Let rest for at least 10 minutes before serving.

Lime Fused Olive Oil

This unbelievably fresh, fragrant citrus-fused olive oil is the perfect companion to Mexican food, dips, spreads, seafood, and most of all, salad dressings. It will brighten any salad when paired with any white balsamic (see page 343 for specific combinations). You'll find **Lime** fused olive oil in the following recipes (and in several recipe variations throughout the book):

I first encountered guacamole in Germany, of all places. I shared a house and kitchen with a woman named Bethany, a Floridian who considered guacamole a staple food. We'd make a big bowl of this to snack on while we talked and talked and dreamed of warmer weather. I love my guacamole a bit chunky, with every ingredient featuring in every bite. The olive oil makes this possible while also making it incredibly creamy. I can't make guac any other way. **MAKES 1 ¹/₂–2 CUPS**

Lime & Cilantro Guacamole

2 large ripe avocados
1 small plum tomato
1 small red onion
1 bunch cilantro
2 Tbsp lime juice
2 Tbsp **Lime** fused olive oil
Sea salt

> If you're a cilantro lover, you're welcome to use **Cilantro & Onion** infused olive oil instead of the **Lime** fused olive oil.

Mash the avocados in a medium-sized bowl. Dice and rinse the tomato to get rid of all the seeds, dice the onion, coarsely chop the cilantro, and add them all to the avocado. Pour in the lime juice and olive oil and mix together in a blender for a creamier finish, or by hand for a chunkier look. (Alternatively, just toss everything in the food processor and pulse to combine.) Add sea salt to taste.

This will keep in the fridge in an airtight container for up to 2 days.

Rice noodle salads are refreshing and filling, and they require minimal effort to prepare at home. If spot prawns aren't in season, regular prawns will suffice. In fact, any protein can be used in this salad. It's the perfect way to use up any leftovers from Quick Whole Roast Chicken (page 66). You could also omit the prawns, double the veggies, throw in some tofu for protein, and make it a veggie salad. **SERVES 4**

Spot Prawn Rice Noodle Salad

⅓ cup **Lime** fused olive oil, divided
Grated zest and juice of 1 lime, divided
Pinch crushed red pepper flakes
12–15 spot prawns, shelled and deveined
8 oz thin rice noodles
2 carrots
½ red bell pepper
½ English cucumber, peeled
½ ripe mango
¼ cup **Lemongrass Mint** or **Honey Ginger** white balsamic vinegar
1 Tbsp smooth peanut butter
1 tsp soy sauce
½ tsp sea salt
1 bunch mint, torn into pieces
1 bunch Thai basil, torn into pieces
¼ cup chopped peanuts (optional)

In a large bowl, whisk together ¼ cup of the olive oil with half of the lime zest and juice, and a pinch of red pepper flakes. Add the prawns and chill in the fridge for 15 minutes.

Meanwhile, bring a saucepan of water to a boil and gently drop in the rice noodles. Remove from the heat and allow to sit for 3–5 minutes, or according to the package directions. Drain and fluff the noodles and place them in a serving bowl.

Slice the carrots, bell pepper, cucumber, and mango into matchsticks.

Heat a medium-sized frying pan or wok and add the prawns and marinade (no oil required). Sauté for 1–2 minutes per side, until the prawns are curled up and bright pink. Be careful not to overcook them. Remove from the heat.

In a small bowl, whisk together the remaining olive oil, the balsamic, peanut butter, and soy sauce. Season to taste with sea salt.

Drizzle half the dressing over the rice noodles and toss to coat.

Top the noodles with the veggies, then the prawns, and drizzle over the remaining dressing. Sprinkle torn mint and basil over top, followed by chopped peanuts, if using, and finish with the remaining lime juice.

My husband is a lover of all things sandwich. Anything between two pieces of bread makes him a happy man. However, if you don't need two slices of bread to make a meal complete, the tenderloin in this Vietnamese-style sandwich can also be sliced over top of the Spot Prawn Rice Noodle Salad (page 71) instead of spot prawns (making it Pork Rice Noodle Salad, I guess) or served with your favorite side dishes. Fresh veggies are just as good as pickled in this. Try julienned carrots, bell peppers, and celery for a delightful crunch. **MAKES 4 SANDWICHES**

Lemongrass Mint Pork Bahn Mi

2 garlic cloves, crushed

4 Tbsp **Lime** fused olive oil, divided

2 Tbsp **Lemongrass Mint** white balsamic vinegar

2 Tbsp soy sauce

1 Tbsp toasted sesame oil

1 tsp Sriracha hot sauce

1 (2 lb) pork tenderloin

4 long crusty buns (or baguette cut into 4 pieces)

¼ cup Simple Aioli (page 20)

Pickled carrot and daikon radish

Torn cilantro leaves

Torn fresh mint leaves

Jalapeño pepper (optional)

In a small bowl or liquid measuring cup, whisk together the garlic, 2 Tbsp of the olive oil, the balsamic, soy sauce, sesame oil, and Sriracha.

Place the tenderloin between two sheets of parchment paper and pound it lightly with a meat mallet. Rinse the tenderloin, pat it dry, and place it in a shallow roasting pan, just big enough to hold it. Drizzle with the marinade and use the back of a spoon to ensure the pork is fully and evenly coated. Flip it over, cover with plastic wrap, and place in the fridge for at least 4 hours, or up to overnight.

Heat a frying pan over medium-high heat. Add the tenderloin and its marinade and fry for 5–7 minutes per side, flipping after 2–3 minutes per side, until seared on all four sides, browned, and cooked through. This will take at least 7–10 minutes. Remove from the pan and let rest on a cutting board for 5 minutes, before carving into thin strips on the diagonal.

While the frying pan is still hot, cut the buns or baguette pieces in half, brush the insides with the remaining olive oil, and place cut side down on the frying pan for about 30 seconds. Place each bun on a serving plate, spread with aioli, and add sliced pork and pickled vegetables.

Top with cilantro, fresh mint, and a few slices of jalapeño, if using.

There are so many ways you can make these bars (see below), but the one constant is the coconut. I love this tropical version, but use whichever fruit and nuts you like best. And if you don't have wheat germ, try flax meal. **MAKES ONE (9- × 13-INCH) PAN**

Tropical Breakfast Bars

2 cups quick-cooking oats

1 cup all-purpose flour

³/₄ cup brown sugar, packed

¹/₂ cup wheat germ

¹/₂ tsp sea salt

¹/₂ tsp ground cinnamon

¹/₂ cup shredded unsweetened coconut

¹/₂ cup diced dried mango

¹/₄ cup diced dried pineapple

¹/₂ cup **Lime** fused olive oil

¹/₂ cup honey

2 eggs, slightly beaten

2 tsp pure vanilla extract

Try either **Lemon** or **Blood Orange** fused olive oil instead of **Lime** here, and use dried cherries, cranberries, blueberries, or figs for the fruit. Or try subbing ¹/₂ cup of the fruit with nuts and seeds.

Preheat the oven to 350°F. Line a 9- × 13-inch baking pan with parchment paper.

In a large bowl, toss the oats, flour, sugar, wheat germ, salt, and cinnamon with the coconut, mango, and pineapple to fully combine.

Add the olive oil, honey, eggs, and vanilla, and mix well. The mixture will be quite sticky when everything is fully combined.

Press the mixture into the prepared pan, using the back of a spoon with a drop of oil rubbed on it to spread it evenly and smooth the top. Bake for 25–30 minutes, until the top is golden.

Slice into 1- × 3-inch bars while still warm and allow them to cool completely in the pan before removing them. Peel off the parchment paper and separate the bars.

Store in an airtight container for up to 1 week, or in the freezer for up to 3 months, wrapped individually in plastic wrap or in an airtight container, with the layers separated by parchment paper.

There is something particularly satisfying about crunchy granola on top of a bowl of Greek yogurt first thing in the morning. And the flavor options are almost endless. See the variations listed below for some suggestions, but this is an ideal recipe for letting your culinary imagination run wild. **MAKES 8 CUPS**

Harvest Granola

4 cups rolled oats

1 cup mixed nuts

1 cup shredded unsweetened coconut

½ cup pumpkin seeds

¼ cup wheat germ

¼ cup flax seeds

¼ cup **extra virgin** olive oil

¼ cup **Maple** dark balsamic vinegar

¼ cup honey

2 egg whites

2 cups cubed mixed dried fruit (cranberries, cherries, blueberries, apricots, etc.)

SUGGESTED VARIETALS
Arbequina, Arbosana, Hojiblanca

Coconut Lime Granola Try combining **Lime** fused olive oil and **Pineapple** white balsamic vinegar with dried tropical fruit such as mango, papaya, and pineapple.

Cranberry Orange Granola Use **Cranberry Pear** white balsamic vinegar and **Blood Orange** fused olive oil with dried apricots and either dried cranberries or dried cherries.

Lemon Mango Granola Use **Lemon** fused olive oil and **Mango** white balsamic vinegar with dried guava and papaya.

Preheat the oven to 325°F. Line a large rimmed baking tray with parchment paper.

In a large mixing bowl, place the oats, nuts, coconut, pumpkin seeds, wheat germ, and flax seeds, and toss to combine.

In a small saucepan, place the olive oil, balsamic, and honey. Heat on low until the honey has dissolved, about 3 minutes. Pour this over the dry granola, tossing to thoroughly coat.

Beat the egg whites in a small bowl until frothy, add to the granola, and mix to evenly coat.

Spread the granola on the prepared baking tray and bake for 15 minutes. Using a large spatula, turn the granola and bake for another 15–20 minutes, until golden and toasted. Remove from the oven and let cool to room temperature. Break up into pieces, place in an airtight container with the dried fruit, and toss to combine. This will keep for 2–3 weeks.

Wild Dill Infused Olive Oil

Packed with flavor, **Wild Dill** infused olive oil is sure to please even herb-skeptics. This is my favorite oil to use on salmon, to make a creamy coleslaw, or to whisk into a ranch dressing. Garden fresh dill has a very short season, so I keep this fresh and delicious olive oil on hand to use anytime I have a dill hankering or I want the flavor of dill to be noticeable but not overpoweringly present. If you're a dill lover, this olive oil will be a staple. You'll find **Wild Dill** infused olive oil in the following recipes (and in several recipe variations throughout the book):

There is something so simple and satisfying about fish tacos. Hearty but not overly filling, these salmon tacos are the perfect weeknight meal to toss together, and—bonus!—they're amazing for lunch the next day. The **Wild Dill** infused olive oil keeps the salmon meat moist and soft and also helps the spices stay put during cooking. For an extra kick of dill, serve this with Creamy Dill Coleslaw (page 78). For an incredible simple salad that will last for a couple of days, replace the scallops in the Lemon Pomegranate Scallops on Greens with the salmon from this recipe. It's a heartier, less decadent protein option than scallops. **SERVES 4**

Salmon Tacos

1 lb salmon fillet

¼ cup + 1 Tbsp **Wild Dill** infused olive oil

2 Tbsp **Sicilian Lemon** white balsamic vinegar

1 Tbsp tomato paste

2 tsp ground cumin

1 tsp ground coriander

12 (each 6-inch) corn tortillas

1 cup shredded red cabbage

3 radishes

1 avocado

½ cup cilantro

1 cup Mango Jalapeño Salsa (page 293)

For a slightly brighter and spicier version, substitute the **Sicilian Lemon** white balsamic with **Honey Ginger**.

If you love cilantro more than dill, feel free to use **Cilantro & Onion** infused olive oil instead of the **Wild Dill**.

Preheat the oven to 400°F. Line a baking tray with parchment paper.

Rinse and pat dry the salmon, and then place it on the prepared baking tray.

In a small bowl, whisk together the ¼ cup olive oil, the balsamic, tomato paste, cumin, and coriander until fully combined. Brush this on the salmon to evenly coat the top. Bake for 15 minutes, until the salmon easily flakes apart and is cooked through. Remove from the oven.

Place the tortillas in a paper bag or wrap them in foil and warm them in the oven.

Toss the shredded cabbage with the remaining 1 Tbsp olive oil. Thinly slice the radishes, slice the avocado, and roughly chop the cilantro.

Remove the tortillas from the oven and place three on each serving plate.

Flake the salmon apart and evenly divide between the tortillas. Top with cabbage, radishes, and a few slices of avocado, then sprinkle with cilantro and a good dollop of salsa. Serve immediately.

Tacos are best enjoyed as soon as they are assembled, although the salmon on its own will keep for up to 3 days in the fridge in an airtight container.

On hot summer days, I crave this simple, cool, and refreshing slaw. I will make literally buckets of it and eat it all, totally unashamedly. I can't get enough. The **Wild Dill** infused olive oil adds a bright yet refreshing touch to the creamy cool yogurt and helps keep the cabbage crisp too. **SERVES 4 (OR 1 IF YOU'RE ME!)**

Creamy Dill Coleslaw

1 small head green cabbage
1 garlic clove
¾ cup Greek yogurt
2 Tbsp **Wild Dill** infused olive oil
1 Tbsp lemon juice
1 tsp sea salt

If you're a basil lover, substitute **Basil** infused olive oil for the **Wild Dill**.

If you're looking for something even more herb-forward, substitute **Rosemary** infused olive oil for the **Wild Dill**.

Love spice? Substitute **Harissa** or **Chipotle** for the **Wild Dill** infused olive oil.

Shred, or thinly slice, the cabbage and toss it to break up its layers. Mince the garlic and place it in the serving bowl. Add the yogurt, oil, lemon juice, and salt and whisk well to combine. Add the cabbage and toss to coat. Let sit for at least 1 hour to allow the flavors to develop.

This is best enjoyed within 2 days of being made. It keeps best in an airtight container in the fridge.

My favorite part of this breakfast dish is the hollandaise, hands down. I love hollandaise, and especially olive oil hollandaise. It is so simple to make and doesn't require melting butter, which means no ladling melting butter from a pot, of course. The trick is twofold: 1) have a pour spout on your olive oil bottle that pours in a steady stream, and 2) whisk as you pour. You can also pour it in a steady stream into a blender with the machine running and it will whip up perfectly in no time. **SERVES 4**

West Coast Eggs Benedict

HOLLANDAISE

4 egg yolks
2 tsp lemon juice
$^{1}/_{2}$ tsp sea salt
$^{3}/_{4}$ cup **Wild Dill** infused olive oil, divided

EGGS BENEDICT

2 Tbsp white wine vinegar
8 eggs
4 English muffins
8 Tbsp **extra virgin** olive oil
8 oz lox or hot- or cold-smoked salmon
2 avocados
1 small shallot

To make the hollandaise, place a saucepan of water to boil on the stove and place a bowl or pot on top to make a double boiler. Turn down the heat, allowing the water to simmer and the bowl on top to warm.

Remove the bowl from the simmering water, add the egg yolks, lemon juice, and sea salt, and whisk until the mixture is light and creamy in color and thick ribbons form as you whisk. Place the bowl back on the pot of simmering water and drizzle in about 1 tsp of the olive oil. Whisk it in, allowing it to completely emulsify with the yolk mixture. It will thicken as the oil is whisked in. Repeat with another 1 tsp of the oil. Next, slowly pour in the olive oil in a very fine stream, whisking constantly to incorporate. If the sauce stops thickening, stop adding olive oil and just whisk for 1–2 minutes, until it begins to thicken again. When that happens, you can resume adding the olive oil slowly. If the water is making the bowl too warm, remove it from the heat and continue adding and whisking, then place back over the heat in order to keep the bowl warm. Whisk until all the olive oil has been added and the sauce is thick and creamy in texture.

For a simple blender version, start in the same way, by warming a bowl over a saucepan of simmering water. After you've added the second teaspoon of olive oil and the sauce is starting to thicken, use a spatula to scrape the entire contents into the bowl of a blender and then start the blender running at medium-low speed. Remove the top of the blender lid so you can pour in the olive oil in a fine stream while the sauce is blending. Continue to blend until all of the olive oil is emulsified and the sauce is thick and creamy.

CONTINUED →

In the saucepan of water used to warm the bowl, add the wine vinegar and bring the liquid back up to a rolling boil before lowering the temperature so the water is very hot but not bubbling. Ensure there are at least 2 inches of water in the pot. Crack the first egg into a ramekin to add it easily to the water. Using a wooden spoon, swirl the water to make a vortex then slip the egg into the water. Using the spoon, fold any strings that may have formed over the yolk and cook for 4 minutes, for a soft to medium egg. Remove from the water with a slotted spoon and place on a plate to drain slightly and set a bit. Repeat with the remaining eggs.

To assemble the eggs benedict, slice the English muffins in half and toast lightly. Drizzle each muffin pair with 1 Tbsp of olive oil and top each half with some lox or smoked salmon. Slice the avocados and shallot and place a few slices of each on top of the salmon. Top with the egg and spoon hollandaise over top. Serve immediately.

This is best enjoyed as soon as it's made, as it doesn't keep well once assembled. The hollandaise will keep for about an hour. If you need to keep it longer, place a piece of plastic wrap over top and press it against the top of the sauce. When you're ready to serve, whisk the sauce and drizzle in 1 Tbsp of olive oil or so to loosen it up a bit and make it creamy again. If the sauce has cooled, place over a pot of boiling water and whisk to warm while whisking in the olive oil, being careful not to overheat, or you'll end up having scrambled eggs on top of your poached ones (sadly I'm speaking from experience!).

Tuscan Herb
Infused Olive Oil

Also known as the taste of the Italian countryside! With its heavenly combination of herbs, including basil, rosemary, and oregano, this oil is exquisite drizzled on pizza or pasta, or as a stand-alone dipping oil. Pair it with **Sicilian Lemon** white balsamic for the perfect base for your new favorite homemade Italian Caesar salad dressing. You'll find **Tuscan Herb** infused olive oil in the following recipes (and in several recipe variations throughout the book):

Delicious, creamy, and extra garlicky if you let it sit in the fridge for 10 minutes, this is the best Caesar dressing I have ever made. Need I say that the best way to enjoy this is with lettuce, cheese, bacon, and croutons? **MAKES ¾ CUP**

Italian Caesar Salad Dressing

2 garlic cloves, minced
1 egg yolk (use soft-boiled/pasteurized egg if you don't want to use raw)
½ cup **Tuscan Herb** infused olive oil
1 Tbsp **Sicilian Lemon** white balsamic vinegar
1 tsp Worcestershire sauce
½ tsp ground black pepper
½ tsp sea salt
Pinch dry mustard

Place all the ingredients in a small bowl, mix well until fully combined, and use immediately.

The perfect addition to a Caesar salad, these croutons are great on top of soup too. I leave the crusts on the bread for extra texture. I like to use a combination of dark rye, white, and whole wheat, but whatever is in the cupboard will do. **MAKES 4 CUPS**

Tuscan Herb Olive Oil Croutons

6 slices fresh or day-old bread
½ cup **Tuscan Herb** infused olive oil
1 tsp sea salt
½ tsp ground black pepper

Preheat the oven to 375°F.

Cut the bread into 1-inch cubes, place them in a large bowl, and toss with the other ingredients.

When the bread is evenly coated, place the cubes on a rimmed baking tray on the middle rack of the oven. Bake for 35 minutes, stirring a couple times to ensure even browning. They will keep in an airtight container at room temperature for 1 week.

This tasty egg dish was a Sunday night staple when I was in university. I'd make two: one for dinner for my roommate and me and the other for breakfast for the week. I love the combination of green onions, peppers, and ham, but it's great with broccoli and shredded chicken too. One thing that I didn't enjoy about my university frittata was that any herbs I tried to mix in always floated to the top and didn't mix into the dish. The **Tuscan Herb** infused olive oil solves that problem. **SERVES 4**

Herb, Ham, & Cheese Frittata

6 eggs
½ cup table (18%) cream or evaporated milk
¼ cup **Tuscan Herb** infused olive oil
½ tsp sea salt
¼ tsp ground black pepper
¼ cup chopped green onions
½ cup chopped red or green bell peppers, or a mix of colors
½ cup diced ham
1½ cups grated cheddar cheese, divided

If **Tuscan Herb** infused olive oil isn't in the cupboard, **Herbes de Provence**, **Rosemary**, **Wild Dill**, and **Basil** are just as tasty and will put a unique twist on this classic.

Preheat the oven to 350°F. Grease a 9-inch pie plate.

In a mixing bowl, beat the eggs, cream, and olive oil. Pour this mixture into the prepared pie plate.

Sprinkle the remaining ingredients over the egg mixture in the order listed, finishing with the cheese. Sprinkle half the cheese on top and poke it down a little so that it's covered with egg mixture. Then sprinkle the rest evenly over top.

Bake for 30–35 minutes, or until a knife inserted in the center comes out clean, to ensure the center is set. If the cheese is browning too quickly, cover it loosely with aluminum foil.

Allow to cool slightly and firm up a bit before serving warm.

This salad is the perfect size for lunch for one, and it doubles easily for a side salad for two for an evening meal. The herbaceous, tangy dressing, created from the **Tuscan Herb** infused olive oil and **Sicilian Lemon** white balsamic vinegar, soaks into the farro and makes it almost taste like pasta. The tomatoes and parsley make this hearty and delicious lunch super healthy too. **SERVES 1**

Mediterranean Farro Salad

½ cup farro
2 Tbsp **Tuscan Herb** infused olive oil
1 Tbsp **Sicilian Lemon** white balsamic vinegar
½ cup chopped flat-leaf parsley
1 cup grape tomatoes, halved
1 Tbsp diced onion
2 Tbsp crumbled feta cheese

For a lighter version, use **Herbes de Provence** or **Basil** infused olive oil. **Wild Dill** is ideal if you're looking for a refreshing feel.

If you're a cilantro lover, substitute the **Tuscan Herb** with **Cilantro & Onion** infused olive oil and use chopped cilantro instead of parsley.

Cook the farro in 1¼ cups boiling water, following the package directions. Let cool then fluff in the saucepan.

In a small bowl, whisk the olive oil and balsamic with the parsley (but keep a little bit of parsley for your garnish!).

Add the farro and toss to combine well. Toss in the tomatoes and onion and continue to mix well. Top with the feta and a sprinkle of parsley.

Enjoy fresh, or let it sit in the fridge overnight to allow the flavors to develop.

Bacon, Cheddar, Egg, Avocado, and Tomato. As any brunch fan in the vicinity of Victoria, BC, will tell you, it's the best breakfast sandwich ever made. Eat often. **MAKES 2 SANDWICHES**

BC-EAT Breakfast Sandwich

½ lb extra-thick bacon
2 eggs
Aged cheddar cheese
4 slices rustic bread or 2 ciabatta buns
2 Tbsp **Tuscan Herb** infused olive oil
1 avocado, sliced
1 large tomato, sliced
Sea salt

In a large frying pan, cook the bacon until crispy. Place it on paper towel to absorb any grease, and set aside.

Leave about 2 Tbsp of the bacon grease in the frying pan. Fry the eggs in this grease over medium heat, breaking the yolks to let them cook fully.

Place the bread on a cookie sheet and preheat the broiler. Drizzle each piece of bread with the olive oil and top with two slices of cheese. Toast under the broiler until the cheese is melted and just starting to bubble.

Top two slices of the bread with bacon, a fried egg, and slices of avocado and tomato. Finish each with a sprinkle of salt and another slice of toasted cheesy bread.

Serve immediately.

The roasted garlic in this Alfredo kicks the whole dish up a notch, especially when combined with the **Tuscan Herb** infused olive oil. I love this with homemade fettuccini, but it's also great with rice and some veggies. Or toss it with some cooked penne in a roasting pan, sprinkle with cheese, and bake for 15 minutes at 350°F for a delicious baked pasta. **SERVES 2**

Tuscan Chicken Alfredo Sauce

1 whole bulb garlic
¼ cup **Tuscan Herb** infused olive oil, divided
2 boneless, skinless chicken breasts
½ tsp sea salt
½ tsp ground black pepper
2 Tbsp all-purpose flour
1½ cups whole milk
¾ cup grated mozzarella cheese
½ cup grated Parmesan cheese

> If **Tuscan Herb** isn't in the cupboard, this recipe works equally well with **Basil** or **Rosemary** infused olive oil, especially if you want a more intense flavor of just the one herb.
>
> If you're a parsley lover, **Milanese Gremolata** infused olive oil is also lovely here, or try **Herbes de Provence** for a French twist.

Preheat the oven to 375°F.

Carefully cut the top off the garlic bulb, only just exposing the tops of the cloves. Place in a small ramekin, and drizzle 2 tsp of the olive oil over the top of the bulb. Cover with parchment paper or aluminum foil and roast for 30 minutes, until the bulb is squishy and soft. Set aside.

Meanwhile, pat dry the chicken, place it in a small roasting pan, season with the salt and pepper, and roast for 20 minutes until the internal temperature is 170°F. Remove from the oven and let rest for a few minutes before slicing.

In a medium-sized saucepan, heat the remaining olive oil over medium heat and mix in the flour. Cook this roux until you have a creamy, smooth paste.

In another saucepan, heat the milk to a simmer, being careful not to let it boil.

Slowly add the hot milk to the roux, whisking constantly. Once all the milk has been added, remove the pan from the heat, squish the bulb of roasted garlic to push the roasted garlic flesh into the sauce, and whisk to fully incorporate. Whisk in the mozzarella and Parmesan cheeses and let them sit for a few minutes to allow them to melt before whisking to incorporate. Meanwhile, chop the chicken into small pieces (about 1-inch chunks are perfect). Whisk the sauce again, add the chicken, and stir. Season with additional salt and pepper if desired.

Basil Infused Olive Oil

The distinctive, raw flavor of fresh basil is infused into a fresh **extra virgin** olive oil that is perfect for tossing with pasta or steamed vegetables, drizzling on fall soups or over soft cheeses, or as a base for a delicious bright pesto. You'll find **Basil** infused olive oil in the following recipes (and in several recipe variations throughout the book):

The **Basil** infused olive oil adds a unique sweet tanginess to this salad and complements the tomatoes and olives, while the **Neapolitan Herb** dark balsamic vinegar adds a zesty freshness and flavor with little heat. This superb combination works really well in this dish. **SERVES 4 (WITH LEFTOVERS)**

Picnic Pasta Salad

1 lb dried farfalle (bow-tie), penne, or
   macaroni (elbow) pasta
½ cup **Basil** infused olive oil, divided
¼ cup **Neapolitan Herb** dark balsamic
   vinegar
2 cups halved cherry tomatoes
1 cup pitted and sliced olives
1 cup chopped cucumber, unpeeled
1 cup chopped bell pepper
2 Tbsp chopped fresh oregano or
   curly-leaf parsley
Sea salt and ground black pepper

Substitute **Tuscan Herb** infused olive oil for the **Basil**, and **Sicilian Lemon** white balsamic for the **Neapolitan Herb** dark balsamic for a sweet and savory version.

For a delicious sweet and herbaceous version, use **Herbes de Provence** infused olive oil instead of the **Basil** and **Apple** white balsamic in place of the **Neapolitan Herb**.

If you're a mushroom lover, add ½ cup of chopped fresh mushrooms, and use **Wild Mushroom & Sage** for the olive oil and **Honey Ginger** white balsamic for the balsamic.

Bring a large saucepan of salted water to a boil, toss in the pasta, and boil according to package directions until not quite al dente. (Try to keep the pasta on the harder side of al dente, as the dressing will also soften it.) Drain the pasta, rinse it under cold water, and place in a large serving bowl. Toss with 6 Tbsp of the olive oil and the entire ¼ cup of balsamic.

Preheat the oven to 325°F.

Place the cherry tomato halves in a single layer on a parchment-covered baking tray. Drizzle with the remaining 2 Tbsp of olive oil, and roast for 25 minutes, turning once to ensure they are evenly roasted. Remove from the oven and let cool slightly.

Add the chopped olives, cucumber, and pepper to the cooled pasta and toss in the roasted tomatoes to ensure that everything is well coated in the dressing. Garnish with the oregano or parsley, and season to taste with salt and pepper.

The tanginess of grapefruit and the sweet crunch of watermelon are just waiting for an invitation to a potluck. This salad is crisp, sweet, and tart all at the same time, with every ingredient shining through. I really love the addition of the jalapeño. In addition to bringing a touch of surprise, it adds intensity to the flavor of the watermelon and the coolness of the mint. **Basil** infused olive oil is my favorite oil for this salad, as it pulls everything together perfectly. **SERVES 4 AS A SIDE**

Grapefruit Watermelon Salad

4 sprigs mint
4 cups cubed watermelon
1 jalapeño, seeded and chopped
1/2 cup crumbled feta cheese, divided
3 Tbsp **Basil** infused olive oil
1 Tbsp **Grapefruit** white balsamic vinegar
Sea salt

For a more savory option, the **Lemongrass Mint** white balsamic is a great substitute for the **Grapefruit**.

Remove the mint leaves from their sprigs and roll each one lengthwise. Cut them into a chiffonade to create ribbons.

Place the watermelon cubes in a serving bowl, toss with the jalapeño and sprinkle with the mint and half the feta. Drizzle with the olive oil and balsamic and toss gently to coat.

Top with the remaining feta and a few pinches of sea salt. Let rest for half an hour before serving to allow the dressing to soak in.

For the more traditional version of this recipe, which uses tomatoes, see page 163. But why wait until tomatoes are in season? Strawberries and basil are such a lovely match, and this version will be more than enough to see you through to peak tomato season. **SERVES 2–4**

Springtime Strawberry Insalata Caprese

1 cup cherry-sized bocconcini cheese
1 pint small sweet strawberries, hulled and
   sliced
2 Tbsp **Basil** infused olive oil
2 Tbsp **Traditional** dark balsamic vinegar
10–15 large fresh basil leaves
Sea salt and ground black pepper

In a large bowl, toss the bocconcini with the strawberries, drizzle with the olive oil and balsamic, and top with the basil leaves. Season to taste with salt and pepper.

For a fun appetizer, thread a toothpick with 1 strawberry, 1 basil leaf, and 1 piece of bocconcini. Arrange on a plate and drizzle with olive oil and balsamic. Sprinkle with salt and pepper to taste.

This personal favorite came via my mentor, Alessandra, one of the most incredible women I know. She raved about it, I rave about it, and you will rave about it. It's hearty, filling, and keeps your hunger under control all afternoon. It's a great addition to a summer barbecue but is also a great winter lunch. It keeps refrigerated extremely well but is best eaten right out of the bowl with the closest fork you can find. **SERVES 2**

Kale Quinoa Salad

½ cup uncooked quinoa
1 small bunch kale (4–6 leaves)
4 Tbsp **Basil** infused olive oil, divided
2 Tbsp **Raspberry** dark balsamic vinegar
2 tsp grainy Dijon mustard
2 tsp honey
1 shallot, diced
½ cup pecans
½ cup dried blueberries
¼ cup crumbled feta cheese

Another herbaceous and refreshing combo is **Herbes de Provence** infused olive oil with **Grapefruit** or **Apple** white balsamic.

For a fruitier version of this salad, substitute **Lemon** fused olive oil for the **Basil** and **Pomegranate** dark balsamic for the **Raspberry**.

For a more herbaceous version, substitute **Rosemary** infused olive oil for the **Basil** and use **Black Cherry** dark balsamic instead of the **Raspberry**.

Bring 1½ cups of water to a boil in a small saucepan over high heat. Rinse the quinoa well, then add it to the boiling water. Stir gently then turn down the heat to medium and simmer, partially covered, for 15 minutes, or until the quinoa is soft and the water has been absorbed.

Remove the stems from the kale and tear the leaves into bite-sized pieces or cut them into ribbons for a prettier presentation. Toss the kale into a serving bowl, drizzle 1 Tbsp of the olive oil over it, and massage the leaves well. As you rub the oil in, the kale will turn from a dull green to a shiny, bright green.

In a small bowl or Mason jar, place the remaining olive oil, balsamic, mustard, and honey to taste. Whisk or shake well to combine.

Fluff the warm quinoa in the pot, drizzle half the dressing over it, and mix well. The warm quinoa will soak up the dressing, which will add lots of flavor to your salad.

Place the quinoa on the kale and gently toss. Sprinkle with the shallot, pecans, blueberries, and feta cheese. Drizzle with the remaining dressing before serving.

You can make this soup in massive batches, omitting the cream, and then freeze it, puréed or unpuréed, for winter. Let it thaw, purée if necessary, and then reheat in a pot on the stove, adding the cream right before serving. **SERVES 4**

Butternut Squash & Apple Bisque

1 medium butternut squash
4 Tbsp **Basil** infused olive oil, divided
2 shallots, minced
2 garlic cloves, minced
2 Golden Delicious apples, peeled and diced
1 bay leaf
2 tsp grated ginger
½ tsp ground turmeric
4 cups chicken stock
1 cup table (18%) cream
Sea salt and ground black pepper
Tuscan Herb Olive Oil Croutons (optional, page 83)

For a softer and less basil-forward version, use **Herbes de Provence** infused olive oil instead of the **Basil**.

Preheat the oven to 375°F. Line a rimmed baking tray with parchment paper.

Peel and slice the squash in half vertically, slice each half (slices should be 1–1½ inches thick), and place on the prepared baking tray. Drizzle with 3 Tbsp of the olive oil, turning to coat each piece well. Roast for 25 minutes.

In a soup pot, sauté the shallots and garlic in the remaining 1 Tbsp of olive oil for a few minutes until tender. Add the squash, apples, bay leaf, ginger, turmeric, and then the chicken stock. Bring to a boil, turn down the heat, and let simmer, covered, for 30 minutes, until the squash and apples are very tender. (You can also throw it into a slow cooker and let it cook on low for 6–8 hours, if you prefer.) Remove the bay leaf.

Let the soup cool slightly and then use an immersion or regular blender to blend it until creamy and smooth. Add the cream and reheat gently, stirring well. Season with salt and pepper to taste, and garnish with a drizzle of olive oil and a sprinkle of croutons, if using.

I first fell in love with soft pecorino over the breakfast table in Marche with my Aunt Maria. Pecorino cheese is actually native to Fano. It is made from ewe's milk and comes in hard and soft varieties. Soft pecorino can be found in most Mediterranean delis and is quite different from hard pecorino, which is similar to Parmesan. It has a lovely subtle sharpness that brightens the spinach and complements the basil in this pesto. However, both Parmesan and Romano work well in this recipe, so don't fret if you can't find soft pecorino. **MAKES 2 CUPS**

Pesto with Soft Pecorino

2 garlic cloves

1 tsp sea salt

3 Tbsp lemon juice

¾ cup baby spinach, large stems removed

¾ cup arugula

½ cup **Basil** infused olive oil

¾ cup finely grated pecorino cheese (or Parmesan or Romano)

Peel and roughly chop the garlic, place it in a large mortar, add the salt followed by the lemon juice, and gently grind with the pestle until the garlic is well mashed.

Wash and dry the baby spinach, tear roughly, and add to the mortar with the arugula. Drizzle in some of the olive oil, mix it in well with a small spatula, and repeat until you've used all the oil and the pesto has become a smooth paste. Mix in the cheese and serve.

This will keep in an airtight container in the fridge for about 1 week. You can also freeze it without the cheese.

Garlic Infused Olive Oil

The name says it all . . . GARLIC! Add to mashed potatoes, roasted vegetables, or hearty soups and stews, or just drizzle it on toast to tantalize your taste buds. You'll find **Garlic** infused olive oil in the following recipes (and in several recipe variations throughout the book):

The preserved lemons in this simple hummus make it extra flavorful. Spread this on flatbread (page 22) or serve with crostini or pita chips. You can make your own preserved lemons, of course, but if you're using store-bought, look for small whole ones. Sliced preserved lemons are generally made from really large lemons and are often a bit bitter. If you don't want to use preserved lemons, use 1 tsp Japanese toasted sesame oil to add a nutty flavor. And the trick to extra smooth and creamy hummus? Peel your chickpeas. Seriously. It's worth the extra effort. **MAKES 2 CUPS**

Olive Oil & Preserved Lemon Hummus

1 (19 oz) can chickpeas, rinsed and drained

½ cup tahini

½ cup Garlic infused olive oil

2 wedges preserved lemon (about 1 inch wide)

Sea salt and ground black pepper

Robust single varietal **extra virgin** olive oil, for drizzling (**Arbosana**, **Coratina**, or **Manzanillo** are lovely here.)

To make a party-perfect hummus, double the recipe and substitute Chipotle infused olive oil for half the Garlic infused olive oil, plus extra for drizzling over top.

Place the chickpeas in a bowl to peel. Take each chickpea and squeeze and rub it gently between your fingers. The chickpea should pop out of its skin. Put the skinned chickpeas in a bowl and discard the skins.

Pulse the chickpeas a few times in a food processor, then add the tahini, Garlic infused olive oil, and preserved lemon with ½ cup water. Blend for 20–30 seconds then scrape down the sides of the bowl. If the hummus is still quite chunky, add about 2 Tbsp of water and blend for another 30–40 more seconds. Repeat if necessary.

When the hummus is creamy and still thick, transfer it to a wide bowl, top with a sprinkle of salt and pepper, and drizzle generously with a robust **extra virgin** olive oil.

This will keep in an airtight container in the fridge for up to 1 week.

As a kid, I never liked salads like this (for some strange reason), but now I love this salad. I don't recommend using fresh garlic in this recipe because it can get very overwhelming, especially if you keep it in the fridge. The **Garlic** infused olive oil and **Sicilian Lemon** balsamic vinegar add a softness that doesn't stomp all over the flavor of the beans. The combination of chickpeas, red kidney beans, and green beans gives it great color. **SERVES 4 AS A SIDE**

Three Bean Salad

1½ cups canned chickpeas, rinsed and drained
1 cup canned red kidney beans, rinsed and drained
1 cup snapped green beans, cooked and cooled
1 Tbsp chopped chives
1 Tbsp finely chopped fresh flat-leaf parsley
¼ cup **Garlic** infused olive oil
¼ cup **Sicilian Lemon** white balsamic vinegar

If you don't have Garlic infused olive oil, **Tuscan Herb, Rosemary**, or **Dill** infused olive oils are lovely here as well.

Toss the chickpeas and kidney beans in a large bowl with the string beans and sprinkle with the fresh herbs.

In a small bowl, whisk together the olive oil and balsamic. Drizzle this dressing over the salad and toss well to coat. Let sit, covered, in the fridge for at least 1 hour before serving to allow the flavors to develop.

Boiling the potatoes before grilling them ensures fluffy, soft centers and crispy outsides with no burning. It takes a few extra minutes but really is worthwhile. The olive oil is absorbed into the partly cooked potatoes, giving them a delicious spicy touch all the way through. These are the perfect accompaniment to sausages or burgers and grilled corn, but they also make wonderful pan fries for breakfast. **SERVES 2 AS A SIDE**

Barbecue Garlic Potato Wedges

½ lb potatoes (russet or Yukon Gold work best here)
3 Tbsp **Garlic** infused olive oil
1 tsp sea salt

For a less garlic-forward version, use **Tuscan Herb** or **Rosemary** infused olive oil instead of the **Garlic**.

For a spicy version, use **Harissa** or **Chipotle** infused olive oil instead of the **Garlic** to add some heat.

Wash and scrub the potatoes and slice them lengthwise into wedges. Place them in a large saucepan of boiling water and boil until just tender but not soft, 5–7 minutes. Drain and rinse with cold water. Pat dry with paper towel.

Heat the grill to high and give it a brush to ensure it is clean. This will prevent the potatoes from sticking. (I guess you should clean the grill before using it anyway!)

Drizzle the wedges with the olive oil and toss to evenly coat. Place on the hot grill for 5–10 minutes, turning 2–3 times to evenly brown and crisp the outside. If roasting in the oven, place the tossed potato wedges on the parchment covered baking sheet and roast for 25–30 minutes until golden and crisp. Place on a serving platter and sprinkle with sea salt.

This is the perfect summer appetizer for a patio party. I admit that they are a bit fiddly to make, but I promise they are well worth the effort. And they keep well in the fridge for a day or two, so you can make them ahead of time. The **Garlic** infused olive oil makes the filling creamy smooth, helps the cheese whip together, and complements the capers really well. It also adds an evenness that minced garlic couldn't provide. **SERVES 4–6 AS AN APPETIZER**

Mediterranean Stuffed Cherry Tomatoes

24 cherry tomatoes
1 (8 oz) package cream cheese
¼ cup crumbled feta cheese
3 Tbsp **Garlic** infused olive oil
2 Tbsp capers
1 Tbsp chopped fresh oregano, plus 24 small leaves for garnish

> If you'd prefer a less intense garlic element, use **Tuscan Herb** instead of the **Garlic** infused olive oil for a full herbaceous flavor and more balance in terms of the garlic. **Rosemary** infused olive oil is also a lovely alternative to the **Garlic**.

Rinse the tomatoes and pat them dry. Slice a sliver from the bottom of each tomato so that they sit upright, then take a sharp small paring knife and cut a small circle around the top of the tomato where the stem attaches. Cut down and in to make a cone shape. Remove this cone and use a small spoon to remove any seeds.

In a medium mixing bowl, mix together the cream cheese, feta, olive oil, capers, and oregano until smooth and well combined.

Transfer the cheese mixture to a piping bag fitted with a small star tip. Fill the tomatoes with cheese mixture and top with an oregano leaf.

Serve immediately or chill until needed.

Wild Mushroom & Sage Infused Olive Oil

This **extra virgin** olive oil is a delicious combination of fresh, herbaceous sage and earthy, savory wild mushrooms. Try it drizzled over steak, mashed potatoes, or soup, or in risotto, stuffing, or aioli. You'll find **Wild Mushroom & Sage** infused olive oil in the following recipes (and in several recipe variations throughout the book):

The traditional version of this recipe is labor-intensive and time-consuming to say the least. This version is much easier to make and just as tasty—and the ravioli keep extremely well in the freezer. Just freeze them on a parchment-lined baking tray, then transfer them to airtight bags to store. You can cook them from frozen, following the directions below. Note that you'll need a ravioli mold for this.   MAKES 40–45 RAVIOLI (ABOUT 4 SERVINGS)

Ricotta Ravioli with Caramelized Shallots

³/₄ cup fresh ricotta cheese

7 eggs, divided

¹/₄ cup finely diced fresh or dried wild mushrooms

¹/₃ cup grated Parmesan cheese

Sea salt

3 cups all-purpose flour, divided

4 shallots

¹/₄ cup **Wild Mushroom & Sage** infused olive oil, divided

1 Tbsp brown sugar

6–8 fresh sage leaves

Ground black pepper

Talk about choice! Try using **Garlic** infused olive oil, with 2 Tbsp chopped fresh rosemary instead of sage, or **Rosemary** infused olive oil with 1 tsp fresh thyme leaves and 1 Tbsp fresh chopped oregano.

If you're feeling rushed (or just lazy), use **Tuscan Herb** infused olive oil without fresh herbs. Chanterelles, morels, and shiitake are all lovely here, but if you're not a fan of wild mushrooms, add ¹/₄ cup more cheese—mozzarella works well—instead.

Line a sieve with cheesecloth and place it over a bowl. Place the ricotta on the cheesecloth, bring up the corners, twist them together, and squeeze firmly to remove any extra water from the cheese. You can also let the cheese drain in the fridge overnight if you'd rather not squeeze it.

In a small mixing bowl, whisk 1 egg, then stir in the diced mushrooms, ricotta, and Parmesan. Season with a bit of sea salt and set aside in the fridge.

In a medium mixing bowl, whisk 1 of the remaining eggs. Add ½ cup of the flour, kneading well with your hands until completely smooth. Repeat with the remaining 5 eggs and the flour. You'll most probably need all of the flour listed, but if you have any left over you can use it for dusting.

Cut the dough into thirds. Use a pasta maker or roll out each section in an 1/8-inch-thick sheet (some people like to roll it between sheets of parchment paper) and flour each side well to keep it soft while making the ravioli.

Line a rimmed baking tray with parchment paper and sprinkle liberally with flour.

Lay a sheet of pasta over a ravioli mold and gently press in the spaces to make little cups for the filling. The sheet needs to be just over twice as long as the mold. Place 1 tsp of ricotta-mushroom filling in each cup and fold the long end of the pasta sheet over top to make the lids. Gently press down on the pasta, then roll a rolling pin over the top. You may need someone to hold down the far side of the mold when rolling the opposite end, so it doesn't flip or jump off the counter. Gently remove the individual ravioli from the mold, dust them with flour, and sit them on the prepared baking tray. Repeat with the remaining pasta and filling.

Carefully slice the shallots into half-moons and place them in a frying pan with half the olive oil. Cook over medium heat for 3 minutes, until soft. Sprinkle with the sugar and continue to cook until they are brown and caramelized, 2–3 minutes. Remove from the heat.

Bring a very large saucepan of well-salted (salted like the sea!) water to a boil, add the ravioli, stirring gently to avoid sticking, and 1 cup of cold, unsalted water. Bring the water back to a boil and add another cup of cold, unsalted water. Bring back to a boil again and strain out the ravioli. This should take 3–4 minutes. Adding the cold water prevents the ravioli from breaking as they cook.

Place the ravioli in a serving bowl.

Place the shallots back on medium heat and add the remaining olive oil. When sizzling, add the sage leaves and let them crisp, about 1 minute. Pour this shallot mixture over the ravioli, toss gently, and serve.

Omelets are truly great breakfast companions, because they can be stuffed with a whole number of delights. I use button mushrooms and peppers here, but try spinach and feta and mushrooms, or goat cheese for a creamy twist. The oil adds a fluffiness to the eggs and helps the herbs fully incorporate into the mixture, giving a smooth, even flavor. Try serving this with Pan-Fried Potatoes (page 23) on the side! **MAKES 1 LARGE OMELET**

Simple Breakfast Omelet

2 Tbsp **Wild Mushroom & Sage** infused olive oil, divided
¼ cup chopped button mushrooms
1 Tbsp chopped green onions
1 Tbsp chopped fresh curly-leaf parsley
3 eggs
2 Tbsp grated white cheddar cheese

In a small omelet pan, or 8-inch frying pan, warm 1 Tbsp of the olive oil over medium heat. Sauté the veggies in the oil until just tender.

Beat the eggs with the remaining 1 Tbsp of oil and pour them over the veggies. Let cook for 1 minute, sprinkle with the cheese, and fold the omelet in half. Let it cook for another minute before serving.

For a different spin, replace the button mushrooms and **Wild Mushroom & Sage** infused oil with the following combinations (in the same volume):

* Bell peppers + **Chipotle** or **Harissa** infused olive oil

* Diced ham or chicken + **Rosemary** infused olive oil

* Smoked salmon, shredded + **Wild Dill** infused olive oil

* Spinach + **Herbes de Provence** infused olive oil

* Tomatoes + **Tuscan Herb** infused olive oil

* Zucchini + **Milanese Gremolata** infused olive oil

Stuffing is too delightful to be reserved for Thanksgiving or Christmas; it deserves to be enjoyed more often. I love to pack this stuffing into muffin tins and serve it with hot beef sandwiches (a great way to use up any leftovers from the Roast Beef with Rosemary Lemon Glaze on page 138). You can also pack it into a crown pork roast or serve it alongside a perfectly roasted turkey. **MAKES 8 CUPS (OR ENOUGH TO STUFF A STANDARD TURKEY)**

Wild Mushroom & Ginger Sausage Stuffing

1 large onion, chopped

2 garlic cloves, minced

2 stalks celery, chopped

1/4 cup plus 2 Tbsp **Wild Mushroom & Sage** infused olive oil

1 lb Italian sausage, casings removed

4 eggs

1 cup vegetable stock

1/4 cup **Honey Ginger** white balsamic vinegar

5 cups fresh bread crumbs

1 cup chopped dried apricots

1/2 cup fresh cranberries

2 Tbsp roughly torn sage leaves

For a less mushroom-forward version, use **Herbes de Provence** infused olive oil instead of the **Wild Mushroom & Sage**, **Apple** white balsamic vinegar instead of the **Honey Ginger**, and chopped apple for the dried apricots.

Preheat the oven to 350°F. Lightly oil a 7- × 11-inch baking dish.

In a small frying pan, sauté the onion, garlic, and celery in the 2 Tbsp olive oil over medium heat until almost translucent, about 2 minutes. Add the sausage meat and brown it in the onion mixture until translucent, about 5 minutes. You shouldn't need to break it up unless you like it really fine.

In a large bowl, beat the eggs with the stock, balsamic, and remaining 1/4 cup of olive oil. Gently mix in the bread crumbs, apricots, cranberries, and sage leaves. Add the sausage mixture and toss to combine, ensuring the bread is well soaked in the egg mixture.

Press the stuffing mixture into the baking dish, cover tightly with aluminum foil, and bake for 45 minutes. Remove the foil and bake uncovered for 7 minutes to let the top crisp. Let stand for 10 minutes before serving.

If you want to try baking this in a muffin tin, just oil the muffin cups and proceed as above, baking for 20 minutes.

This salad is perfect for mushroom lovers. Any and all of your favorite wild mushrooms can be used in this salad. The **Honey Ginger** balsamic vinegar brightens the rich, mellow flavor of the mushrooms, and the barley adds body and a delightful nutty texture. **SERVES 4**

Warm Pearl Barley Salad with Wild Mushrooms

2 1/2 cups vegetable stock
3/4 cup uncooked pearl barley
1/2 cup **Honey Ginger** white balsamic vinegar
1/3 cup **Wild Mushroom & Sage** infused
   olive oil
2 tsp Dijon mustard
Coarse salt and ground black pepper
2 cups fresh wild mushrooms, cleaned and
   stems removed
2 cups baby spinach, large stems removed
1/2 cup crumbled goat cheese

Fill a saucepan with vegetable stock and bring to a boil over medium-high heat. Rinse the barley well in a fine mesh strainer, add it to the boiling stock, and turn down the heat to low, stirring once to ensure the barley isn't sticking. Let the barley simmer, covered, for 15–20 minutes, or until all the water has been absorbed. Remove from the heat and fluff with a fork.

In a small bowl, place the balsamic, olive oil, Dijon, and salt and pepper to taste. Whisk until emulsified into a dressing.

In a large frying pan set off the heat, toss the mushrooms with half the dressing. Sauté the mushrooms over medium heat until tender and most of the dressing has evaporated, about 15 minutes.

In a large bowl, fluff the cooked barley with the remaining dressing.

Toss the spinach in with the mushrooms to heat and wilt only slightly, then add to the barley.

Top with crumbled goat cheese before serving.

Roasted acorn squash is particularly lovely because the squash becomes its own bowl, leaving you with very little clean-up—tasty and practical. This recipe is pictured with the Honey-Glazed Chicken on page 53. **SERVES 4 AS A SIDE**

Wild Mushroom & Sage Roasted Acorn Squash

1 acorn squash

4 Tbsp **Wild Mushroom & Sage** infused olive oil

2 Tbsp **Honey Ginger** white balsamic vinegar

1 tsp flaky sea salt

If you're looking for some tang to go with the sweetness, a robust single varietal **extra virgin** olive oil, like **Coratina** or **Manzanillo** or a robust **Picual** with **Blackberry Ginger** dark balsamic is a delicious combo.

This is a great recipe if you're feeling experimental. Try **Blood Orange** fused olive oil with either **Cranberry Pear** white balsamic or **Cinnamon Pear** dark balsamic for a fruity twist.

Preheat the oven to 375°F.

Using a large knife cut the squash in half vertically, remove seeds, and rinse the flesh. Place the squash cut side down on a cutting board and slice into 1-inch-thick slices.

Prepare a baking sheet with parchment paper and arrange the squash in a single layer.

In a small bowl, whisk together the oil and vinegar and using a basting brush, coat the squash evenly with a third of the marinade, then turn the pieces over and brush again.

Place the baking sheet in preheated oven and roast for 15-20 minutes. Remove from oven, turn the pieces of squash over again, baste with the olive oil and vinegar glaze, then drizzle the remaining on top and into the center of the squash. Roast an additional 15 minutes. Remove from oven and sprinkle with sea salt. Serve immediately.

Chipotle Infused Olive Oil

Chipotle peppers are known more for their smokiness than their heat, making this oil a perfect pairing for Mexican dishes. Drizzle this over anything in need of an extra zap of flavor, whether it's Mexican or not: tacos, salsa, roasted potatoes, aioli, you name it. You'll find **Chipotle** infused olive oil in the following recipes (and in several recipe variations throughout the book):

This marinade can serve multiple purposes. You can use it as directed to marinate steak, or you can mix it into ground beef for burgers. Actually, it's a great base for all things ground beef. Try tossing it into a frying pan and heating until its onions are sizzling, then add 1 lb of ground beef and brown it to make an amazing base for a rich chili or ragout, or the beginnings of a taco salad. This is also delicious drizzled on burgers, brushed on salmon, or paired with steak topped with blue cheese. **MAKES ³/₄ CUP**

Espresso Chipotle Grill Marinade

¹/₄ cup **Chipotle** infused olive oil
¹/₄ cup **Espresso** dark balsamic vinegar
2 Tbsp lime juice
2 Tbsp minced red onion
1 Tbsp minced garlic
1 Tbsp Dutch-process cocoa powder
2 tsp sea salt
1 tsp ground black pepper

Chocolate or **Red Apple** dark balsamic can also be used for this marinade. I prefer the **Red Apple** to marinate pork; **Chocolate** is great for both pork and beef. **Pomegranate** dark balsamic is lovely with lamb, and for a more complex flavor, use **Harissa** infused olive oil instead of the **Chipotle**.

Mix all the ingredients well and place them in a resealable plastic bag or plastic container with up to 2 lb of your favorite meat, poultry, or even vegetables. Marinate in the fridge for 1–2 hours, or up to overnight for meat.

This marinade will keep in an airtight container in the fridge for up to 1 week.

This salad is a real all-rounder: it's fun, it's bright, it's smoky, it's creamy, it's spicy, and it's hearty too. If you're not keen on eating pork, try chicken or prawns instead. Buttermilk is great here because of its natural thickness and tangy flavor. If you don't have any, you can also make your own version by adding 1 Tbsp lemon juice to whole or 2% milk to make ½ cup total; let it sit for about 5 minutes before using. **SERVES 4**

Spicy Pork Salad with Chipotle Buttermilk Dressing

1 (2–3 lb) pork tenderloin

2 Tbsp **Chipotle** infused olive oil

1 tsp sea salt

1 tsp ground black pepper

½ cup buttermilk

¼ cup Chipotle Aioli (page 20)

1 Tbsp grainy Dijon mustard

2 Tbsp diced red onion

1 garlic clove, minced

1 head red leaf lettuce, trimmed and
    chopped

2 plum tomatoes, chopped and rinsed to
    remove seeds

¼ cup frozen corn kernels, thawed and
    dried

½ cup grated cheddar cheese

If you want to tone down the spice of the dressing, use **Rosemary**, **Wild Dill**, or **Garlic** infused olive oil for a more classic feel. Or you can use traditional aioli rather than chipotle.

Preheat the oven to 450°F. Line a baking dish large enough to hold the tenderloin with parchment paper.

Lightly pound the tenderloin with a meat mallet until it is 1 inch thick. Place it in the prepared baking dish, drizzle with the olive oil, and sprinkle with the salt and pepper. Rub everything in to evenly coat the tenderloin.

Bake, uncovered, for 15–20 minutes, turning once so it cooks evenly. Insert a meat thermometer to ensure it is done (145°F). Remove from the oven and let rest for 10 minutes.

Meanwhile, prepare the dressing. In a medium bowl, whisk the buttermilk, aioli, and Dijon with the red onion and garlic. Season to taste with salt and pepper, and let it sit for a few minutes to allow the buttermilk to coagulate and the flavors to develop.

In a large bowl, or in individual serving bowls, toss the lettuce, tomatoes, corn, and cheese. Reserve 1 Tbsp of the buttermilk dressing and drizzle the rest over the salad. Toss to combine.

Cut the pork into 1-inch cubes, sprinkle them over the salad, and drizzle with the reserved 1 Tbsp of dressing. Serve immediately.

I love harvest time: Farmers' markets are abundant with colorful produce, the kitchen table fruit bowl is overflowing, and the garden is exploding with tasty ingredients. Roasting tomatoes is a great way to use up some of the season-end produce, and this salsa is the perfect vehicle to showcase them. Try this alongside Lime & Cilantro Guacamole (page 69) and Mango Jalapeño Salsa (page 293) for a lovely trio of dips. **MAKES 3 CUPS**

Roasted Tomato Salsa

1 lb Roma or cherry tomatoes
2 green or red bell peppers
1 large onion
3–4 garlic cloves
2 Tbsp **Chipotle** infused olive oil (or more to taste)
2 Tbsp lime juice
Sea salt

Extra virgin olive oil, **Lime, Cilantro & Onion**, or **Garlic** would all work well with this recipe. Try Harissa if you want a bit of a spicy kick!

Preheat the oven to 375°F. Line a large rimmed baking tray with parchment paper.

Wash and rinse the tomatoes, slice them in half, and lay them cut side up on the baking tray. Slice the bell peppers in half lengthwise, remove the seeds, slice each half in half, and place them cut side down on the baking tray.

Roughly chop the onion and place it on the baking tray. Peel the garlic cloves but leave them whole. Place them on the baking tray as well.

Drizzle all the vegetables with the olive oil and roast for 20 minutes. Turn the broiler to high and set the baking tray 5 inches from the element for 3 minutes to ensure the peppers and onions are well blistered. Remove the baking tray from the oven and let the roasted vegetables cool for 5 minutes.

Transfer the veggies to a blender or food processor, pour in the lime juice, and blend to the desired consistency. Add salt to taste. Place the salsa in a serving bowl and allow to cool completely in the fridge before serving. For an extra kick, drizzle with a touch more **Chipotle** infused olive oil.

Herbes de Provence Infused Olive Oil

A traditional blend of French herbs is the foundation for this lovely, delicate infused olive oil. With its perfect balance of savory, thyme, bay leaf, and lavender, this oil is incredibly versatile and will add a fresh French flavor to almost any dish. It pairs perfectly with **Apple** white balsamic vinegar—try this combo tossed on fresh greens for a simple salad. For more of my favorites, browse through this entire section. You'll find **Herbes de Provence** infused olive oil in the following recipes (and in several recipe variations throughout the book):

If there is a soup or broth that will keep me healthy and make me feel better when I'm sick, it's this. I love a good hearty rich bone broth, sometimes with a few onions added. It makes a lovely base for soups and stews and is incredible in sauces as well. Between the nutritional benefits of a bone broth and those of the olive oil, this is as healthy as all get out. The key to a good bone broth? Simmer it for at least 10 hours. Time to dig out the slow cooker! **MAKES APPROXIMATELY 5 QUARTS**

Simple Bone Broth

2 lb beef bones
¼ cup **Herbes de Provence** infused olive oil
1 leek
2 carrots
1 celery stalk
1 unpeeled garlic bulb
1 tomato
2 bay leaves
1 sprig thyme
1 tsp sea salt

Extra virgin olive oil, **Tuscan Herb**, **Garlic**, **Basil**, and **Wild Dill** are all great options if **Herbes de Provence** isn't in the cupboard.

Preheat the oven to 425°F. Line a rimmed baking sheet with parchment.

Spread the bones on the prepared baking sheet. Drizzle with olive oil and then use a pastry brush to coat them well on all sides.

Roast for 1 hour, until deeply brown and fragrant. Place the bones and any drippings in the bowl of your slow cooker and fill to within an inch of the top with water.

Slice the ends off the leek and add it, whole, to the water, along with the whole carrots and celery. Slice the bulb of garlic in half and add, along with the whole tomato, herbs, and salt. Cook on low heat for at least 10 hours, or up to 24. If the water starts to evaporate, top up the slow cooker with fresh water to keep it full.

Turn off the slow cooker and allow the broth to cool slightly. Strain it through a fine mesh sieve, removing any bits of garlic skin. Compost the vegetables and leftover bones.

Serve warm.

You can store the broth in an airtight container in the fridge for up to 5 days. For an easy addition to soups and stews, freeze it in ice cube trays then transfer the cubes to a resealable plastic bag for up to 6 months. As the broth cools it will become quite gelatinous. There's no need to panic about this. When you reheat the broth it will liquefy again, or you can add a bit of water and whisk it while it warms up to encourage it to soften and melt into broth again.

My friend Brad calls Brussels sprouts mutant cabbages, because let's be real, they really do look like tiny cabbages. For some reason, though, this vegetable tends to get picked on more than most. I think it's time we gave them the respect they deserve. So, let's slather them in tasty olive oil and balsamic vinegar, and roast them so they caramelize perfectly, turning these ugly ducklings into the swans of the vegetable world. **SERVES 4 AS A SIDE**

Roasted Brussels Sprouts

4 cups Brussels sprouts
½ cup **Herbes de Provence** infused olive oil
2 Tbsp **Apple** white balsamic vinegar
1 tsp sea salt
½ tsp fresh cracked black pepper

Preheat the oven to 400°F. Line a rimmed baking sheet with parchment paper.

Trim the base stem of the Brussels sprouts and remove any coarse or wilted outer leaves. Slice the sprouts in half and place them in a large bowl. Drizzle with the olive oil and vinegar and toss well to coat, massaging the olive oil into the sprouts as you do so. Spread the sprouts evenly on the prepared baking sheet and drizzle with any remaining olive oil and vinegar lying at the bottom of the bowl. Sprinkle the salt and pepper over top.

Roast for 30–35 minutes, turning once, halfway through cooking. They will be golden and crisp and caramelized on the outside, soft and fork-tender in the center. Remove from the oven and serve immediately.

The sprouts will keep in an airtight container in the fridge for up to 4 days and can easily be reheated and crisped up in the oven for 15 minutes at 400°F or in a frying pan.

Perfect for a summer cookout, this marinade is not only wonderful with chicken breasts, thighs, and wings, it also works beautifully on salmon. Try using it as a sauce to smear on chicken while it's cooking, or as a dressing for potato salad. If you're using homemade buttermilk (see page 43), remember to let it sit for 5 minutes before adding it to the marinade. **SERVES 4**

Creamy Herbed Chicken

½ cup buttermilk
¼ cup **Herbes de Provence** infused olive oil
2 Tbsp grainy Dijon mustard
1 Tbsp lemon juice
4 boneless, skinless chicken breasts
1 Tbsp chopped fresh dill

Rosemary, Wild Dill, Milanese Gremolata, Cilantro & Onion, and Basil are all great options if Herbes de Provence isn't in the cupboard

In a small bowl, whisk together the buttermilk, olive oil, Dijon, and lemon juice. Let sit for 10 minutes to thicken.

Place the chicken in a large resealable plastic bag. Pour in the marinade and shake gently to coat the chicken well. Place the bag flat in the fridge for 1–4 hours.

Preheat a barbecue to 400°F–450°F.

Remove the chicken from the marinade. Grill for 10 minutes per side, until cooked through and the internal temperature has reached 165°F. Transfer to a serving plate and garnish with the fresh dill.

Harissa Infused Olive Oil

Harissa originates from North Africa and the Middle East. Serrano and cayenne peppers, garlic, caraway, coriander, and cumin are crushed together to form a paste, which creates an incredibly spicy and delicious infused olive oil. Try this with stir-fries, or for glazing chicken, or for adding a delicious kick to hummus (see page 63). You'll find **Harissa** infused olive oil in the following recipes (and in several recipe variations throughout the book):

Risotto normally has delicate flavors, but this version has a delightful brightness thanks to the spicy **Harissa** infused olive oil. The sweet potatoes make the dish extra creamy and complement the spice. I love serving this for lunch on a cold winter weekend. It's comfort food at its best. **SERVES 4**

Harissa Roasted Sweet Potato & Spinach Risotto

1 large sweet potato
1/4 cup + 2 Tbsp **Harissa** infused olive oil, divided
6 cups chicken or vegetable stock
6–8 strands saffron
2 shallots, minced
1 tsp ground cumin
1 tsp ground coriander
1 1/2 cups Arborio rice
1/2 cup **Mango** white balsamic vinegar
2 cups baby spinach, large stems removed
1/2 cup grated Parmesan cheese
Sea salt

Preheat the oven to 375°F. Line a rimmed baking tray with parchment paper.

Cut the sweet potato in half lengthwise and brush with the 2 Tbsp of olive oil. Place the potato cut side down on the prepared baking tray and bake for 20 minutes. Flip the potato over and bake for an additional 20 minutes, until fork-tender. Remove from the oven and let cool.

In a large saucepan, bring the stock to a simmer and add the saffron. Cover and keep it at a simmer.

In a large frying pan over medium heat, sauté the minced shallots, cumin, and coriander in the remaining olive oil until soft but not golden, about 3 minutes. Add the rice and mix to coat it evenly with olive oil. Stir constantly, until the rice is shiny and translucent.

Add the balsamic, using it to deglaze the pan, and scrape up any bits of shallot that may have stuck.

Keeping the heat on medium, when the vinegar has all but evaporated, slowly start to add the warm broth, 1/2 to 3/4 cup at a time, stirring well after each addition to ensure that the rice is absorbing the broth slowly and consistently. Add the next addition of broth just when the pan is almost dry. It's important to stir constantly.

Once 4 1/2 cups of the broth have been added, the rice should be starting to look plump. Taste to see if it is still firm. If the rice is ready, scoop out the sweet potato flesh from the skin, add it and the spinach to the rice, and mix in the Parmesan cheese. If the rice has a touch of crunch, slowly add one final 1/2 cup of broth, stirring constantly, and then proceed with the sweet potato, baby spinach, and Parmesan.

Place the risotto in a serving bowl or individual plates, sprinkle with a touch of sea salt, and drizzle lightly with more olive oil. Serve immediately.

This snack was a happy accident. One evening I left some chickpeas in the oven and only remembered them at cleanup time. My husband started eating them off the tray while we cleaned up and declared them "really good!" They then became a staple movie night snack for us. Roasting them with the oil helps them crisp up and adds just enough zip to make them nice and spicy. **MAKES 1 ½ CUPS**

Roasted Chickpeas

1 (19 oz) can chickpeas, drained and rinsed
2 Tbsp **Harissa** infused olive oil
1 tsp ground cumin
½ tsp sea salt

For a fresh herb flavor, substitute **Milanese Gremolata**, **Wild Dill**, or **Herbes de Provence** olive oil in place of the **Harissa**.

Substitute **Chipotle** for the **Harissa** if you want something a little smokier-tasting.

Use **Cilantro & Onion** infused olive oil instead of **Harissa** and add a dash of lime juice for a Mexican flair.

Preheat the oven to 425°F. Line a rimmed baking tray with parchment paper.

Place the chickpeas on the parchment paper, drizzle them with the olive oil, and roll them around to coat well. Sprinkle with the ground cumin and salt.

Roast for 25–30 minutes, or until golden brown and crisp. Remove from the oven and let sit for 1–2 minutes. Gently pick up the corners of the parchment paper, let all the chickpeas roll into the center, then pick up the sides gently and pour them into a serving bowl. These are best eaten warm the night you make them, but you could store them for a couple of days in an airtight container in the fridge and quickly crisp them up in the oven or a frying pan to eat later.

Roasting the carrots in the **Harissa** infused olive oil deepens the flavors and enriches this soup. You can also make this with squash (any type except spaghetti) or yams or a combination of both. It's a great way to use up root vegetables! And you can make it in large quantities and freeze it for cold winter days. **SERVES 4–6**

Spicy Roasted Carrot Soup

4 large carrots or 6 medium sized
3 Tbsp **Harissa** infused olive oil, divided, plus more for drizzling
1 large onion, chopped
1 garlic clove
1 Tbsp ground cumin
1 tsp ground coriander
1 tsp ground cinnamon
½ tsp sea salt
½ tsp ground black pepper
4 cups vegetable stock
1 cup table (18%) cream
¼ cup Greek yogurt
2 Tbsp fresh chopped chives
1 tsp ground nutmeg
1 tsp dried chili flakes

If you'd prefer a less spicy version, the **Chipotle** infused olive oil is a lovely choice. **Rosemary**, **Garlic**, and **Cilantro & Onion** are also delicious here as well.

Preheat the oven to 375°F. Line a rimmed baking tray with parchment paper.

Peel the carrots, cut them into 2- to 3-inch pieces, and spread them across the prepared baking tray. Drizzle 2 Tbsp of the olive oil over top and roast until tender, 25 minutes.

Meanwhile, in a large saucepan over medium heat, sauté the onion, garlic, cumin, coriander, and cinnamon in the remaining 1 Tbsp olive oil until the onion is soft but not brown. Add the cooked carrots, salt, and pepper and mix well to combine.

Add the vegetable stock and simmer, covered, over medium heat for 30 minutes. Remove from the heat and allow to cool.

Place the soup in a blender in batches and purée as smoothly as you like. Return the soup to the pot, add the cream, and simmer to warm through.

To serve, garnish with a dollop of Greek yogurt and some chives, nutmeg, and chili flakes.

In many ways there isn't a more classic Canadian cocktail than this constant favorite on the brunch table. Roasting the vegetables in the **Harissa** infused olive oil creates the most amazing base for the drinks. This is batched for a crowd, but you can always half or quarter the recipe if needed, or double it as well. This cocktail lends itself well to fun garnishes, from pickled beans and cucumber dills to bacon, to the classic stalk of celery, which can get pretty adventurous. This recipe is a classic version, although if you'd prefer bourbon, that's okay too! **SERVES 8**

Spicy Caesar Pitcher

BASE

6 large tomatoes
3 large red bell peppers
2 garlic cloves
1 red onion
2 Tbsp **Harissa** infused olive oil
2 tsp celery seed
½ tsp sea salt
½ tsp fresh cracked black pepper
1 cup clam juice
8 oz vodka
⅓ cup lime juice (2–3 limes)
1 Tbsp Worcestershire sauce
8 lime wedges
2 Tbsp celery salt
8 stalks celery for garnish

For a more herbaceous cocktail, substitute **Rosemary** or **Basil** infused olive oil or a robust **extra virgin** olive oil for the **Harissa**. If you still want some spice, add a dash of tabasco sauce along with the Worcestershire sauce.

To add a touch of sweetness, substitute **Sicilian Lemon** white balsamic vinegar for the lime juice.

Preheat the oven to 375°F.

Line a roasting pan or rimmed baking tray with parchment paper.

Slice the tomatoes into wedges and spread evenly over the baking sheet, skin side down. Slice the peppers into quarters and nestle with the tomatoes. Crush the cloves of garlic and chop the red onion into quarters and add to the pan. Drizzle with the olive oil and sprinkle with celery seed, salt, and pepper.

Roast for 30 minutes, until the vegetables are well roasted and the tips of the tomatoes and edges of the peppers are starting to crisp and char a little. The pan will be filled with juices. Remove from the oven and let rest for 5 minutes.

Pour the entire contents of the pan, including the juices, into a blender and purée until very smooth. Add in the clam juice and blend again. Pour into a large Mason jar or pitcher and place in the fridge to cool completely until ready to use.

When you're ready to make the cocktails, place the vodka, lime juice, and Worcestershire sauce in a large pitcher and mix well. Top with 2 cups of the Caesar base and stir to combine.

Cut a small slit in each of the lime wedges and run the wedge around the rim of a glass. Reserve the lime wedges. Place the celery salt in a shallow dish and shake so it is evenly distributed. Carefully dip the rims of 8 Tom Collins glasses in the salt, allowing it to stick. Fill glasses half full of ice. Add the Caesar mix and a stalk of celery and lime wedge for garnish.

Rosemary Infused Olive Oil

Bright and packed with flavor, **Rosemary** infused olive oil is a pantry staple in my house. A note of caution, though: A little goes a long way since the flavor is present and strong. Perfect for marinades, tossing with fresh pasta, adding to sauces, or drizzling over mashed potatoes, this olive oil is as versatile as it is delicious. One thing I find challenging when using fresh rosemary, is that the smell is lovely and oh so fragrant when I'm chopping it, but because the leaves are quite coarse, I find that fresh intense flavor doesn't transfer well. This olive oil lets the flavor transfer perfectly and prevents bits of rosemary getting stuck in my teeth too! You'll find **Rosemary** infused olive oil in the following recipes (and in several recipe variations throughout the book):

There is just something lovely about a Cobb salad, maybe because it contains so many of my favorite things—avocado, bacon, and blue cheese (you can use aged cheddar if blue cheese isn't your favorite)—and is packed with protein. Not only will you enjoy this salad, but you can also rest assured that it won't leave you feeling hungry an hour later. The creamy avocado dressing made with **Rosemary** infused olive oil is like an herbaceous green goddess dressing that complements every component of the salad. It's easily made ahead, so make a big batch to keep on hand in the fridge. **SERVES 4**

Classic Cobb Salad with Creamy Avocado Dressing

SALAD

½ lb bacon
4 boneless skinless chicken breasts
¼ cup **Rosemary** infused olive oil
1 tsp sea salt
1 tsp cracked black pepper
4 eggs
1 head leaf lettuce
1 red onion
1 avocado
2 tsp lime juice
1 cup halved cherry tomatoes
1 cup blue cheese

DRESSING

¼ cup **Rosemary** infused olive oil
¼ cup Greek yogurt
1 avocado, roughly chopped
2 Tbsp lime juice
1 tsp creamy Dijon mustard
1 garlic clove, crushed
2 tsp fresh flat-leaf parsley
2 sprigs thyme, leaves only

Basil or **Garlic** infused olive oil are also delicious here for a less florally flavor.

If rosemary isn't your favorite herb, or you simply find it too strong, feel free to substitute **Herbes de Provence** or **Wild Dill** infused olive oil. The **Wild Dill** will give a ranch feel to the dressing.

Preheat the oven to 400°F. Line a rimmed baking tray with parchment paper.

To make the salad, on one half of the baking tray lay out the bacon in strips so they just touch but don't overlap. On the other half, place the chicken breasts. Drizzle each chicken breast with the olive oil and sprinkle with the salt and pepper.

Bake for 20 minutes, until the bacon is crisp and browned and the chicken is cooked through, the juices run clear, and the flesh is no longer pink. Remove from the oven and set aside.

While the chicken is cooking, place a small saucepan of cold water on the stove. Add the eggs and bring to a rolling boil. Boil for 4 minutes and then immediately remove from the heat, strain, and rinse under cold water. Let the eggs rest in the cold water for at least 10 minutes.

Prepare four serving plates. Wash and spin dry the head of lettuce, then tear it into bite-sized pieces and divide them evenly between the plates. Finely chop the onion and arrange it in a row on top of the lettuce. Chop the avocado into cubes and drizzle them with the lime juice before placing them next to the onion in a second row. Chop the chicken into bite-sized pieces and break up the bacon into large bits. Add to the salad along with the cherry tomatoes, blue cheese, and hard-cooked eggs, placing each ingredient in consecutive rows. Or if you want to save time, loosely arrange all the ingredients over the salad so it looks full and overflowing with toppings.

To make the dressing, place the olive oil, yogurt, roughly chopped avocado, lime juice, and mustard

in a blender and purée until completely blended.
Add the garlic, parsley, and thyme leaves to the bowl,
and blend again so that's it absolutely lump-free and
smooth, smooth, smooth. Pour over the salad and
serve immediately.

The dressing will keep in the fridge for up to 2 days in
an airtight container, but it's best that you eat the salad the
day you make it.

This simple fresh pasta sauce is particularly easy to put together when the garden is overflowing with tomatoes, or your local market is selling tomatoes by the case for the same price as one tomato costs in January. The **Rosemary** infused olive oil brightens the sauce and ensures the flavor is consistent and doesn't dull when stored. Double or triple this recipe and stock up for the winter months. **SERVES 4**

Heirloom Tomato Pasta Sauce

1 onion
6 cloves garlic
¼ cup **Rosemary** infused olive oil
1 tsp sea salt
2 Tbsp **Neapolitan Herb** dark balsamic vinegar
12–14 large heirloom tomatoes
2 tsp granulated sugar
¼ cup fresh chopped flat-leaf parsley
6–8 basil leaves
4 sprigs oregano
2 sprigs thyme

Garlic, **Basil**, **Tuscan Herb**, and **Milanese Gremolata** infused olive oils are all delicious in this sauce in place of the **Rosemary** infused olive oil.

Chop the onion and crush the garlic, leaving the cloves in large pieces.

In a large heavy-bottomed saucepan, twice the size you think you'll need, heat the olive oil over medium heat. Add the onion and garlic and sauté for 3–4 minutes, until starting to caramelize and turn golden. Sprinkle with the salt, allowing the onion and garlic to sweat, then deglaze the pan with the balsamic, scraping up any bits from the bottom.

Remove from the heat while you prep the tomatoes. Bring a pot of water to a boil. Cut a small X in the base of each tomato. You don't want to cut too deep but you do need to pierce the skin. Slip one or two tomatoes at a time into the boiling water and boil for 5–10 seconds. Remove with a slotted spoon and repeat with the remaining tomatoes. The skins will slip off very easily after they have been blanched.

Quarter the tomatoes. Working in batches, place the tomato quarters in the bowl of a blender or food processor, or use a food mill if you don't have either of those. Pulse or grind a few times to break up the tomatoes and release the juices. Pour the tomatoes into the saucepan. Add the sugar and stir to combine. Remove the herbs from their stems, reserving 2–3 basil leaves, and roughly chop before adding to the tomatoes. Stir to combine.

Place the saucepan back on medium heat and bring to a rolling boil. Turn down the heat to low and simmer, uncovered, for 3–4 hours, or until the sauce is the desired thickness. You can stir this once or twice to check that it's not sticking to the pot, but this sauce is an independent little devil and it's happier if you stand back and let it look after itself.

Remove from the heat and serve immediately over fresh pasta or rice, garnished with the reserved basil leaves. Alternatively, let it cool to room temperature and then store in an airtight container, topped with the remaining basil leaves. This will store in the fridge for up to 1 week or in the freezer for up to 6 months. Discard the basil leaves after the sauce has thawed, as they'll be sad, limp, and generally unappealing.

This brings back vivid memories of my mom basting a roast beef with her herbed compound butter. It was always a bit of an ordeal, putting the spit together and getting everything ready, but oh, it was worth the work and the wait. Roasting this in the oven reduces the work, but it doesn't reduce the flavor. The oil creates a beautiful crust and keeps the meat moist and the flavor even, without any burning. You can also make this in the slow cooker by cooking on low for 6–8 hours. **SERVES 4**

Roast Beef with Rosemary Lemon Glaze

2 lb potatoes (Yukon Golds are classic, but russets work well too)
2 large red onions
1 lb carrots, peeled
¼ cup **Rosemary** infused olive oil
2 Tbsp lemon juice
1 Tbsp grated lemon zest
2 tsp Dijon mustard
1 (4–5 lb) beef roast (rump or round are best)
1 tsp sea salt
½ tsp black pepper

For a less rosemary-forward version of this recipe, although I do love the rosemary personally, either **Herbes de Provence** or **Milanese Gremolata** infused olive oil would be a lovely substitute.

Preheat the oven to 325°F.

Scrub the potatoes and roughly chop them into 2-inch pieces. Cut the onions in half and roughly chop the carrots.

In a small bowl, whisk together the olive oil, lemon juice and zest, and Dijon. Place the potatoes in the bottom of a large roasting pan. Place the roast on top of the potatoes. Nestle the remaining vegetables around the roast, but not on top of it, and pour the olive oil mixture over top. Season with the salt and pepper.

Cover the roasting pan tightly with aluminum foil and top with a lid or a second layer of foil. Roast for 2 hours, baste with the cooking juices, and bake for another 30–40 minutes, until a meat thermometer reads 160°F. Turn off the oven.

Once the roast is cooked, place it on a carving board to rest for 10 minutes. Place the veggies on an ovenproof dish and set them in the oven to keep warm.

Carefully pour the cooking juices into a small saucepan and bring to a simmer over medium heat. Allow the liquid to reduce by half to make a glaze.

Carve the meat, place it on a serving platter, nestle the vegetables around it, and drizzle half the glaze over everything. Place the remaining glaze in a small pitcher to enjoy alongside.

Milanese Gremolata Infused Olive Oil

This is a traditional Italian infused olive oil made from crushing fresh lemon zest, minced garlic, Italian (flat-leaf) parsley, and a cool finish of mint in a mortar to release their pungent essential oils. The following recipes in this book call for this amazing infused oil, but it is so versatile. Try it on chicken, too! You'll find **Milanese Gremolata** infused olive oil in the following recipes (and in several recipe variations throughout the book):

This snack is seriously addictive. Using the **Milanese Gremolata** infused olive oil with a touch of extra garlic allows the full flavor of the oil to be absorbed and roasted into the cereal. Crisp, crunchy, and exploding with flavor, this snack will disappear in no time. **MAKES 6 CUPS**

Milanese Gremolata Nibbles

3 cups Cheerios
2 cups Shreddies
1 cup pretzels
1 cup **Milanese Gremolata** infused olive oil
2 Tbsp **Garlic** infused olive oil
Sea salt

Preheat the oven to 200°F. Line a rimmed baking tray with parchment paper.

In a medium bowl, toss the cereals with the pretzels. Pour the olive oils over top, mixing to thoroughly coat everything.

Spread evenly on the prepared baking tray, sprinkle with salt, and bake for 2 hours, stirring every 30 minutes, until golden. Let cool on the pan until still warm but cool enough to handle, then transfer to a serving bowl.

The **Milanese Gremolata** infused olive oil gives an Italian twist to this classic Greek salad, packed with ripe tomatoes, salty feta, and cool cucumber. The mint in the infused olive oil makes this salad as refreshing as it is flavorful, and it tames both the parsley-forward aspect of the infused olive oil and the lemon kick. This version is perfect for anyone who isn't a big fan of oregano. **SERVES 6 AS A SIDE**

Lemon Mint Greek Salad

4 Roma tomatoes
2 English cucumbers
1–2 red onions
1 cup olives (your choice)
1 cup cubed feta cheese
¼ cup **Milanese Gremolata** infused olive oil
2 Tbsp **Sicilian Lemon** white balsamic vinegar
½ tsp sea salt
¼ tsp cracked black pepper

If you're looking for more classic Greek flavors, use **Garlic** infused olive oil, **Oregano** white balsamic, and **Lemongrass Mint** instead of the options listed above.

Chop the tomatoes into quarters. Cut the cucumbers and red onions into 1-inch dice. Place them all in a serving bowl with the olives and cubed cheese, toss with the olive oil and balsamic, and season with the salt and pepper. You can serve this immediately, but it really comes into its own if you place it in the fridge for an hour to let the flavors meld.

Tabbouleh salad is a year-round staple for us. Lovely and fresh, this salad is filled with more herbs than grain. I prefer to use Israeli couscous, which is larger than regular couscous, because it stands up better to the volume of herbs. The **Milanese Gremolata** infused olive oil and **Lemongrass Mint** white balsamic vinegar make for a perfect flavor combination as the dressing, but the variations are also delicious and a fun way to switch up this staple salad. It keeps in the fridge for at least a week, so don't hesitate to make a double batch. **SERVES 4**

Couscous Tabbouleh Salad

1 ½ cups chicken or vegetable stock
1 cup Israeli couscous
½ small red onion, finely chopped
1 Roma tomato, finely chopped
2 cups fresh curly-leaf parsley
½ cup fresh mint leaves
1 lemon, grated zest and juice
2 garlic cloves, minced
½ cup **Milanese Gremolata** infused olive oil
½ cup **Lemongrass Mint** white balsamic vinegar
Sea salt and ground black pepper

For a spicy version, swap in the **Harissa** infused olive oil and **Mango** white balsamic vinegar for something fresh and contemporary, or use **Pomegranate** dark balsamic for a more traditional rich and spicy flavor.

To create a more classically Italian flavor profile, try a combination of **Tuscan Herb** infused olive oil and **Sicilian Lemon** white balsamic, which is basil-, garlic-, and rosemary-forward, instead of the **Milanese Gremolata** and **Lemongrass Mint**, which is brimming with parsley, mint, and lemon.

Bring the stock to a boil in a medium saucepan and add the couscous. Remove from the heat, cover with a lid, and let stand for 15–20 minutes, until all the stock is absorbed. Fluff the couscous with a fork and transfer it to a baking sheet or a plate where you can spread it out, so it can cool more quickly.

In a large serving bowl, combine the cooled couscous, onion, tomato, parsley, mint, and lemon juice, and toss well to combine.

In a separate bowl, whisk together the lemon zest, garlic, olive oil, balsamic, and salt and pepper to taste.

Drizzle the dressing over the salad and mix well to combine. Let sit for at least 30 minutes in the fridge before serving.

This keeps for 1 week in an airtight container in the fridge.

This dish is lovely for Easter dinner, but really it tastes great any time of year. Serve it alongside Barbecue Garlic Potato Wedges (page 103) or Wild Mushroom & Sage Roasted Acorn Squash (page 112). **SERVES 4**

Milanese Gremolata Rack of Lamb

1 rack of lamb (4 ribs, about ½ lb each)
½ cup **Milanese Gremolata** infused olive oil, divided
¼ cup **Sicilian Lemon** white balsamic vinegar
2 Tbsp creamy Dijon mustard
1 Tbsp tomato paste
Sea salt and ground black pepper

Herbed Rack of Lamb Substitute the **Milanese Gremolata** with **Rosemary** infused olive oil and the **Sicilian Lemon** white balsamic with **Neapolitan Herb** dark balsamic.

Sweet and Tangy Rack of Lamb Substitute the **Milanese Gremolata** with **Harissa** infused olive oil and the **Sicilian Lemon** white balsamic with **Pomegranate** dark balsamic.

In a roasting pan, arrange the ribs fat side up in a single layer. Pierce the meat with a knife to allow the marinade to penetrate.

In a small bowl, whisk ¼ cup of the olive oil with the balsamic, Dijon, and tomato paste until emulsified. Brush some of this marinade over the ribs and drizzle the rest over top. Cover with a tight-fitting lid or aluminum foil and let sit in the fridge for 8–24 hours.

Preheat the oven to 425°F. Line a roasting pan or rimmed baking tray with aluminum foil.

Arrange the ribs on the prepared pan, drizzle generously with the residue marinade, and season to taste with salt and pepper. Roast the lamb, uncovered, for 15 minutes. Brush the ribs with the remaining ¼ cup of olive oil and roast for another 15–20 minutes, until all the ribs register at least 135°F.

Serve immediately!

Cilantro & Onion Infused Olive Oil

For the cilantro lovers of the world, this is your dream olive oil. The perfect pairing for Mexican food, I use it in salsa and guacamole, roasted chicken or fish for tacos, and in a variety of Indian and South East Asian dishes. Sauté your onions in this before making a simple green curry and cilantro will infuse every bite of the dish. Whisk it into some yogurt and dollop it on a spicy curry for a quick two-ingredient raita. I'm realizing as I write this that I pull this oil out of the cupboard much more often than I thought. You'll find **Cilantro & Onion** infused olive oil in the following recipes (and in several recipe variations throughout the book):

I first fell in love with cilantro cumin rice during my days of frequenting a local Mexican restaurant a bit too often in university. Their burritos were addictive for one reason: this rice, with its whole cumin seeds and fresh cilantro flavor. I had to recreate it at home, of course. The **Cilantro & Onion** infused olive oil permeates every part of this dish, evens out the flavor, and keeps the grains of rice soft, ensuring they don't stick together. **SERVES 2**

Cilantro Cumin Rice

2 tsp whole cumin seeds
1 white onion
2 garlic cloves
¼ cup **Cilantro & Onion** infused olive oil
1 tsp sea salt
1 cup basmati or jasmine rice
2 tsp lime juice
¼ cup chopped fresh cilantro leaves

Dry-toast the cumin seeds over medium heat in a small frying pan for 2–3 minutes. Shake the pan frequently to move the seeds around and ensure they toast evenly. Watch them closely, as they can burn quickly. As soon as their fragrance is strong and they are a deep brown color, remove them from the heat.

Mince the onion and garlic. In a medium-sized saucepan over medium-high heat, sauté them in the olive oil until just translucent. Stir in the salt. Add the rice and toasted cumin seeds. Sauté until the rice is translucent and well coated in the olive oil. Add 2 cups of water to the pot. Bring to a boil, cover, and turn down the heat to low. Allow the rice to fully absorb the water, about 20 minutes. Remove from the heat, stir to check the bottom of the pot to ensure all the water has been absorbed, and then fluff with a fork. Stir in the lime juice and then the cilantro. Serve immediately.

This will keep in an airtight container in the fridge for up to 3 days.

This quick dinner is easy to toss together at the last minute, but it will look like you've been slaving in the kitchen for hours. It makes the best lunches, because the flavors continue to develop overnight in the fridge, and often I find it's even better the next day. It also freezes extremely well. Serve this over Cilantro Cumin Rice (page 148) for an extra cilantro kick. **SERVES 4**

Chickpea Tikka Masala

4 garlic cloves

1 small green chili

1 tsp sea salt

1 red onion

¼ cup **Cilantro & Onion** infused olive oil

1 tsp black or yellow mustard seeds (optional)

2 Tbsp **Lemongrass Mint** white balsamic vinegar

1 (28 oz) can whole plum tomatoes

2 tsp whole coriander seeds

1 tsp cumin seeds

3 tsp ground turmeric

2 tsp garam masala

1 tsp ground cardamom

1 (6 oz) can tomato paste

1 (16 oz) can chickpeas, drained and rinsed

1 cup plain yogurt

½ cup whipping (35%) cream

½ cup fresh cilantro leaves, divided

For a simple Chicken Tikka Masala, use 3 cups cooked cubed or chopped chicken instead of the chickpeas. Leftovers from the Quick Whole Roast Chicken (page 66) or Apricot & Lemon Pulled Chicken (page 307) are perfect for this.

If you like spice, substitute **Harissa** infused olive oil for the **Cilantro & Onion**.

If you're looking for a more traditional flavor, a robust **extra virgin** olive oil is incredible here.

Crush and roughly chop the garlic. Seed and roughly chop the chili pepper. Place the garlic and chili pepper in a mortar, add the salt, and grind to a fine paste with the pestle. Alternatively, sprinkle the garlic and chili with salt and chop together to create a very fine mince.

Chop the onion into four rounds.

Heat the olive oil in a large frying pan over medium-high heat. Add the mustard seeds, if using, and swirl them around the pan. When they start to pop, add the onions and let them begin to caramelize, about 3–5 minutes. Stir just enough to prevent them from sticking. Add the garlic-chili mixture and stir to combine. Deglaze the pan with the balsamic, scraping up any bits that have stuck to the bottom.

Open the can of tomatoes, but don't remove the lid fully. Pour the juice from the can into the pan, then gently crush the tomatoes in your hand before adding them to the pan. Stir to combine and bring to a strong simmer.

In a small frying pan, toast the coriander and cumin until well toasted and extra fragrant. Place these in your mortar and use the pestle to grind them to a fine powder (or blitz them in a spice blender if you have one). Add all the spices (toasted and untoasted) to the tomato mixture and stir to combine, continuing to simmer the mixture, uncovered. Simmer for 10 minutes to allow the flavors to develop and the sauce to reduce slightly.

Spoon in the tomato paste and then the chickpeas. Simmer for 5 minutes to warm the chickpeas through.

Remove from the heat, stir in the yogurt, cream, and half the cilantro, then transfer to a serving dish or serving plates, and garnish with the remaining cilantro leaves.

Refreshing and so simple, this salad is lovely on a hot summer day for lunch or as a side dish as part of a picnic. The olive oil keeps it cool and creamy and the balsamic prevents the avocado from browning: a match made in vegetable heaven! **SERVES 2**

Cucumber Avocado Salad

1 English cucumber

2 avocados

2 Tbsp **Cilantro & Onion** infused olive oil

1 Tbsp **Grapefruit** white balsamic vinegar

1 Tbsp lemon juice

2 tsp honey

1 tsp sea salt

2 Tbsp torn cilantro leaves for garnish

Basil infused olive oil with the **Grapefruit** white balsamic is a sweet combo, and basil is one of my all-time favorite herbs to pair with fresh acidic grapefruit.

Herbes de Provence fused olive oil and **Apple** white balsamic are also a favorite combination for this dish. The sweetness of the balsamic and the complexity of the herbs elevate the simple cool cucumber and creamy avocado.

If you're a dill lover, try the **Wild Dill** infused olive oil with **Sicilian Lemon** white balsamic for a light refreshing combination that is perfect with barbecued salmon.

Peel the cucumber to make stripes about ½ inch wide, leaving ½ inch of peel in between each peeled piece. Chop into thin rounds and then into half-moons, and place in a serving bowl. Slice the avocados in half and carefully remove the pit. Make a cross-hatched pattern with a paring knife in the flesh of each avocado half and then turn the peel inside out to release the cubes from the skin. You may need to pull them gently. Add avocado cubes to bowl.

In a small bowl, whisk together the olive oil, balsamic, lemon juice, honey, and salt. Pour this over the cucumber and avocado, and toss to coat well. Place in the fridge to chill or serve immediately.

This will keep for up to 2 days in an airtight container in the fridge.

MARINADES

Marinades have two purposes: to impart flavor and to tenderize. They also happen
to make it easy to enjoy tasty meals every night of the week. Most marinades can be
whipped up in record time and can be stored in the fridge for a few days, so all you have
to do is grab some meat, pour homemade marinade over it, and let it soak up the flavors
while you get on with your day.

WHAT MAKES A SUCCESSFUL MARINADE?

A carefully chosen acid can transform a marinade from good to spectacular. Lemon
juice, wine, and vinegar all contain just enough acidity to begin to break down meat
and tenderize it beautifully. The flavor of the acid should complement the flavors in
the rest of your meal so that it all ties together. I've put together a table for you to use
as a flavor guide but play with your favorite marinade recipes and experiment with
different flavor combinations. (If your favorite marinade recipe doesn't include oil—
and not all marinades use oil—don't be tempted to add any.)

MEAT	BALSAMIC VINEGARS PAIRINGS
Chicken	Peach, Sicilian Lemon, Lemongrass Mint
Pork	Apricot, Mango, Grapefruit, Fig, Black Cherry, Blackberry Ginger
Lamb	Pomegranate
Beef	Neapolitan Herb

HOW MUCH MARINADE DO I NEED?

The volume of marinade you'll need depends not only on the quantity but also the type of food. Expect to use around ½ cup marinade for four chicken breasts, steaks, pork chops, or fish fillets. You'll need around ¾ cup if you're marinating four lamb chops or four servings' worth of veggies, shrimp, or meat for kebabs. If in doubt, use more than you think you need.

MARINATING TIMES

Marinating times vary greatly. Steak can sit in its marinade for up to 24 hours and can even be frozen in it. Chicken and pork don't need quite as long, with 2 hours being ample for chicken and 3 hours for pork. Seafood, especially shellfish, should not be allowed to marinate for too long, as it can become very chewy. Around 10–15 minutes is plenty to marinate seafood. It's also very porous, so it soaks up the flavors quickly. Vegetables only need about 30 minutes to marinate and are typically best cooked or roasted directly in the marinade.

QUICK & EASY MARINADES

For quick and easy meals, use the olive oil and balsamic combinations in the same volumes as the oil and balsamic in the Basic Marinade recipe (below). The variations all use 1 Tbsp Dijon, unless otherwise stated.

BASIC MARINADE

Combine ½ cup **extra virgin** olive oil with ¼ cup balsamic. Whisk in 1 Tbsp Dijon mustard and 2 Tbsp of finely chopped garlic.

LEMONY MINT MARINADE FOR LAMB

A combination of **Milanese Gremolata** infused olive oil and **Lemongrass Mint** white balsamic is wonderful on any cut of leg of lamb or lamb chops. (See the full recipe on page 144.)

LEMON ROSEMARY MARINADE FOR BEEF

Use **Rosemary** infused olive oil and lemon juice in place of vinegar for this steak marinade. (See also the recipe on page 138.)

TANGY SESAME MARINADE FOR TUNA OR SALMON

Use Japanese toasted sesame oil and **Honey Ginger** white balsamic in this marinade. Serve with an Asian-influenced dipping sauce (on page 155).

BLACKBERRY GINGER MARINADE FOR PORK

Use any robust **extra virgin** olive oil with **Blackberry Ginger** dark balsamic for this. It's fantastic on pork chops and pork tenderloin. (See page 171 for a more detailed version of this.)

FRESH & FRUITY MARINADE FOR FISH OR SHELLFISH

Use **Lime** fused olive oil and **Pineapple** white balsamic and omit the garlic and substitute diced red onion. This is great on mild-tasting fish such as snapper, and delicious on shrimp or prawns. Make sure to whip up a bit of Tropical Quick & Easy Dipping Sauce (recipe on page 155) to serve alongside whatever you end up marinating in this combo.

CITRUS MARINADE FOR CHICKEN OR FISH

Use **Blood Orange** fused olive oil and **Grapefruit** white balsamic. This is really nice for barbecued chicken and amazing on halibut. Or try using it to marinate fruit before grilling (just omit the Dijon and garlic). Serve alongside goat cheese drizzled with honey for dessert.

QUICK & EASY DIPPING SAUCES

Seafood doesn't need to be marinated for very long, if at all, because it picks up flavors quickly and is generally mild-tasting. A great alternative is to serve a bit of dipping sauce in individual containers to deliver an extra dose of flavor. Make as much as you need for your crowd according to these guidelines.

ASIAN-INFLUENCED

1 Tbsp Garlic infused olive oil + 1 tsp Japanese toasted sesame oil + 2 tsp Honey Ginger white balsamic (and a touch of spicy mustard!). Serve alongside sushi or any seafood of your choice, or with seared Ahi tuna belly marinated in a tangy sesame marinade (see page 289).

TROPICAL

2 Tbsp Lime fused olive oil + 1 Tbsp Pineapple white balsamic. Great with oysters, scallops, shrimp or prawns, or crab. Use a fresh and fruity marinade (see page 154) to lightly marinate oysters before frying them. Serve hot with this dipping sauce. Unbelievably good.

GARLIC BUTTER

2 Tbsp Butter infused olive oil + 1 tsp of Garlic infused olive oil. Use instead of melted garlic butter when you're serving up crab, shrimp or prawns, and lobster. And no warmers necessary!

LEMON GARLIC

2 Tbsp Garlic infused olive oil + 1 tsp Sicilian Lemon white balsamic. Fantastic on any seafood or roasted veggies.

SPICY

2 Tbsp Harissa infused olive oil + 2 tsp Mango white balsamic. Use this on fish, crab, or shrimp and prawns.

SWEET AND SAVORY

2 Tbsp Basil infused olive oil + 2 Tbsp Peach white balsamic. Delicious on halibut, cod, or shrimp or prawns.

Dark Balsamic Vinegars

Traditional balsamic vinegars are a product of Modena, Italy. They are made from a caramelized reduction, called a "must," created from crushed white grapes, usually Trebbiano and Lambrusco. The grape juice, pulp, and skins are caramelized in copper kettles set over an open wood fire. This grape must is fermented in wooden barrels and aged, gradually becoming the vinegar we know and love.

As it ages, the balsamic gains character and texture, partly because it is moved into a new barrel every two years. Traditional dark balsamics are grouped into three age categories according to how long they have been left to age: young (3–5 years), middle-aged (6–12 years), and old (12–110+ years!). Technically, to be officially classified as "balsamic vinegar," the oldest vinegar in the barrel needs to be at least 12 years old.

The taste of a quality aged dark balsamic is rich and full. Its acidity is 4–5%, so it's less acidic than traditional red or white wine vinegars and has a healthy balance between sweetness and acidity. Just a drop on a strawberry or on a sliver of Parmesan cheese is transformative. It is an incredible cooking tool, and can enhance the flavor, richness, and complexity of a dish. Don't ever underestimate the power of a quality dark balsamic vinegar.

This recipe is extremely easy—it's just balsamic vinegar, reduced so that it's thick and concentrated. It takes less than a minute to make! And you can put it on absolutely anything. **MAKES ¹/₂ CUP**

Dark Balsamic Crème

¹/₂ cup any dark balsamic vinegar

Any dark balsamic vinegar is delightful done this way. Try **Strawberry** dark balsamic crème drizzled over ice cream, **Maple** dark balsamic crème brushed over grilled salmon, **Wild Blueberry** dark balsamic crème drizzled over waffles, or **Fig** dark balsamic crème drizzled over goat cheese. Get the idea?

In a shallow saucepan or 8-inch frying pan, slowly bring the vinegar first to a simmer over medium heat. As it reaches a boil, gently swirl the balsamic over the bottom of the pan a few times—three swirls should do the trick. As you gently swirl the vinegar, you'll notice it going from moving around the pan quickly to leaving a trail behind. As soon as you see an even trail being left behind, remove the pan from the heat and let cool to room temperature. You'll have a thick crème. This process will take 20–30 seconds at most. Don't take your eyes off it for a second! You might find—as I have on occasion—that you have balsamic pull taffy on the stove rather than the glaze you were planning for, especially once it has cooled. If you pull it off the heat too soon, just warm it for a little longer to thicken. If it is too thick, warm it again and add a little more balsamic to incorporate, but don't let it boil. This will thin it to a drizzling consistency.

This is best used at room temperature. If it's stored in the fridge, it will thicken to the consistency of molasses—and it moves as slowly as molasses when it comes to returning to a room-temperature consistency. I prefer to drizzle it warm or just above room temperature if I'm using it on a warm salad, roasted vegetables, or a meat dish, so it drizzles smoothly and easily and doesn't cool down the rest of the dish. When I'm drizzling it over ice cream, cheese, or any other cold dish, I use it at room temperature, so it doesn't warm up the dish too much but is still of drizzling consistency.

This reduction will last basically indefinitely at room temperature. Store it in a cupboard in an airtight container, such as a Mason jar. I tend to keep a jar of it beside my honey pot and quadruple this recipe to make 2 cups at a time.

Traditional

So smooth you could sip it after dinner! This thick, full-bodied balsamic vinegar is incredible drizzled over strawberries, cheese, or even ice cream. You'll find **Traditional** dark balsamic vinegar in the following recipes (and in several recipe variations throughout the book):

Pork roasts are a dream: cheap, easy to cook, delicious, and versatile. I'm using loin here, but use whichever cut you prefer. You might have to adjust the cooking time slightly, depending on the cut, so factor that into your schedule. **SERVES 4–6**

Garlic Pork Roast with Balsamic Vinegar

1 (5–6 lb) pork loin roast
2 lb baby potatoes, scrubbed
6 garlic cloves
1 large onion
2 cinnamon sticks
15 whole cloves
¾ cup robust **extra virgin** olive oil
¼ cup **Traditional** dark balsamic vinegar
1½ tsp ground black pepper
Sea salt

For an extra kick of garlic, use the **Garlic** infused olive oil in place of the **extra virgin** olive oil.

For a herbaceous option, use the **Rosemary**, **Wild Dill**, **Cilantro & Onion**, or **Basil** in place of the **extra virgin** olive oil.

Pomegranate, **Fig**, **Oregano**, or **Lemongrass Mint** would all be lovely here in place of **Traditional** dark balsamic vinegar.

Preheat the oven to 350°F.

Rinse the pork roast with warm water and pat it dry. Place it in a roasting pan just large enough to hold the roast and nestle the potatoes and garlic tightly around it. Chop the onion into large slices or wedges and nestle them in with the potatoes. Tuck a cinnamon stick right beside the roast on each side. Poke the cloves into the top of the roast, spacing them evenly.

Pour the olive oil and balsamic over the roast, allowing them to drizzle down over the onion and potatoes. Season with the pepper and some salt to taste, cover tightly with aluminum foil or a lid, and place in the oven.

Bake for 1–1½ hours until the internal temperature of the pork reaches 155°F–160°F. When it's almost but not quite at the required temperature, remove the foil and cook for 10 minutes to allow the roast to brown on top. If you're looking for a really crispy crust, turn the broiler on for the last 3–5 minutes of cooking. This will also brown the potatoes a bit more and give them a crispy top.

Remove from the oven. Tent the pork in the pan with aluminum foil and allow to rest for about 10 minutes before cutting. Remove the cloves and cinnamon sticks before serving. Serve the potatoes, onion, and garlic in a separate bowl, or alongside the roast on a large serving platter. Serve with drippings on the side or make them into a simple gravy. (You can mash up some of the garlic to add to the gravy if you like.)

This salad is fresh, bright, and colorful—it's sunshine in a bowl. If you have a hankering for a strawberry-filled caprese salad, head over to page 95. **SERVES 2–4**

Colorful Heirloom Insalata Caprese

1 cup cherry-sized bocconcini cheese
1 pint heirloom cherry/grape tomatoes in an assortment of colors
2 large heirloom tomatoes, sliced
2 Tbsp medium to robust **extra virgin** olive oil
2 Tbsp **Traditional** dark balsamic vinegar
10–15 large fresh basil leaves
Sea salt and ground black pepper

For a variation that is incredibly delicious and will definitely catch guests off guard, use **Basil** infused olive oil and **Chocolate** dark balsamic in this recipe.

Picual is my favorite cultivar to use in caprese salads because of its unique green tomato notes. If fresh basil isn't in season, use **Basil** infused olive oil instead of the single varietal **extra virgin** olive oil.

While **Traditional** dark balsamic vinegar is my favorite option for capreses, try **Neapolitan Herb** or **Fig** dark balsamic or **Sicilian Lemon** white balsamic to switch things up a little.

In a large bowl, toss the bocconcini cheese with the tomatoes, drizzle with the olive oil and balsamic, and top with the basil leaves. Season to taste with salt and pepper.

For a fun appetizer, thread a toothpick with 1 tomato, 1 basil leaf, and 1 piece of bocconcini. Arrange on a plate and drizzle with olive oil and balsamic.

Sprinkle with salt and pepper to taste.

Take caramel corn to a new level by adding balsamic to give it some depth. This is an ideal treat to make ahead and put in jars to hand out as favors or homemade Christmas gifts. If you don't have **Butter** infused olive oil, you can use a mild **extra virgin** olive oil with an FFA of less than 0.2 (see page 13). **MAKES ABOUT 4 CUPS**

Balsamic Caramel Popcorn

3 Tbsp **Butter** infused olive oil, divided
¼ cup popcorn kernels
¾ cup granulated sugar
2 Tbsp honey
2 Tbsp **Traditional** dark balsamic vinegar
¼ tsp baking soda
½ tsp flaked sea salt such as fleur de sel or Maldon sea salt (optional)

If **Butter** infused olive oil isn't in the cupboard, a medium-robust **extra virgin** olive oil will work beautifully.

Dragon's Breath Balsamic Caramel Corn
If you like spice, try popping the corn in **Harissa** infused olive oil to make your mouth tingle.

Lime Black Pepper Balsamic Caramel Corn
For a savory but less spicy version than dragon's breath, use **Lime** fused olive oil to pop the popcorn and add 1 tsp of cracked black pepper after you add the baking soda to warm up the dish and complement the caramel too.

Preheat the oven to 325°F. Line a rimmed baking tray with parchment paper.

Heat 2 Tbsp of the olive oil in a heavy-bottomed saucepan over medium-high heat. To check the temperature, add a couple kernels, cover, and let them pop for 3–5 minutes. Add the remaining kernels, cover, and remove the saucepan from the heat for 30 seconds. Shake it slightly, return it to the heat, and crack the lid just enough to allow the steam to escape. Once the corn is popping rapidly, shake the pot with the lid partially on until there are 5–7 seconds between pops. Pour the popcorn into a large bowl.

Place the remaining 1 Tbsp oil, the sugar, honey, and balsamic in a nonstick saucepan and stir to dissolve the sugar. Bring to a low boil—stronger than a simmer but not going crazy like a full boil—and cook, without stirring, until the caramel darkens, 3–5 minutes. Carefully add the baking soda—it will foam up!—and stir it in. Pour the syrup over the popcorn and stir quickly to cover all the kernels. Pour onto the baking tray and spread out evenly. Bake for 15–20 minutes, sprinkle with the sea salt, if using, and break it up into smaller pieces when cool enough to handle.

You can store this in an airtight container for about 1 week, but it's at its absolute best on the day you make it. When I make it, it doesn't even last a day!

Fig

This balsamic is beautifully harmonious, with a rich, full flavor that can only come from figs. This is the perfect accompaniment to a single cultivar, but it is equally beautiful on its own, drizzled on goat cheese and fresh salads. You'll find **Fig** dark balsamic vinegar in the following recipes (and in several recipe variations throughout the book):

FIG   167

This is a lovely light summer dessert. You can serve it in dessert cups, alongside pound cake, or on graham crackers. The balsamic adds a beautiful color to the cream. It's easy to switch up with whatever balsamic you've got on hand; just try to match the flavor to the berries or fruit you're using. I like to use fresh figs when they're in season, but since that's rare, I've provided many options! **SERVES 8**

Whipped Mascarpone with Summer Fruit

1 cup whipping (35%) cream
4 Tbsp granulated sugar, divided
1 cup mascarpone cheese
1 cup fresh berries or fruit (or you can use a mix of strawberries, raspberries, blackberries, cherries, blueberries, or whatever is in season)
2 Tbsp **Fig** dark balsamic vinegar

For a tropical twist, substitute **Coconut**, **Mango**, or **Pineapple** white balsamic in place of the **Fig**, use mango, pineapple, apricots, and peaches for the fruit, and garnish with ¼ cup of toasted, sweetened, shredded coconut.

Substitute **Strawberry**, **Raspberry**, **Black Cherry**, or **Chocolate** dark balsamic or **Vanilla**, **Plum**, or **Apricot** white balsamic for the **Fig** dark balsamic. All are equally delicious.

In a cold mixing bowl, whip the cream. When the cream is almost stiff, whip in 3 Tbsp of the sugar. When the cream is stiff, fold in the mascarpone cheese and place in the fridge, uncovered, for 15 minutes to chill.

In a separate bowl, place the berries, drizzle with the balsamic, and then sprinkle with the remaining 1 Tbsp sugar. If you're using cherries or strawberries, chop them roughly so the fruit is in smaller chunks; raspberries, blackberries, and blueberries can be left whole.

Stir the fruit to ensure everything is well coated in balsamic and allow to macerate for another 5–10 minutes.

Take the whipped cheese out of the fridge and gently fold in the balsamic macerated berries to create a swirl effect before serving.

This is a quick and easy appetizer. Fresh chèvre is best here as its flavor is rich, creamy, and not too sharp, but play around with blue, feta, or cream cheese to put your own spin on it. **SERVES 4 AS AN APPETIZER**

Chèvre Crostini

8–10 baguette slices, ¹⁄₂ inch thick
2 Tbsp fresh **extra virgin** olive oil
¹⁄₂ cup chèvre
¹⁄₂ cup arugula or baby kale
2 Tbsp **Fig** dark balsamic vinegar

To make this very herbaceous, I love to use **Neapolitan Herb** dark balsamic with a robust **extra virgin** olive oil such as **Manzanillo** or **Picual**.

Try **Blood Orange** fused olive oil and **Chocolate** dark balsamic vinegar for a rich twist, or **Tuscan Herb**, **Herbes de Provence**, or **Rosemary** infused olive oil and **Sicilian Lemon** white balsamic for something a bit fresher-tasting.

Smoked Salmon Chèvre Crostini To fancy-up this simple recipe and make a smoked salmon version, use **Wild Dill** infused olive oil on the crostini, add a small piece of lox to each piece of baguette along with the cheese and arugula, and top with **Pomegranate** dark balsamic.

Preheat the broiler to high.

Place the baguette slices on a cookie sheet. Drizzle with the olive oil and toast under the broiler until crisp and golden, about 2 minutes.

Top each piece of baguette with a generous spread of goat cheese and then arugula, and drizzle with the balsamic.

FIG 169

This recipe developed from a conversation with my mentor and close friend, Alessandra, about some figs she'd had at a cocktail party and wanted to recreate. We put our heads together and this is the result. The sweet but tangy balsamic soaks into the figs, the salty prosciutto complements the sweetness of the figs, and the creamy chèvre completes the equation. **SERVES 4 AS AN APPETIZER**

Roasted Chèvre Stuffed Figs

½ cup creamy chèvre
2 Tbsp honey
12 fresh figs
12 slices prosciutto
2 Tbsp Fig dark balsamic vinegar, divided
Cracked black pepper

Herb and Prosciutto Roasted Figs Use fresh cheese—a mascarpone or ricotta would be ideal—instead of the chèvre and whip 1 Tbsp of Herbes de Provence infused olive oil into it before adding it to the figs. Traditional dark balsamic also works well in place of the Fig dark balsamic in this variation.

Honey-Roasted Chèvre Stuffed Figs Use Honey Ginger white balsamic instead of the Fig dark balsamic.

Preheat the oven to 375°F. Line a rimmed baking tray with parchment paper.

In a small bowl, whip the chèvre with the honey until smooth and creamy.

Wash and rinse the figs. Slice off the top and bottom of each one so they will sit upright on a cutting board without falling over. Make four evenly spaced vertical slices down each fig, slicing down about three-quarters of the way. (I find scissors are easier to use than a knife for this.) With a small spoon, gently open the fig slightly. Place a small spoonful of chèvre inside each fig.

Gently wrap each fig in prosciutto and fold over the bottom to keep it in place. Put the figs on the prepared baking tray and drizzle with 1 Tbsp of the balsamic.

Bake for 10–15 minutes, until the prosciutto is crisp, the figs are just starting to brown on top, and the chèvre is golden and gooey.

Remove from the oven, drizzle with the remaining 1 Tbsp balsamic, and finish with cracked pepper to taste.

Blackberry Ginger

This complex aged balsamic vinegar combines the gentle heat of ginger and the ripe sweetness of blackberry—and doesn't quite taste like either of them. These flavors work wonderfully well together over pancakes or ice cream, in jelly, and with pork, beef, and Asian-style dishes. You'll find **Blackberry Ginger** dark balsamic vinegar in the following recipes (and in several recipe variations throughout the book):

A pan sauce is a lovely thing. Not quite gravy, closer to a chutney, pan sauces are warm and perfect with pork. After you've seared the pork, reserve the juices and use them in the sauce. This recipe is pretty versatile, as you'll see from the list of variations. **SERVES 4**

Pork Tenderloin with Balsamic Pan Sauce

1 (2–3 lb) pork tenderloin
3 Tbsp **extra virgin** olive oil, divided
1/2 tsp sea salt
1/4 tsp cracked black pepper
Leaves from 10 sprigs thyme, divided, or 1/2 tsp dried thyme, divided
1 shallot, thinly sliced
1/3 cup chicken stock
1 small Golden Delicious apple, peeled and diced
1 cup cranberries (fresh or frozen)
1/4 cup **Blackberry Ginger** dark balsamic vinegar
1/2 tsp grainy Dijon mustard

For a fully savory version, use a mixture of 2 cloves of minced garlic, 2 Tbsp fresh rosemary, 1 Tbsp fresh oregano, and 1 Tbsp fresh sage instead of the cranberries, and **Neapolitan Herb** dark balsamic in place of the **Blackberry Ginger**.

If apple is your favorite fruit, replace the cranberries with an additional apple, and use **Apple** white balsamic vinegar in place of the **Blackberry Ginger**.

Apricot Use apricots instead of cranberries, **Apricot** white balsamic with fresh or dried mint instead of the thyme, and **Basil** infused olive oil instead of **extra virgin**.

Blueberry Use blueberries instead of cranberries, **Wild Blueberry** dark balsamic instead of **Blackberry Ginger**, **Rosemary** infused olive oil instead of **extra virgin**, and fresh or dried rosemary instead of the thyme.

Cinnamon Pear Double the apple, omit the berries, and use **Cinnamon Pear** dark balsamic and fresh nutmeg.

Preheat the oven to 425°F.

Wash the pork tenderloin with hot water and pat it dry. Drizzle it with 1 Tbsp of the olive oil, then season with the salt, pepper, and half of the thyme, rubbing them well into the tenderloin.

In a medium-sized heavy-bottomed frying pan over medium-high heat, add 1 Tbsp of the olive oil and sear the pork until well browned all over, about 3 minutes per side. Don't rush this step. Transfer the tenderloin to a roasting pan, leaving the juices in the frying pan, and roast for 10–12 minutes, or until the meat reaches 140°F. Remove from the oven and let rest for 5 minutes before slicing.

In the frying pan the pork was seared in, cook the shallot in the remaining 1 Tbsp olive oil on medium-high for 2–3 minutes until softened, then deglaze the pan with the chicken stock. Add the apple and cranberries and cook for 3 minutes, scraping the drippings from the bottom of the pan. Add the balsamic, Dijon, and remaining thyme and turn down the heat to medium-low. Simmer the sauce for 10 minutes, until reduced and thickened slightly. Season to taste with more salt and pepper and drizzle over the pork to serve.

I dream of having a pantry stocked with homemade chutneys, dressings, and sauces, but who has the time? Luckily, this fabulous Asian-inspired sauce doesn't take too long to cook up. It's sweet and spicy, and goes well with any combination of veg and meat, or even just veg. At least once a month I double this recipe and pop it in the fridge to use often. **MAKES ABOUT 1 CUP**

Blackberry Ginger Stir-Fry Sauce

¼ cup **Blackberry Ginger** dark balsamic
   vinegar
1 shallot, minced
2 Tbsp cornstarch
2 Tbsp brown sugar
2 Tbsp lime juice
2 Tbsp grainy Dijon mustard
1 Tbsp Sriracha sauce
1 Tbsp Worcestershire sauce
2 tsp ground ginger
2 tsp dried parsley
1 tsp dried thyme

Black Cherry Stir-Fry Sauce For a fruitier version of this sauce that also subs amazingly as a steak or pork chop marinade, use **Cherry** dark balsamic instead of the **Blackberry Ginger**.

Honey Ginger Stir-Fry Sauce Substitute **Honey Ginger** white balsamic for the **Blackberry Ginger** for a lighter and slightly sweeter version of this sauce.

Whisk all the ingredients in a small bowl or place them all in a Mason jar and shake well.

To use, pour about 1 Tbsp per 1 cup of veggies into a hot frying pan filled with lightly sautéed vegetables. Bring to a boil and turn the vegetables to coat evenly. Cook until the sauce has thickened.

This will keep in an airtight container in the fridge for about 1 month.

Coffee cakes are my weakness. If there's one on the counter, it's gone within minutes. This blackberry breakfast buckle is a favorite during August when blackberries are on every street corner—literally!—where I live in Victoria, BC, Canada. When blackberries aren't in season, raspberries, blueberries, and rhubarb are all a great second choice. **MAKES ONE (8- × 8-INCH) SQUARE OR ONE (9-INCH) ROUND CAKE**

Blackberry Breakfast Buckle

CAKE
2 cups fresh blackberries
2 Tbsp **Blackberry Ginger** dark balsamic vinegar
¼ cup mild and creamy **extra virgin** olive oil
1 egg
⅔ cup granulated sugar
2 cups all-purpose flour
2 tsp baking powder
1 tsp baking soda
¾ cup 2% milk

STREUSEL TOPPING
¼ cup all-purpose flour
¼ cup brown sugar, packed
1 tsp ground ginger
½ tsp ground nutmeg
2 Tbsp **Lemon** fused olive oil

This cake is equally good with **Traditional** dark balsamic, but for a floral take on it, look for **Lavender** dark balsamic.

Preheat the oven to 350°F. Grease an 8- × 8-inch baking pan or 9-inch springform pan.

In a small bowl, toss the blackberries with the balsamic. Set aside.

In a medium-sized mixing bowl, beat the olive oil with the egg until frothy. Whisk in the sugar. Sift in the flour, baking powder, and baking soda and gently fold to combine. Add the milk to loosen the batter and use a wooden spoon to fully incorporate.

Fold in half of the blackberries and vinegar, being careful not to break too many of the berries. Pour the batter into the prepared pan. Dot the batter with the remaining blackberries and drizzle with any juices from the bowl. Gently tap the cake pan on the counter to remove any air bubbles.

In a small bowl, mix together the streusel ingredients to form a crumbly mixture.

Sprinkle the batter with the streusel and bake for 35 minutes, or until a toothpick inserted in the center of the cake comes out clean.

As soon as the cake comes out of the oven, run a knife around the outside to loosen it from the edges of the pan. Let sit in the pan for 10 minutes then serve warm with a hot cup of Earl Grey tea.

Espresso

This balsamic lives up to its name: It'll wake you up. Its amazing taste of rich, dark-roasted espresso is a great complement to steak, salads, cheesecake, and ice cream. Try pairing it with **Chipotle** infused olive oil or **Blood Orange** fused olive oil for a unique salad dressing. You'll find **Espresso** dark balsamic in the following recipes (and in several recipe variations throughout the book):

I've been blessed with many special people in my life—mentors, friends, grandmas—and we have all bonded in the kitchen. It's where community is created and connections are made. When I lived in Kansas City, I stayed with an amazing family on a farm, and Grandma Atwell lived right next door. She taught me so much, including the importance of making Sunday lunch a time when the whole family gets together to share a meal and stories from their week. This beef brisket often landed on the table for those Sunday lunches. We would put it together on Saturday evening in the slow cooker and the house would smell heavenly in the morning. Leftovers make lovely lunches. **SERVES 6–8**

Kansas City–Style Slow Cooker Beef Brisket

1 (4–5 lb) beef brisket
2 Tbsp celery seed, divided
1 tsp sea salt, divided
2 garlic cloves, minced, divided
4 Tbsp liquid smoke, divided
4 Tbsp **Espresso** dark balsamic vinegar, divided
20 whole black peppercorns
2 cups Espresso Barbecue Sauce (page 178)

Line your slow cooker with parchment paper and allow the parchment edges to fall over the side.

Cut the brisket in half so that it will fit into the slow cooker. Place one piece in the slow cooker and sprinkle the top of it with 1 Tbsp of the celery seed, ½ tsp salt, 1 minced clove of garlic, 2 Tbsp of the liquid smoke, and 2 Tbsp of the balsamic.

Place the second piece of brisket on top and sprinkle with the remaining celery seed, salt, garlic, liquid smoke, and balsamic. Sprinkle with the peppercorns, fold the edges of the parchment paper over top to cover everything, and place the lid on the slow cooker. Cook on low for 8–10 hours.

Remove the lid of the slow cooker, peel back the parchment paper, and scrape off the peppercorns. Using two forks, shred the meat into chunks. It should be extremely tender and just falling apart.

Carefully pull out the parchment paper, allowing the meat to fall into the slow cooker. Add the barbecue sauce and coat the meat thoroughly and evenly. Turn the slow cooker to high for 30 minutes or continue to cook on low for 1½ hours, to heat the sauce and meat together.

If you've ever lived in the Midwest, you're completely spoiled as far as barbecue sauce is concerned. However, I'm pretty confident this recipe can stand up to the competition. It's lovely on beef, pork, or chicken, and I also use it in the Maple Baked Beans (page 213) and Kansas City–Style Slow Cooker Beef Brisket (page 177), and any other time it's required— and sometimes even when it isn't. The **Espresso** dark balsamic vinegar adds a delicious layer of deep, roasted notes to the sauce. The sweetness of the vinegar makes the sauce taste smooth and not too sharp and brings an almost nutty note. **MAKES 6 CUPS**

Espresso Barbecue Sauce

1 large onion, diced

2 garlic cloves, minced

1 small red or serrano chili pepper, seeded and diced

2 Tbsp robust, fresh **extra virgin** olive oil

2 cups tomato ketchup

2 cups tomato sauce

1 cup brown sugar, packed

1 cup **Espresso** dark balsamic vinegar

½ cup molasses

1 Tbsp liquid smoke (optional)

3 tsp smoked paprika

2 tsp celery seed

1 tsp ground cinnamon

Sea salt and ground black pepper

In a large saucepan, sauté the onion, garlic, and chili in the olive oil until the onion is translucent and soft, 3–5 minutes. Add the remaining ingredients and stir well to combine.

Bring the sauce to a boil then turn down the heat to a simmer and cook, uncovered, until thick, about 30 minutes. The longer this sauce simmers and reduces, the more intense the flavor. Feel free to use this immediately, but the flavors really meld if you let it sit overnight.

Keep this in airtight jars in the fridge for up to 4 months.

Apple Balsamic Barbecue Sauce Use **Red Apple** dark balsamic instead of the **Espresso** for the perfect version for pork.

Chocolate Balsamic Barbecue Sauce Use **Chocolate** dark balsamic instead of the **Espresso** for an even richer version.

Maple Balsamic Barbecue Sauce Use **Maple** dark balsamic instead of the **Espresso** for a sweeter option.

In my early days of experimenting with different infused balsamic vinegars, this recipe was a game-changer. These steaks were so intensely good, thanks to just one ingredient, that I had to press forward with my flavor experiments. Here, the **Espresso** dark balsamic vinegar not only adds incredible flavor to the steaks, but also naturally candies the outside of the meat. When you flip your steak, the balsamic candy seals in the juices and keeps the meat extra tender. I use three flips: two to sear and seal each side, and a third to add the cheese. **SERVES 2**

Espresso Blue Steaks

2 grilling steaks
½ cup **Espresso** dark balsamic vinegar
½ cup crumbled blue cheese (any type)

In a large bowl or baking dish, place the steaks and drizzle them with the balsamic. Let them sit for at least 1 hour, flip, and let rest for another hour, or up to overnight.

Heat the grill to at least 500°F.

Reserving the balsamic in which they marinated, place the steaks on the grill. Drizzle each one with 1 Tbsp of the reserved balsamic.

Let the steaks sit on the grill for 3 minutes for rare-medium and 5 minutes for well done, then flip, and drizzle each steak with another 1 Tbsp each of the reserved balsamic. Repeat until the steaks reach the desired doneness. After the final flip, sprinkle with the blue cheese.

Serve immediately on a bed of garlic mashed potatoes or alongside grilled veggies and Barbecue Garlic Potato Wedges (page 103).

This oil-free marinade is simple to make but has complex, delicious flavors. It's obviously great for marinating fresh meat, but it's also wonderful for freezing with meat. Just add it to the freezer bags of meat so that it marinates while freezing and then thawing. Note that you can't use the marinade on a fresh piece of meat once it's thawed out because of the risk of cross-contamination. I remove all the marinade from thawed-out meat before cooking it, just to be safe. (All the flavor has already been absorbed anyway.) **MAKES 1 CUP**

Espresso Grill Marinade

2 garlic cloves
½ small onion
½ cup **Espresso** dark balsamic vinegar
1 Tbsp Pommery or Dijon-style mustard
2 tsp Worcestershire sauce
2 tsp cracked black pepper

Mix all the ingredients well in a blender until smooth. This will keep in an airtight container in the fridge for up to 2 weeks.

Pork Ribs Marinade Double the recipe and use **Red Apple** or **Neapolitan Herb** dark balsamic in place of the **Espresso** and add 2 Tbsp lemon juice and 2 Tbsp brown sugar.

Simple Salmon Marinade Add ¼ cup fresh chopped dill and use **Pomegranate** dark balsamic in place of the **Espresso**.

Spicy Chicken Grill Marinade Add 2 Tbsp hot sauce and use **Apple** or **Apricot** white balsamic vinegar instead of the **Espresso**.

I believe short ribs are a seriously underrated meat. Easy to prepare and great for crowds, they are especially tender when braised. I like to stack them upright in a slow cooker and cook them all day on low. This recipe doubles easily if you're serving a crowd. Serve these with Pan-Fried Potatoes (page 23), Whipped Feta Dip (page 262), Lime & Cilantro Guacamole (page 69), and Roasted Tomato Salsa (page 117) for a delicious appetizer for a larger group. **SERVES 4**

Beer & Balsamic Braised Beef Short Ribs

2–3 lb trimmed beef short ribs
2 Tbsp robust **extra virgin** olive oil
1 large onion
4 garlic cloves
⅓ cup **Espresso** dark balsamic vinegar
2 Tbsp tomato paste
2 cups stout-style dark beer
4–6 cups beef stock

Many of the dark balsamic vinegars are great alternatives for this recipe, but it's important to match them up with the right style of beer or wine in place of the stout. Here are my favorite swap-outs:

Beer & Blackberry Balsamic Braised Beef Short Ribs Lager and **Blackberry Ginger** dark balsamic

Chocolate Braised Beef Short Ribs Porter and **Chocolate** dark balsamic

Maple Infused Braised Beef Short Ribs Milk stout and **Maple** dark balsamic

Simple Fig Balsamic Beef Braised Short Ribs Merlot and **Fig** dark balsamic

Simple Wine Braised Beef Short Ribs Shiraz and **Pomegranate** dark balsamic

Traditional-Style Balsamic Braised Beef Short Ribs Cabernet or Carménère and **Traditional** dark balsamic

In a frying pan, brown the short ribs on all sides in the olive oil, searing well. Don't rush this step; it should take about 10 minutes per batch. Remove from the frying pan and place in a small roasting pan, just big enough to hold everything comfortably, bone side up, or stack them in a slow cooker.

Chop the onion and garlic, add to the frying pan, and sauté until soft and golden, 5–7 minutes. Add the balsamic and tomato paste to deglaze the pan, scraping any bits from the bottom. Pour this mixture over the short ribs. Add the beer and enough beef stock to completely cover the meat.

OVEN METHOD Preheat the oven to 325°F. Cover the ribs tightly with two layers of foil to prevent any steam from escaping, and place in the oven for 3 hours.

SLOW COOKER METHOD Place the lid on the slow cooker and cook the ribs on low for 6–8 hours.

TO FINISH Remove from the oven or slow cooker and let rest in the cooking vessel for 15 minutes. Pile high on a serving platter, reserving the drippings. Remove 2 cups of the drippings from the roasting pan or slow cooker and place in a small saucepan. Bring to a boil then simmer for about 5 minutes to reduce and use as a gravy if desired.

Black Cherry

Rich and sweet black cherries are combined with aged balsamic vinegar to produce a sweet, fragrant, and very rich-tasting product. This balsamic has character! It is a perfect complement to salads that feature cheese, especially feta, goat, and blue. It pairs well with the lighter single varietal **extra virgin** olive oils and really shines alongside the **Blood Orange** and **Lemon** fused olive oils. You'll find **Black Cherry** dark balsamic vinegar in the following recipes (and in several recipe variations throughout the book):

This barbecue sauce is lovely on pork with some goat cheese crumbled on top. The richness of the cherries makes it quite different from your typical barbecue sauce. If you're looking for something closer to a typical sauce, add some liquid smoke and chili powder. If cherries aren't available, you can use plums and switch the vinegar to a Black Currant or Violet balsamic. **MAKES 3 CUPS**

Black Cherry Balsamic Barbecue Sauce

½ cup red onion
2 garlic cloves
2 Tbsp fruity **extra virgin** olive oil
1 cup crushed tomatoes
1 cup chopped pitted cherries
½ cup brown sugar, packed
½ cup **Black Cherry** dark balsamic vinegar
¼ cup molasses
1 Tbsp Worcestershire sauce
¼ cup dark rum
2 tsp cracked black pepper
1 tsp sea salt

Finely chop the onion and garlic. In a heavy-bottomed saucepan over medium heat, sauté the onion and garlic in the olive oil until soft. Add the tomatoes and cherries and stir to combine. Add the sugar, balsamic, molasses, Worcestershire sauce, rum, pepper, and salt. Bring to a boil and then turn down to a simmer, stirring once or twice, and until thick, about 20 minutes.

Remove from the heat and allow to cool. Purée the sauce until smooth and store it in an airtight container in the fridge for up to 2 weeks.

Apple Balsamic Barbecue Sauce Replace the cherries with 1 cup of unsweetened apple sauce and the **Black Cherry** dark balsamic with **Apple** white balsamic.

Plum Balsamic Barbecue Sauce Use sliced fresh pitted plums instead of the cherries and **Plum** white balsamic instead of the **Black Cherry** dark balsamic.

I somehow never appreciated appetizers until my husband I were married, and now I know what I was missing. These puffs are a must as a straight appetizer or as part of an appetizer dinner. If Gorgonzola isn't your thing, feel free to switch it up for goat cheese or feta. The **Black Cherry** dark balsamic complements the natural tang of the blue cheese and adds a delicious richness to the puffs. **MAKES 12 PUFFS, SERVES 4 AS AN APPETIZER**

Baked Gorgonzola Puffs

1 sheet puff pastry (store-bought is fine)
2 Tbsp fruity, robust **extra virgin** olive oil
1 cup crumbled Gorgonzola
⅓ cup chopped walnuts
1 Tbsp chopped fresh rosemary leaves
2 Tbsp Black Cherry dark balsamic vinegar
Cracked black pepper

Apricot Baked Gorgonzola Puffs Use Herbes de Provence infused olive oil in place of the **extra virgin** and Apricot white balsamic in place of the Black Cherry.

Harvest Baked Gorgonzola Puffs Use Blood Orange fused olive oil in place of the **extra virgin** and Maple or Cinnamon Pear dark balsamic in place of the Black Cherry.

Roasted Plum Gorgonzola Puffs Use Lime fused olive oil in place of the **extra virgin** and Plum white balsamic in place of the Black Cherry.

Savory Baked Gorgonzola Puffs Use Rosemary infused olive oil in place of the **extra virgin** and Neapolitan Herb dark balsamic in place of the Black Cherry.

Preheat the oven to 350°F.

Roll out the pastry to a ¼-inch-thick square. Using a pizza cutter, trim the edges, if necessary, and cut it into 12 squares. Brush each square with the olive oil. Place each square, olive oil side down, into a muffin tin and gently shape so that the corners are poking up and the bottom is pressed down.

Divide the Gorgonzola evenly between the pastry cups and top with a sprinkle of walnuts and fresh rosemary. Drizzle with the balsamic and sprinkle with cracked black pepper.

Bake for 10–12 minutes, until the pastry has puffed up and is golden brown. Serve immediately.

These simple yet delicious grilled chops are easy to put together when company arrives unexpectedly—or decides to stay longer than planned! This recipe lets you pull off an incredible meal without hiding in the kitchen for hours. It's easily doubled or tripled. **SERVES 4**

Glazed Barbecue Pork Chops

4 butterfly pork chops
Sea salt and ground black pepper
¼ cup **Black Cherry** dark balsamic vinegar
1 Tbsp grainy Dijon mustard

Apple-Glazed Barbecue Pork Chops
Substitute **Apple** white balsamic for the **Black Cherry** dark balsamic.

Sweet Sesame Barbecue Pork Chops
Substitute **Apricot** or **Plum** white balsamic for the **Black Cherry** dark balsamic and tahini for the Dijon.

Heat the grill to 500°F.

Wash the pork chops, pat them dry, and season with salt and pepper.

In a small bowl, whisk together the balsamic and Dijon to make a glaze.

Place the pork chops on the grill and use a pastry brush to quickly brush one-quarter of the glaze over the chops. Grill for 3–5 minutes, depending on the thickness of the chops, with the lid of the barbecue down, giving the balsamic a chance to caramelize. Flip the chops and brush them again with one-quarter of the glaze. Flip two more times until the glaze is finished and the chops are well browned and cooked through. Serve immediately with salad and plenty of sunshine.

Hot Fudge. Need I say more? Well, actually, I do need to tell you that the addition of the dark balsamic here only makes it better. Serve over ice cream, with warm brownies, or even as a frosting for Black Forest cake. **MAKES 2 CUPS**

Black Cherry Hot Fudge

¾ cup whipping (35%) cream
½ cup granulated sugar
¼ cup **Black Cherry** dark balsamic vinegar
8 oz unsweetened chocolate, chopped
Pinch of fine sea salt

There are many variations for this! Instead of the **Black Cherry** dark balsamic, you can opt for:

❋ **Classic Hot Fudge** Use **Vanilla** white balsamic

❋ **Double Chocolate Hot Fudge** Use **Chocolate** dark balsamic

❋ **Mocha Hot Fudge** Use **Espresso** dark balsamic

❋ **Raspberry Hot Fudge** Use **Raspberry** dark balsamic

❋ **Rich & Sweet Hot Fudge** Use **Fig** dark balsamic

❋ **Strawberry Hot Fudge** Use **Strawberry** dark balsamic

In a heavy-bottomed saucepan, whisk together the whipping cream, sugar, and balsamic. Bring to a gentle simmer over medium heat and be careful not to let the cream boil. When the mixture is just starting to release steam, remove from the heat and add the chopped chocolate. Let sit for 5 minutes without stirring and then whisk until the chocolate is fully combined.

Transfer to a clean Mason jar or other glass container and let cool to room temperature. It will thicken as it cools, so feel free to microwave it for 10 seconds to warm it up when you want to use it.

You can store this in an airtight container for up to 1 month in the fridge—although, let's be honest: it never lasts that long!

Cherry pie is a summer staple at our house, and this version takes the old-time favorite to the heavens. A glacé is a single-crust pie with a glossy top, and in this case the single crust keeps the gorgeous cherries on display, making this as good to look at as it is to eat. Use black sweet cherries—Bing, if possible—rather than sour cherries to make this pie decadent; the balsamic adds richness to the pastry. **MAKES ONE (9-INCH) PIE**

Cherry Glacé

PASTRY

2 cups cake and pastry flour

2 tsp baking soda

1/2 tsp sea salt

3/4 cup **Lemon** fused olive oil

1 egg

1 Tbsp **Sicilian Lemon** white balsamic vinegar

FILLING

4 cups fresh black cherries, rinsed and pitted

1/4 cup **Black Cherry** dark balsamic vinegar

1/2 cup brown sugar, packed

3 Tbsp cornstarch

You can use **Peach** or **Apricot** white balsamic in place of the **Sicilian Lemon** in the pastry.

Blueberry Glacé Substitute 4 cups fresh blueberries in place of the cherries and **Wild Blueberry** dark balsamic instead of the **Black Cherry**.

Stone Fruit Glacé Substitute 2 cups peeled, sliced peaches + 1 cup sliced plums + 1 cup sliced apricots in place of the cherries, and use **Apricot** or **Plum** white balsamic instead of the **Black Cherry** dark balsamic.

Strawberry Glacé Substitute 4 cups sliced fresh strawberries for the cherries and use **Strawberry** dark balsamic instead of the **Black Cherry**.

To make the pastry, in a bowl, sift the flour with the baking soda and salt. Make a well in the bottom of the bowl and drizzle in the olive oil. Mix gently with a pastry blender or two knives until it resembles coarse oatmeal.

Crack the egg into a 1 cup measure, beat it slightly with a fork, and add the Sicilian Lemon balsamic, continuing to beat until it is frothy and white. Fill the measuring cup with ice-cold water and gently mix into the flour.

Using your hands, blend until the ingredients are fully incorporated. Try not to knead it too much. Press the pastry into a ball, wrap it in plastic wrap or a tea towel, and place it in the fridge for 30 minutes. While the pastry is cooling, prepare the filling. Place cherries in a medium-sized saucepan and add the Black Cherry balsamic. Put the lid on and simmer the cherries over medium heat for 10–15 minutes, until they begin to soften.

In a small bowl, whisk the sugar and cornstarch until no lumps remain. Add 1/2 cup cold water, mixing to incorporate, then add to the cherry mixture.

Bring to a hard boil over high heat and continue to boil over medium-high heat, stirring constantly, until the juices are clear and the sauce is starting to thicken.

Preheat the oven to 350°F.

Take the pastry from the fridge and roll it out into a 10-inch circle. Place it in a 9-inch pie plate and trim the edges, letting the pastry hang 1/2 inch over the side of the plate. Prick the pastry with a fork or line it with pastry weights to prevent it from bubbling while baking. Bake for 10 minutes, until golden brown and cooked through. Pour the hot cherry mixture into the warm pie shell and allow it to set, uncovered, for 4–6 hours in the fridge. Enjoy with a dusting of icing sugar and a scoop of ice cream!

Strawberry

This dark balsamic is both sweet and tart and has a bright, mouthwatering flavor. In addition to being used as a vinegar, it can be used as a condiment on fruit salads and desserts, such as cheesecake, ice cream, or chocolate pudding. Try pairing it with a mild fruity **extra virgin** olive oil to set off an awesome spinach salad. You'll find **Strawberry** dark balsamic vinegar in the following recipes (and in several recipe variations throughout the book):

Trifle is such a fun dessert. It's easy to put together but it's still great for a special occasion and I find it tastes even better the next day. The **Strawberry** dark balsamic adds a depth to this trifle, turning it into a creamy, rich dessert to be savored, rather than something that gives you a sugar rush and makes your cheeks tingle. **SERVES 4–6**

Individual Chocolate Trifles with Stewed Balsamic Strawberries

2 cups washed, rinsed, hulled, and sliced strawberries, plus a few more for garnish

¼ cup **Strawberry** dark balsamic vinegar

1 chocolate pound cake or 8- × 8-inch pan brownies

1 cup whipping (35%) cream

1 Tbsp icing sugar

For extra chocolate goodness, use **Chocolate** dark balsamic instead of the **Strawberry**.

Individual Chocolate Trifles with Stewed Balsamic Blueberries Use **Vanilla** white balsamic and 2 cups of blueberries instead of the **Strawberry** dark balsamic and strawberries. Chocolate and blueberries are a flavor combination I always feel is underrated or forgotten. It's so delicious!

Individual Chocolate Trifles with Stewed Balsamic Raspberries Use **Raspberry** dark balsamic and 2 cups of fresh raspberries instead of the **Strawberry** dark balsamic and strawberries for another classic chocolate-fruit pairing. You might want to run the sauce through a mesh strainer to remove the raspberry seeds for this option.

Place the strawberries in a saucepan over medium heat with the balsamic, bring to a simmer, and cook for 5 minutes, until the strawberries are soft and the juice easily coats the back of a spoon. You'll have about 1 cup of stewed strawberries.

Cut up the pound cake or brownies into 1-inch cubes or chunks. Whip the cream with the icing sugar until soft peaks form.

Place some cake in the bottom of 4 parfait glasses. Top with 2 heaping Tbsp of the strawberries and a dollop of whipped cream. Repeat with the remaining ingredients, finishing with a dollop of whipped cream and some fresh strawberries on top.

Panzanella salads are a great excuse to have a salad with more croutons than anything else. Hearty, delicious, and filling, they are the ultimate summer food when filled with fresh garden vegetables. The combination of **Strawberry** dark balsamic vinegar and **Basil** infused olive oil pairs beautifully with the Parmesan cheese, bell peppers, sweet strawberries, and peppery arugula. This is a great way to use up slightly stale or day-old bread, although fresh works just fine as well. **SERVES 2 AS A SIDE**

Arugula Panzanella Salad

2 slices crusty sourdough or round bread
1 cup sliced strawberries
½ red or yellow bell pepper, sliced
4 Tbsp **Basil** infused olive oil, divided
4 Tbsp **Strawberry** dark balsamic vinegar, divided
1 bunch arugula
2 Tbsp shaved Parmesan Cheese
Sea salt and cracked black pepper

Lime fused olive oil has an even more summery note than the **Basil**.

Wild Blueberry dark balsamic works well in place of the **Strawberry** if you swap out the Parmesan for feta.

Preheat the oven to 400°F. Line a rimmed baking tray with parchment paper.

Cut the bread into 1-inch cubes and spread them evenly on the baking tray with the strawberries and bell pepper. Drizzle with 3 Tbsp of the olive oil and 3 Tbsp of the balsamic, shaking the pan to evenly distribute. Roast for 10 minutes, turning the bread halfway through to ensure it's evenly toasted.

Wash and rinse the arugula and roughly tear the leaves. Place the arugula in a serving bowl, and drizzle with the remaining olive oil and balsamic. Toss the leaves to coat evenly.

When the strawberries and peppers are just soft and the bread is well toasted, add them to the arugula, scraping any juices from the parchment into the salad bowl. Top with the Parmesan and season to taste with salt and pepper.

This fudge is not only easy to make, it also looks beautiful. It's great for a light summer treat or a simple make-ahead dessert. The balsamic makes the already delicious strawberries more like candy than fruit. **MAKES ONE (8- × 4-INCH) LOAF PAN**

Strawberries & Cream Fudge

CANDIED STRAWBERRIES

½ cup dried strawberries

½ cup granulated sugar

¼ cup **Strawberry** dark balsamic vinegar

FUDGE

2 Tbsp + 1 tsp **Blood Orange** fused olive oil

2 cups granulated sugar

1 cup table (18%) cream

¼ cup white or golden corn syrup

Creamy Maple Walnut Fudge Substitute large walnut pieces for the dried strawberries and use **Maple** dark balsamic in place of the **Strawberry**.

Festive Fudge Substitute ¾ cup of sweetened dried cranberries for the dried strawberries, use **Cranberry Pear** or **Vanilla** white balsamic instead of the **Strawberry** dark balsamic, and add ¼ tsp of cinnamon when you're mixing in the 2 Tbsp of **Blood Orange** fused olive oil for the fudge component.

Tropical Fudge Substitute dried mango, papaya, and pineapple for the dried strawberries, **Coconut** or **Mango** white balsamic for the **Strawberry** dark balsamic, and **Lime** fused olive oil for the **Blood Orange** fused olive oil in the fudge component.

To make the candied strawberries, place the strawberries in a saucepan over medium heat, making sure to cut any of the large strawberries in half. Add the sugar and balsamic and stir constantly until the sugar has melted and the strawberries are soft, about 5 minutes. Bring just to a boil and then turn down the heat; simmer, uncovered, for 5 minutes until the liquid is thick and the strawberries are candied, stirring to avoid sticking. Allow to cool to room temperature while you make the fudge.

Line an 8- × 4-inch loaf tin with parchment paper and drizzle 1 tsp of the olive oil over it, using your hands to coat the paper with the oil.

Pour the sugar, cream, and corn syrup into a heavy-bottomed saucepan. Stirring constantly, bring to a simmer over medium heat. When the mixture starts to boil, stop stirring. Let it boil gently for 10–12 minutes until it reaches 240°F on a candy thermometer or soft ball stage (see page 226).

Remove from the heat and stir in the 2 Tbsp olive oil. Using a handheld or stand mixer, beat the fudge on high speed until it is no longer glossy, 5–7 minutes.

Pour the fudge into the prepared pan and smooth the top gently with an oiled spatula. Carefully place the candied strawberries in the fudge and press gently so the tops are just poking out.

Place in the fridge, uncovered, and allow to set for at least 3 hours, or overnight. Remove from the fridge, lift the fudge out of the pan, and peel back the parchment paper. Using a sharp knife, cut the loaf into 1-inch-wide bars, and cut each bar into four pieces.

Store in an airtight container for up to 1 week.

Raspberry

This balsamic is bursting with the flavor of whole, fresh raspberries. It is rich, sweet, tangy, and well balanced. Try it with your favorite **extra virgin** oil (it's incredible paired with **Lemon** fused olive oil) on fresh greens and crumbled goat cheese or as a glaze on pork tenderloin. You'll find **Raspberry** dark balsamic vinegar in the following recipes (and in several recipe variations throughout the book):

These easy cheesecake treats are great for taking to work as a lunch treat, or for summer patio parties. I tend to use Nilla wafers for the base, but that's just a personal preference. Or try using chocolate cookies—I like Fudgee-Os or Oreos. **MAKES 12**

Cheesecake Treats with Raspberry Swirl

1 cup whole, fresh raspberries
2 Tbsp **Raspberry** dark balsamic vinegar
2 eggs
¼ cup granulated sugar
1 Tbsp **Lemon** fused olive oil
1 cup cream cheese
12 round vanilla wafer cookies

Keep the fresh raspberries and use **Pomegranate** or **Maple** dark balsamic for a richer, more complex twist.

Use 1 cup sliced fresh peaches instead of the raspberries, and **Vanilla**, **Plum**, **Apricot**, or **Honey Ginger** white balsamic instead of the dark balsamic.

Preheat the oven to 350°F. Line a muffin tin with cupcake papers.

In a small saucepan over medium heat, mash the raspberries slightly with a wooden spoon. Add the balsamic and mix well. Bring just to a boil, remove from the heat, and let cool.

In a mixing bowl, beat the eggs with the sugar and oil until frothy. Add the cream cheese in batches, mixing well between each addition, to form a creamy, smooth mixture.

In the bottom of each cup, place one wafer cookie. Spoon cream cheese mixture on top to fill the paper case halfway, add 2 Tbsp of the raspberry mixture, and top with more cream cheese mixture. The cupcake papers should be two-thirds full. Using a toothpick, swirl the raspberry mixture into the cheesecake, starting in the center and working your way out in a spiral motion.

Bake for 12 minutes, until puffed and the edges are just golden. Let cool completely in the pan before enjoying!

Where I live, we have so many wild berries. Being able to forage is something I never take for granted, and it is something I miss during the winter months. This syrup is one simple way to capture that summer freshness. Adding a splash of **Raspberry** dark balsamic vinegar enhances the flavor and brightens the syrup as well. Any neutral spirit will work here, which is why I chose vodka, as it doesn't impart any flavors to the syrup and it allows the berry flavor to retain its integrity. **MAKES 3 CUPS**

Raspberry Cocktail Syrup

2 cups fresh raspberries
1 cup high-proof (at least 80 proof) vodka
1 cup granulated sugar
2 Tbsp **Raspberry** dark balsamic vinegar

Apricot Cocktail Syrup Substitute freshly chopped apricots for the raspberries and use **Apricot** white balsamic instead of the **Raspberry** dark balsamic.

Blackberry Cocktail Syrup Substitute fresh blackberries for the raspberries and **Blackberry Ginger** dark balsamic for the **Raspberry**.

Blueberry Cocktail Syrup Substitute fresh blueberries for the raspberries and **Blueberry** or **Maple** dark balsamic for the **Raspberry**.

Cranberry Cocktail Syrup Substitute fresh cranberries for the raspberries, increase the sugar by 1/2 cup, and use **Cranberry Pear** white balsamic for the **Raspberry** dark balsamic.

Peach Cocktail Syrup Substitute freshly chopped peaches for the raspberries and use **Peach** white balsamic instead of the **Raspberry** dark balsamic.

Plum Cocktail Syrup Substitute chopped fresh plums for the raspberries and **Plum** white balsamic vinegar for the **Raspberry** dark balsamic.

Pomegranate Cocktail Syrup Substitute 2 1/2 cups of pomegranate arils for the raspberries and **Pomegranate** dark balsamic for the **Raspberry**.

Wash the raspberries well and shake dry. Place them in a mixing bowl and mash until they are broken up and the consistency is very pulpy, thick, and juicy. Add the vodka and stir to mix evenly with the berries, then cover and let sit overnight on the counter. Transfer the bowl to the fridge and let steep there for another 2 days, or up to 1 week. Each day remove the bowl from the fridge and stir gently to ensure the berries have fully extracted all their juices. At the end of the steeping time, strain the mixture into a Mason jar through a fine mesh strainer or a cheesecloth to remove any residue pulp and the seeds.

In a small saucepan over medium heat, heat the sugar with 1/2 cup of water and the balsamic, stirring until the sugar is fully dissolved. Remove from the heat and allow to cool to room temperature. Pour this mixture into the raspberry liqueur in the Mason jar and stir to combine.

Add a splash of this to gin and tonic, champagne, or a vodka soda for a refreshing drink that will immediately take you back to warm summer days.

Store in the fridge in an airtight container for up to 3 months.

This is another of those recipes that remind me of my childhood. My mom used to make it for almost every special family meal, and I always was the lucky one who was allowed to lick the pot. My aunt calls it "eating clouds"—it really is just that fluffy. The raspberries make it tart and sweet and give it the perfect texture. This is easily doubled and put into a 9- × 13-inch pan. The balsamic adds a new dimension, brightening the raspberries and the fluffiness of the egg whites. **SERVES 6**

Raspberry Fluff

1¹/₂ cups graham cracker crumbs
¹/₃ cup icing sugar
¹/₃ cup **Lemon** fused olive oil
4 cups whole raspberries (fresh or frozen)
1 package raspberry Jell-O
4 egg yolks
2 Tbsp **Raspberry** dark balsamic vinegar
4 egg whites
1 cup granulated sugar

To be honest, I've tried this recipe with so many different kinds of fruit and Jell-O and none of them work. This version is the best way to make it.

Grease an 8- × 8-inch baking pan.

In a medium bowl, mix together the cookie crumbs, icing sugar, and olive oil and press into the bottom of the prepared pan. Chill for at least 15 minutes.

Place the raspberries, Jell-O, egg yolks, and balsamic in a large saucepan over medium heat. Stir until slightly thick and coming just to a boil. Remove from the heat, pour into a large bowl, and chill for about 2 hours. It will thicken as it chills.

Beat the egg whites until stiff peaks form. Add the sugar, 2–3 Tbsp at a time, whipping after each addition. Fold the egg whites gently into the chilled raspberry mixture, being careful not to overmix. Big clumps of egg whites are totally fine—this mixture should not be smooth. Pour over the crumb crust. Chill, uncovered, for a minimum of 6 hours, or up to overnight.

Pomegranate

Incredibly sweet and succulent, this velvety, rich balsamic vinegar has endless culinary possibilities. Try glazing salmon with a pomegranate balsamic reduction (see page 263 for inspiration). It also makes a perfect pair with **Wild Dill** infused olive oil (no kidding!) or **Lemon** fused olive oil. You'll find **Pomegranate** dark balsamic vinegar in the following recipes (and in several recipe variations throughout the book):

If you've never cooked with long peppers before, you're in for a treat. Originally from India, they are also commonly grown in Indonesia and many tropical South Asian countries. They have a slightly smoky yet sweet and spicy flavor and just shine alongside the tangy pomegranate molasses and balsamic. The initial roasting at a high temperature creates a crispy crust. This is ideal for a special breakfast; simply pop it in the oven before you go to bed and 8 hours later you'll wake up to a heavenly smell! **SERVES 6–8 WITH LEFTOVERS**

Overnight Pomegranate-Glazed Ham

1 (8–10 lb) bone-in ham
1 Tbsp sea salt
2 long peppers
1 sprig thyme, leaves only
¼ tsp ground nutmeg
½ cup pomegranate molasses
¼ cup **Pomegranate** dark balsamic vinegar

If **Pomegranate** dark balsamic isn't in the cupboard, **Traditional** works equally well. For a fruitier version, try **Black Cherry** or **Red Apple**.

Wash the ham in hot water, pat dry, and place it fat side up in a roasting pan so it fits snugly. Rub the salt in on all sides and let rest, uncovered, at room temperature for 1 hour.

Preheat the oven to 450°F.

Using a large mortar and pestle, grind up the long peppers to a fine powder. Add the thyme leaves and nutmeg and grind together to mix. Add the molasses and balsamic. Mix well to combine and then smear evenly all over the ham.

Roast for 15 minutes at 450°F, then turn down the heat (without opening the oven door) to 200°F and roast for 6–8 hours, depending on the size of ham.

Let rest for 10 minutes before slicing.

Figs have such a short season that if you blink you'll miss them. This recipe is a great way to preserve the flavor of fresh delicious figs. The **Pomegranate** dark balsamic helps the figs caramelize but also tempers the extreme sweetness they can have. Serve over ice cream, spread on toast with cream cheese, or dollop on pork chops hot off the grill. **MAKES ABOUT 2 CUPS**

Stewed Figs

1 lb fresh figs
¼ cup **Pomegranate** dark balsamic vinegar
3 Tbsp granulated sugar

> Use **Fig** dark balsamic for extra fig flavor.
>
> Use **Strawberry** dark balsamic, or **Vanilla** or **Plum** white balsamic for sweeter variations.

Wash and pat dry the figs. Slice off the ends. Quarter the figs if they are small or roughly chop if they are larger and then place them in a saucepan over medium heat with the balsamic, sugar, and 2 Tbsp water.

Using a wooden spoon, gently crush the figs to extract some of the juices and stir to mix them with the balsamic and sugar.

Bring to a simmer and keep at a simmer, stirring frequently, until the figs are soft, and the juices have reduced to a thick syrup, about 20 minutes.

Spread on toast or over ice cream, or serve with a log of goat cheese and crackers for an easy and delicious appetizer.

These will keep in an airtight container in the fridge for up to 1 month.

Lemon is delicious, yes, but the zippy freshness that only limes can give is second to none. This limeade is perfect with the **Pomegranate** dark balsamic and blueberries for a tart freshness. If you can't find wild blueberries, good old standard highbush blueberries will work just fine. For a more tropical ice pop recipe, see page 277. **MAKES 10 ICE POPS**

Wild Blueberry & Pomegranate Limeade Ice Pops

2 cups wild blueberries (frozen work well)
¼ cup **Pomegranate** dark balsamic vinegar
¼ cup honey
1 cup lime juice (about 8 limes)

Blackberry & Lime Ice Pops For a tart, refreshing pop, substitute blackberries for the blueberries and use **Traditional** dark balsamic in place of the **Pomegranate**.

Raspberry & Lime Ice Pops If you're looking for a slightly sweeter version, swap out the blueberries for raspberries, increase the honey to ½ cup, and use **Raspberry** dark balsamic in place of the **Pomegranate**.

Strawberry & Lime Ice Pops A favorite on any day, I love to make these in the heat of July and dunk them in white rum for an adult version. Substitute strawberries for the wild blueberries, use **Strawberry** dark balsamic in place of the **Pomegranate**, and add a pinch of sea salt and white pepper to the berries while cooking for an extra pop of flavor.

Wild Blueberry & Lime Ice Pops For a fully blueberry flavor, use **Wild Blueberry** dark balsamic in place of the **Pomegranate**.

In a saucepan over medium heat, bring the blueberries, balsamic, and honey to a simmer until soft and cooked through, about 10 minutes.

Place in a food processor and blend until smooth. Pour through a fine mesh strainer into a large bowl to remove any extra skin and seeds. Add the lime juice and 1½ cups cold water, mixing well.

Pour into ice pop molds or small 3–4 oz paper drinking cups, such as Dixie cups, and place an ice pop stick in the middle of each.

Freeze for at least 6 hours. To remove from the molds, dip in near-boiling water for 5 seconds to loosen slightly. Eat immediately. Any uneaten ones can be wrapped in parchment paper, placed in resealable plastic bags, and returned to the freezer for later.

Wild Blueberry

This beautiful balsamic is tart, sweet, and perfect on a salad. Pair it with any single varietal **extra virgin** olive oil to enjoy maximum blueberry flavor or toss it with **Lemon** fused olive oil for a nice, crisp twist. Try it drizzled over sliced peaches, cantaloupe, fruit salad, or ice cream. For an extra-special treat, drizzle it over fresh hot pancakes made with **Blood Orange** fused olive oil (see variation on page 210) and add a dollop of mascarpone cheese. A delight for the senses! You'll find **Wild Blueberry** dark balsamic vinegar in the following recipes (and in several recipe variations throughout the book):

The trick to this recipe? Don't peek at the dumplings while they are cooking. The steam from cooking the blueberries also cooks the dumplings, and if it escapes, the dumplings will be soggy inside and won't set. This is a perfect winter evening dessert. **SERVES 4–6**

Blueberry Dumplings

4 cups fresh or frozen blueberries

¼ cup **Wild Blueberry** dark balsamic vinegar

¼ cup honey

2 cups all-purpose flour

2 tsp baking powder

¼ cup **Lemon** fused olive oil

Try this with your favorite berries or stone fruits in season.

Mango Coconut Lime Dumplings Substitute chopped frozen mango for the blueberries, add ½ cup coconut milk plus 2 Tbsp lime juice in place of the water to simmer, and use **Coconut** white balsamic in place of the **Wild Blueberry** dark balsamic.

Mango Dumplings Substitute chopped frozen mango for the blueberries and **Mango** white balsamic for the **Wild Blueberry** dark balsamic.

Plum Dumplings Substitute sliced prune plums or halved red or yellow plums for the blueberries and **Plum** white balsamic for the **Wild Blueberry** dark balsamic.

In a large saucepan over medium heat, bring the blueberries, balsamic, honey, and ½ cup of water to a simmer, uncovered. Stir to ensure the honey has dissolved and the berries are soft. Slowly bring to a gentle boil.

In a mixing bowl, sift together the flour and baking powder, drizzle in the olive oil, and mix well with your hands or a pastry blender to form an oatmeal-textured mixture.

Slowly add 1 cup of water, ¼ cup at a time, to form a very sticky dough.

While the berries are cooking—they must be boiling for this to work—remove the saucepan lid and use a large spoon to place 4–6 large dollops of dough on the top of them. Replace the lid and let sit for 15 minutes. *Do not peek!* After 15 minutes, and only after 15 minutes, remove the lid, spoon the dumplings into serving bowls, and top with a scoop of the berries. Enjoy as is, or with a drizzle of olive oil or a dollop of whipped cream. For a fun breakfast, top with yogurt.

Looking for a sweet, refreshing, summer drink after a long day in the berry patch? Look no further. This quick spritzer is so easy to make and so refreshing. **SERVES 2**

Berry Fizz Spritzer

2 cups mixed berries (blueberries, blackberries, raspberries, strawberries)
2 Tbsp **Wild Blueberry** dark balsamic
  vinegar
2 Tbsp honey
1 cup ice
2 cups soda water

Use the same fruit, but with **Pomegranate**,
Black Cherry, **Strawberry**, or **Raspberry**
dark balsamic vinegar instead of the
Wild Blueberry.

Peach Fizz Spritzer Use fresh peaches
instead of the mixed berries and
use **Apricot**, **Peach**, or **Plum** white
balsamic instead of the **Wild Blueberry**
dark balsamic.

Pineapple Fizz Spritzer Use fresh pineapple
instead of the mixed berries and **Coconut**,
Pineapple, or **Vanilla** white balsamic instead
of the **Wild Blueberry** dark balsamic.

In a blender, purée the berries, balsamic, honey, and ice. Divide between two glasses and top up each glass with 1 cup of club soda.

Add a straw and a few fresh berries threaded onto a drink umbrella.

Pancakes are typically a weekend lunch/dinner food for our family. This recipe makes just enough for two super-hungry people, or four normally hungry people, with bacon or sausage and maybe a fried egg. Breakfast for not-breakfast is always a wonderful thing. If you don't have buttermilk combine 2% milk with 2 Tbsp of **Peach** white balsamic vinegar (rather than the more traditional lemon juice) to make 2 cups. **SERVES 2–4**

Wild Blueberry Pancakes

PANCAKES
2 cups all-purpose flour
¼ cup granulated sugar
2 tsp baking powder
1 tsp baking soda
1 tsp sea salt
½ cup **Lemon** fused olive oil
2 cups buttermilk
2 eggs
1 cup wild blueberries

WILD BLUEBERRY SYRUP
½ cup maple syrup
2 Tbsp **Wild Blueberry** dark balsamic vinegar
¼ cup wild blueberries

TO SERVE
½ cup whipping (35%) cream (optional)

Swap out the **Lemon** fused olive oil for **Blood Orange** and omit the wild blueberries.

Try fresh raspberries instead of wild blueberries in both the pancake batter and the syrup and use **Raspberry** dark balsamic instead of the **Wild Blueberry** in the syrup.

Use **Maple** dark balsamic instead of the **Wild Blueberry** and omit the blueberries for a rich and delicious syrup.

To make the pancakes, in a large bowl, sift the flour, sugar, baking powder, baking soda, and salt. Make a well in the center and pour in the olive oil and then the buttermilk. Give them a little stir just to start combining them and then whisk in the eggs. Continue to whisk until fully combined and bubbling. Gently fold in the blueberries.

Heat a nonstick frying pan and pour in ¼ cup of batter. When bubbles start to appear, flip the pancake and cook for an additional 30–45 seconds. Repeat with the remaining batter.

To make the syrup, combine the maple syrup and balsamic in a small saucepan over medium heat. Add the blueberries, stir to combine, and continue stirring until the syrup is warm. Top with whipped cream, if using, and drizzle the syrup over the warm pancakes to serve.

The syrup will keep in the fridge in an airtight container for a few weeks.

Maple

This balsamic is outrageously good. It's sweet and delicious, and it's basically like a caramelized maple syrup. Think pancakes, waffles, glazing bacon, pork chops, ice cream, dressings, marinades, chocolate, cake, and fruit. You'll find **Maple** dark balsamic vinegar in the following recipes (and in several recipe variations throughout the book):

When I was growing up, my family loved to eat pumpkin soup on cold, rainy days. I've added a sweet maple walnut topping that pairs with it perfectly. If fresh pumpkin isn't close by, sweet potatoes, butternut squash, or a combination of them plus some carrots can be substituted. The soup itself is delicately spiced, letting the pumpkin be just pumpkin. **SERVES 6**

Pumpkin Soup with Pear Walnut Topping

SOUP

1 pie pumpkin, about 2–3 lb or enough for 6 cups of cubed pumpkin

2 Tbsp **Garlic** infused olive oil

1 small onion, chopped

3 cups vegetable broth

1 Tbsp **Maple** dark balsamic vinegar

1 tsp ground ginger

½ tsp ground cinnamon

½ tsp ground nutmeg

1 cup table (18%) cream

TOPPING

1 Bartlett pear, peeled and diced

¼ cup walnut pieces

2 Tbsp brown sugar

2 Tbsp **Maple** dark balsamic vinegar, plus more for drizzling

1 Tbsp lemon juice

To make the soup, peel and chop the pumpkin into 2-inch cubes.

In a soup pot, heat the olive oil over medium heat and sauté the onion until soft and translucent. Add the pumpkin, stock, balsamic, ginger, cinnamon, and nutmeg and bring the soup just to a boil. Turn down the heat and simmer, covered, until the pumpkin is tender, 20–25 minutes. Remove from the heat and let cool.

To make the topping, place the pear, walnuts, sugar, balsamic, and lemon juice in a small saucepan over medium heat. Mix together and heat, stirring until the sugar has dissolved and the pear is just starting to soften, about 5 minutes.

Working in batches, purée the soup in a blender, or use an immersion blender in the pot, until it is smooth and creamy. Return to the soup pot and heat it through. Stir in the cream before serving.

Finish with a dollop of pear walnut topping in the center and a light drizzle of balsamic around the edges of the bowl.

I have a thing for black beans. It doesn't matter what the dish is, if it contains black beans, I'll love it. And maple is a natural match for beans. A pot of these simmering on the stove is sure to make anyone's stomach growl when they catch a whiff of them. Top with an extra drizzle of **Maple** dark balsamic vinegar, serve with corn bread and Kansas City–Style Slow Cooker Beef Brisket (page 177), and please save some for me! **SERVES 4 AS A SIDE**

Maple Baked Beans

4 strips bacon
1 (19 oz) can navy beans
1 (19 oz) can black beans
1 cup **Espresso** barbecue sauce (page 178)
½ cup ketchup
¼ cup **Maple** dark balsamic vinegar
¼ cup brown sugar, packed
1 Tbsp chili powder

Cut the bacon into 1-inch pieces and sear in a large pot until crispy. Rinse and drain the beans well and add them to the pot with the barbecue sauce, ketchup, balsamic, and ½ cup water. Stir in the brown sugar and chili powder, cover, bring to a boil over medium-high heat, then turn down the heat and simmer, slow and low, for 30 minutes, stirring often until the sauce is thick and the beans have softened.

Apple Baked Beans Substitute unsweetened apple sauce for the ketchup and **Apple** white balsamic or **Red Apple** dark balsamic for the **Maple** dark balsamic.

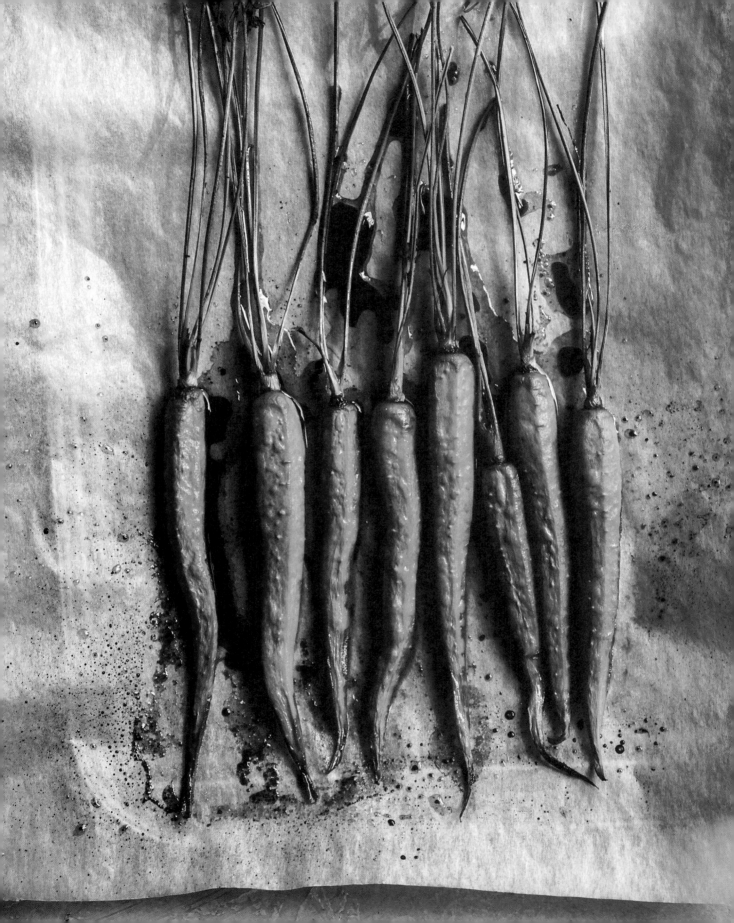

Carrots are already so sweet and flavourful that they really don't need much to make them extra special. A drizzle of honey, maple syrup, or balsamic vinegar, or even a squeeze of orange juice, and you have a delightful side dish on your hands. In this recipe, the balsamic caramelizes them into carrot heaven. Cut them into rounds or little ovals to ensure the edges are nice and crisp, or cut into matchsticks for a soft inside and candied outside, whichever works for you. **SERVES 4 AS A SIDE**

Caramelized Maple Carrots

6 large carrots
¼ cup **Lemon** fused olive oil
¼ cup **Maple** dark balsamic vinegar

Caramelized Maple Yams Substitute two medium-sized yams or sweet potatoes for the carrots and cook as directed.

Cinnamon Pear Roasted Carrots Substitute **Cinnamon Pear** dark balsamic for the **Maple** for an autumnal version.

Honey Ginger Roasted Carrots Substitute **Honey Ginger** dark balsamic for the **Maple** for a warm, comforting side dish.

Pomegranate Roasted Carrots Substitute **Pomegranate** dark balsamic for the **Maple** and garnish with pomegranate arils and a few mint leaves.

Sweet & Fruity Roasted Carrots Substitute **Plum** or **Apricot** white balsamic for the **Maple** dark balsamic.

Preheat the oven to 375°F. Line a rimmed baking tray with parchment paper.

Peel and chop the carrots into rounds, ovals, or matchsticks, depending on what texture you want. Or you can keep them whole. Arrange them in a single layer on the prepared baking tray. Drizzle with the olive oil and balsamic.

Roast for 25 minutes and then turn them to coat them in the balsamic and oil glaze. Bake for another 15 minutes and serve warm.

Making pumpkin pie from a real pumpkin rather than canned is absolutely worth the extra time. Roasting the pumpkin with the spices gives this pie a rich, deep flavor. The balsamic soaks into the pumpkin, so every bit is maple-y roasted goodness. It's not your average pumpkin pie—the balsamic cuts the sweetness and makes the flavor smooth and rich, and the roasted spices make it almost a bit nutty. **MAKES TWO (9-INCH) PIES**

Maple-Roasted Pumpkin Pie

Prepared pastry (page 283)
1 pie pumpkin, about 3–4 lbs
4 Tbsp **Maple** dark balsamic vinegar
2 Tbsp creamy, mild **extra virgin** olive oil
1 cup brown sugar, packed, divided
2 tsp ground cinnamon
1 tsp ground nutmeg
1 tsp ground ginger
¼ tsp ground cloves
½ tsp sea salt
4 large eggs
1½ cups whipping (35%) cream

If you're not a maple fan, you're welcome to use **Traditional** or **Red Apple** dark balsamic here. If you're feeling extra adventurous, the **Blood Orange** fused olive oil is an incredible option for the olive oil.

Preheat the oven to 375°F. Line two 9-inch deep pie plates with the pastry. When the oven is fully heated, bake the pastry for 10–15 minutes or until the edges of the crust are just starting to brown. Remove from oven and set aside.

Using a very large knife or cleaver, cut the pumpkin in half vertically and remove the stem. Use a metal spoon to remove the seeds, scraping the centers clean. Place the pumpkin halves, cut side down, directly on the center rack of the oven and bake for about 25 minutes, until they start to soften. You can pierce the skin to test it.

Remove the pumpkin from the oven and place the halves cut side up on a baking tray. In the cavity of each half of the pumpkin, place equal amounts of the balsamic and olive oil, then the sugar, cinnamon, nutmeg, ginger, and cloves, finishing with the salt. Return the pumpkin to the oven and bake for an additional 30 minutes until the pumpkin flesh is fork-tender. Remove from the oven and let cool on a rack for 10 minutes.

Using a metal spoon, carefully scrape out the pumpkin flesh and mix it into the balsamic mixture. Once it has started to combine, transfer it to a large bowl, scraping the skin clean and mixing the flesh well with the balsamic mixture. You should have 3 cups of baked pumpkin.

Whisk in the eggs and cream, then beat well by hand or with a mixer until the mixture is smooth and creamy.

Pour the pumpkin batter into the prepared pie shells and bake for 45 minutes. Let cool for a few minutes before serving.

This is a great way to use up stale bread. You can make this in advance and let it soak overnight for brunch the next day. If you're not into raisins, try cranberries, chopped walnuts, or pecan pieces. If you don't have **Lemon** fused olive oil, any mild and creamy single varietal **extra virgin** olive oil will do (see pages 16–17). **SERVES 4–6**

Apple Bread Pudding with Maple Caramel Sauce

BREAD PUDDING

4 cups cubed dry bread (about 8 slices)
2 apples, peeled, cored, and diced
½ cup golden raisins
4 eggs
1 cup whole milk
¼ cup **Lemon** fused olive oil
½ cup brown sugar, packed
1 tsp sea salt

MAPLE CARAMEL SAUCE

1 cup granulated sugar
2 Tbsp **Maple** dark balsamic vinegar

A mild creamy **extra virgin** olive oil such as **Arbequina** or **Arbosana** is delightful here; **Blood Orange** fused olive oil is also delicious.

Instead of the **Maple** dark balsamic, use **Apple** white balsamic for an extra-apple-forward version, or **Traditional** dark balsamic for an even richer version.

To make the pudding, in an 8-inch round pie plate, or 8- × 8-inch baking pan, evenly distribute the cubed bread, apples, and raisins.

In a mixing bowl, whisk the eggs, milk, and olive oil with the brown sugar and salt. Pour this over the bread, making sure that all the bread is covered. Tilt the pan slightly and press down on any pieces that are poking out to keep them submerged. Cover tightly with plastic wrap and let sit in the fridge for at least 2 hours, or up to overnight.

Preheat the oven to 350°F. Remove the bread pudding from the fridge to allow it to warm up a bit before putting it in the oven.

Bake, uncovered, for 35 minutes. Insert a toothpick in the center of the pudding. If it comes out clean, the liquid has set, and you can take it out of the oven and let stand for 5 minutes. If necessary, bake for another 5 minutes.

Meanwhile, prepare the sauce. In a deep saucepan, dissolve the sugar in ¼ cup water over medium heat. Pour in the balsamic and bring to a rolling boil. *Do not stir!* Allow the sauce to caramelize and darken, about 2–3 minutes. As it boils, you'll smell a delightful nuttiness coming from it. Remove from the heat, pour into a serving jug, and enjoy on your warm bread pudding.

This pie is like an upside-down caramel pie. For most pies, you toss the brown sugar, spices, and apples together and bake it, but with this one, you make a spiced caramel sauce with the **Maple** dark balsamic vinegar and pour it on top of the apples. The sauce oozes into the apples as the pie bakes, glazing them and creating a thick sauce in the shell with the juices, so when it cools, the caramel is all through the pie. Serve with a scoop of vanilla ice cream. Golden Delicious, Crispin, Cortland, or Spy are all tried and tested varieties of apple for this. **MAKES ONE (9-INCH) PIE**

Maple-Glazed Apple Pie

8–10 tart pie apples
Prepared pastry (page 283)
¼ cup all-purpose flour
1 cup dark brown sugar, packed
¼ cup **Maple** dark balsamic vinegar
2 tsp ground cinnamon
1 tsp ground nutmeg
¼ cup mild, fruity **extra virgin** olive oil

If you'd prefer a richer, more apple-forward version, **Red Apple** dark balsamic or **Apple** white balsamic are lovely alternatives to the **Maple**.

Preheat the oven to 425°F.

Peel, core, and slice the apples (kind of thinly but not too thinly so they still have some substance to them). Roll out half the pastry and place it in a 9-inch pie plate. Sprinkle the flour over the pastry and toss in the apples.

Place the sugar in a small saucepan with the balsamic, cinnamon, and nutmeg. Bring to a rolling boil over medium-high heat for 30 seconds and then remove from the heat.

Whisk in the olive oil and slowly pour the mixture over the apples, ensuring they are evenly coated.

Roll out the top crust, place it over the apples, and seal the edges. Pierce the crust with a fork to allow steam to escape while cooking.

Bake at 425°F for 15 minutes and then turn down the oven temperature to 375°F. Bake for an additional 45 minutes, until the crust is brown and the apples are soft. Let cool completely before serving—at least 3 hours—so that the juices don't run when you cut it.

Hot apple cider is so heartwarming. It lightens a gathering and facilitates the most delightful conversation. The **Maple** dark balsamic vinegar in this recipe adds a beautiful aroma to the cider and a subtle sweetness that is unmatched by any other ingredient. Serve alongside Maple-Glazed Apple Pie (page 219) or Red Apple Beef Bourguignon (page 244) for a hearty meal. **SERVES 4 IN LARGE MUGS**

Hot Apple Cider

3 cups apple cider or apple juice
2 cups cranberry juice
¼ cup **Maple** dark balsamic
¼ cup dark brown sugar, packed
3 cinnamon sticks, plus more for garnish
1 orange
10 whole cloves

For a lighter version, use **Apple** or **Plum** white balsamic instead of the **Maple**.

For a sweeter variation, use **Vanilla** white balsamic instead of the **Maple**.

For an intense apple flavor, substitute **Red Apple** dark balsamic for the **Maple**.

In a large stockpot, bring the apple cider or juice, cranberry juice, balsamic, sugar, and cinnamon sticks to a simmer. Quarter the orange, poke each quarter with a few of the cloves, and add to the pan. Let simmer for 20–30 minutes. Serve warm with a cinnamon stick in each mug for garnish, if desired.

Chocolate

This balsamic has a rich, deep intensity. You can drizzle it over vanilla gelato or macerate fresh berries in it. Oh, and please, please try it in turkey mole and watch your guests be amazed! It's complex and delicious, creamy and sweet, deep and rich. You'll find **Chocolate** dark balsamic vinegar in the following recipes (and in several recipe variations throughout the book):

Fluffy, light, and so moist, these cupcakes win praise every time. The **Chocolate** dark balsamic vinegar reacts with the baking soda, giving their wonderful texture, and its richness adds a lovely complexity to their flavor profile. The cream cheese chocolate frosting adds a lovely brightness, taking these from basic to brilliant. **MAKES 24 CUPCAKES**

Double Chocolate Cupcakes

CUPCAKES
4 eggs
1 ½ cups granulated sugar
¾ cup **Blood Orange** fused olive oil
1 cup all-purpose flour
¾ cup unsweetened cocoa powder
1½ tsp baking powder
1 tsp baking soda
½ tsp sea salt
¾ cup buttermilk (see page 43)
¼ cup **Chocolate** dark balsamic vinegar

FROSTING
1 (8 oz) block cream cheese (at room
    temperature)
½ cup unsalted butter
4 cups icing sugar
½ cup unsweetened cocoa powder
¼ tsp sea salt
2 Tbsp **Chocolate** dark balsamic vinegar

Make these substitutions for both the cupcakes and their frosting.

Substitute a mild **extra virgin** olive oil if **Blood Orange** isn't in the cupboard, or if chocolate and orange isn't your favorite flavor combination.

Black Forest Cupcakes Use **Black Cherry** dark balsamic instead of the **Chocolate** and garnish with a fresh or preserved cherry on top of the frosting.

Fruity Chocolate Cupcakes Substitute **Pomegranate**, **Raspberry**, or **Strawberry** dark balsamic in place of the **Chocolate** for a rich, fruity version. Garnish with the appropriate fruit.

Mocha Chocolate Cupcakes Substitute **Espresso** dark balsamic vinegar for the **Chocolate**.

Preheat the oven to 350°F. Line two muffin tins with paper liners.

To make the cupcakes, in a large bowl, whisk together the eggs and sugar until fluffy and a pale creamy color. Whisk in the olive oil until fully combined, 1–2 minutes.

Sift the flour, cocoa powder, baking powder, and baking soda over top the wet ingredients and then sprinkle in the salt. Stir to combine with a wooden spoon or spatula. There should be no ribbons of flour in the batter. Fold in the buttermilk and balsamic to form a very thin batter. Avoid overmixing, as this will make the cupcakes tough. (This batter is unusually thin, so don't panic.)

Fill the prepared muffin cups half full with batter. Bake for 18–20 minutes, until a toothpick inserted in the center comes out with only a few light crumbs attached and is not wet at all. Remove the tins from the oven and carefully take the cupcakes out of the cups. Place them on a wire rack to cool completely before frosting.

To make the frosting, using a stand mixer or handheld beaters, mix the cream cheese and butter together until fully combined and creamy. Add the icing sugar 1 cup at a time, beating well between each addition, and then beat in the cocoa powder followed by the sea salt. With the mixer running, slowly add the balsamic and then beat on high to create a light, air-filled frosting.

Transfer the frosting to a piping bag fitted with the tip of your choice and frost the cooled cupcakes. Garnish with sprinkles if desired and serve.

These will keep in an airtight container for up to 3 days on the counter. The cupcakes can also be frozen without their frosting for up to 3 months. Ice the cupcakes once they are completely thawed and any condensation has evaporated.

The **Chocolate** dark balsamic vinegar has a major impact here, but in a discreet way—you know something is making the beef taste unusually phenomenal, but you can't quite put your finger on what's creating the magic. Ground chicken or turkey are also delicious in this instead of beef. **SERVES 4**

Chocolate Chili

2 large onions

2 Tbsp robust **extra virgin** olive oil

1 lb ground beef

$1/3$ cup **Chocolate** dark balsamic vinegar

Sea salt and ground black pepper

6 tomatoes, diced

4 cups assorted canned beans (kidney, black, navy, chickpeas, etc.), rinsed and drained

$1^1/2$ cups tomato juice

2 Tbsp chili powder

2 tsp smoked paprika

1 tsp ground cumin

1 bay leaf

Use **Espresso** or **Pomegranate** dark balsamic vinegar, or **Oregano** white balsamic vinegar for a different yet equally delicious flavor profile.

Dice the onions and sauté them in the olive oil in a frying pan over medium heat until translucent. Add the ground meat and begin to brown it. Once the meat is broken up and beginning to brown, add the balsamic and season to taste with salt and pepper. Cook until the juices have almost evaporated and the meat is evenly browned.

SLOW-COOKER METHOD Transfer the beef to a slow cooker and add the tomatoes, beans, tomato juice, chili powder, paprika, cumin, and bay leaf. Stir to combine. Cook on low for 6 hours. Remove the bay leaf before serving.

STOVETOP METHOD Once the meat is evenly browned, add the tomatoes, beans, tomato juice, chili powder, paprika, cumin, and bay leaf. Stir to combine. Bring to a boil, turn down the heat to medium-low, and simmer, uncovered, for 25–30 minutes. Remove the bay leaf before serving.

Fudge is delicious and decadent, yet relatively simple to make at home. This recipe can be made in about 20 minutes, and most of that time is spent watching a pot boil. The options for this are endless, so experiment with your favorite oil-balsamic combos (although you might want to take it easy on anything garlicky). You can add ¾ cup nuts, chocolate chips, or chopped candy canes for a special treat. When I had our retail store, a special tip from the staff was: if you are "extra in love with balsamic," use ½ cup of it!

MAKES ONE (8- × 8-INCH) PAN

Easy Chocolate Balsamic Fudge

2½ cups granulated sugar
⅔ cup Dutch process cocoa powder
1 cup half-and-half (10–12%) cream
¼ cup **Chocolate** dark balsamic vinegar
1 tsp sea salt, divided
2 Tbsp **Blood Orange** fused olive oil

Instead of the **Chocolate** dark balsamic, use **Strawberry** for a fruity version, **Fig** for a sweeter version, or **Pomegranate** for an intensely rich and deeply flavored fudge.

Milk Chocolate Balsamic Fudge Use **Vanilla** white balsamic instead of the **Chocolate** and cut the cocoa powder in half for a creamier, sweeter version.

Mocha Fudge Use **Espresso** dark balsamic instead of **Chocolate** for a mocha spin-off.

Line an 8- × 8-inch baking pan with parchment paper. (Or, if you like really thick fudge, use an 8- × 4-inch loaf pan.)

In a heavy-bottomed saucepan, mix together the sugar and cocoa powder. Mix in the half-and-half and balsamic, and warm over medium heat, stirring until the sugar has dissolved. As soon as it reaches a boil, stop stirring. Allow the fudge to boil gently but consistently until it reaches 240°F on a candy thermometer, 5–7 minutes. To test without using a candy thermometer, fill a small bowl with ice-cold water. Using a spoon, allow one drop of chocolate fudge to drip into the bowl of water. When it holds together in a drip and doesn't incorporate into the water, you're almost there. Squish the ball between your fingers. If it doesn't disintegrate, it's ready. But it shouldn't be hard or crunchy—if it turns to a rock-like drop, you'll have to start over.

Remove the saucepan from the heat and mix in ½ tsp of the salt, followed by the olive oil. Beat with a hand mixer or in a stand mixer until the fudge is no longer glossy, 5–7 minutes (it will take longer by hand). If you're adding in any extras (chocolate chips, nuts, candies, etc.), fold them in now with a metal spoon.

Pour the mixture quickly into the prepared pan. Lightly oil the back of a spoon or spatula, use it to smooth the top of the fudge, and sprinkle with the remaining ½ tsp salt. Let the fudge set for at least 2 hours at room temperature or for 1 hour in the fridge.

When the fudge is set, use the parchment paper to remove it from the pan then use a sharp knife to slice it into squares. It will keep in an airtight container for up to 1 week.

Cinnamon Pear

This delightful vinegar is warm and spicy and very versatile. Not only is it beautiful drizzled over fresh fruit as a dessert topping, it also shines when drizzled over Brie or Camembert, roasted vegetables, or even oatmeal. You'll find **Cinnamon Pear** dark balsamic vinegar in the following recipes (and in several recipe variations throughout the book):

I once lived on oatmeal; being a student probably had something to do with that. This is my favorite oatmeal recipe, although, ironically, it only came to me once I'd left university. It's like an oatmeal pie, and it was created by one of my closest friends, Nadia. Thank you, Nadia! The balsamic adds the sweetness of maple syrup but with the molasses-like flavor of Demerara sugar. You don't need too much of it, either. **SERVES 4**

Baked Oatmeal

1 apple (any type)
2 cups quick-cooking oats
½ cup raisins (any type)
½ cup chopped walnuts, divided
1 cup 2% milk
1 Tbsp **Cinnamon Pear** dark balsamic vinegar, plus more for drizzling
2 Tbsp brown sugar
Greek yogurt, to serve

Dried cranberries are also a delicious substitute for the raisins.

If allergies aren't an issue, you can go wild with any combination of nuts, seeds, and dried fruit that appeals to you.

If you have a nut allergy, substitute pumpkin seeds and sunflower seeds or dried cranberries for the walnuts.

Try using **Maple** or **Red Apple** dark balsamic, or **Apricot** or **Plum** white balsamic instead of the **Cinnamon Pear**.

Peel and core the apple and chop it into bite-sized pieces. Place the pieces in a 9-inch pie plate or cast iron pan with the oats, raisins, and ¼ cup of the walnuts, stirring to combine. Pour the milk and balsamic into the pie plate, add 2 cups water, and gently stir to combine. Cover with plastic wrap and place in the fridge overnight.

In the morning, remove the plastic wrap and preheat the oven to 350°F.

Bake the oatmeal for 20–25 minutes, until all the remaining liquid has been absorbed, the oats are soft, and the top is golden.

Cut into slices and serve hot with the remaining walnuts, a sprinkle of sugar, a drizzle of balsamic, and a dollop of Greek yogurt.

When that first crisp morning arrives at the beginning of September, all I want to do is get to the market to pick up some pears and some Brie so I can eat this for dinner. During the holiday season I make this caramelized pear topping in massive quantities and store it in the fridge for last-minute guests. It's quick and easy, and it even lands on toast or oatmeal (as long as no one is watching). Make sure to use a mild and fruity olive oil. **SERVES 4 AS AN APPETIZER**

Caramelized Pear on Warm Brie

2 green onions

2 Tbsp mild and fruity **extra virgin** olive oil

1 pear

¼ cup brown sugar, packed

¼ cup apple juice (or apple cider)

2 Tbsp **Cinnamon Pear** dark balsamic vinegar

1 (4 oz) round of Brie

¼ cup chopped walnuts

If **Cinnamon Pear** isn't in the cupboard, use **Apple** white balsamic or **Cranberry Pear** to add a lovely tartness to this dish.

Wash and trim the green onions. Finely chop them, separate the greens from the whites, and set aside.

In a small saucepan over medium-high heat, sauté the whites of the green onions in the olive oil until just soft, about 1 minute.

Peel, core, and roughly chop the pear into ½-inch pieces. Add the pear, sugar, apple juice, and vinegar. Slowly bring to a boil over medium-high heat, stirring constantly, then turn down the heat to medium. Simmer on medium heat, allowing the pear to caramelize and thicken, 10–12 minutes.

Preheat the oven to 350°F.

Place the Brie in an ovenproof serving dish or Brie baker. Pour the pear and caramel over top and sprinkle with the walnuts. Bake for 10 minutes, just to soften the Brie.

Sprinkle with the green parts of the green onions. Serve warm with a fresh baguette, crostini, or crackers.

This salad is super colorful, making it a fun dish for special occasions or a cheerful, hearty, and lovely side dish for any day of the year. Combining the sweetness of the beets with the richness of the balsamic and the earthiness of the cinnamon creates the perfect balance with the creamy goat cheese in this salad. (Chèvre is too soft for this. You'll need a firmer, but still creamy, cheese that will crumble fairly easily.) **SERVES 2–4**

Roasted Beet Salad with Cinnamon Pear Balsamic & Goat Cheese Crumble

3 cups peeled, cubed beets (red or golden)
¼ cup **Cinnamon Pear** dark balsamic vinegar
1 cup torn baby kale
Sea salt and ground black pepper
¼ cup crumbled goat cheese
½ cup toasted walnut pieces

Although the **Cinnamon Pear** dark balsamic is definitely my favorite balsamic option for this recipe, **Pomegranate** dark balsamic or **Plum** white balsamic are just as delicious.

Place the beets in a saucepan of water (if you're using golden, yellow, and red beets, use two saucepans, as the red beets will stain the golden ones) and bring to a rolling boil over high heat. Turn down the heat to medium-high and simmer for 30–40 minutes, until fork-tender. Drain off the water.

Preheat the oven to 350°F. Line a rimmed baking tray with parchment paper.

Arrange the beets in a single layer on the prepared baking tray and drizzle liberally with the balsamic. Toss gently to coat.

Bake for 10 minutes, then turn. Roast for another 10 minutes, until the beets are evenly roasted and the balsamic has reduced to a thick glaze.

Arrange the baby kale on a serving plate and season to taste with salt and pepper. Arrange the beets on the kale and top with the goat cheese. They're delicious warm but will continue to caramelize as they cool. Top with the walnut pieces.

Neapolitan Herb

Deep and herbaceous, this balsamic vinegar is for all the savory lovers out there. The delightful mix of garlic, sage, thyme, oregano, and other southern Italian herbs in this balsamic makes it an instant marinade, dressing, and flavor-booster all wrapped into one delicious product. Drizzle over tomatoes before roasting them, add to sautéed onions, soak steak or pork in it before grilling . . . Honestly, this versatile balsamic is something you'll be reaching for daily. You'll find **Neapolitan Herb** dark balsamic vinegar in the following recipes (and in several recipe variations throughout the book):

I love roasted tomatoes, especially with **Neapolitan Herb** balsamic vinegar, which makes them almost turn to candy, as the juices reduce along with the balsamic and make the simplest yet most epic sauce. Tossed on linguini, this is my absolute go-to end-of-summer pasta, just as the evenings are growing cooler and I'm starting to crave comfort food but produce is at its peak. **SERVES 4**

Slow-Roasted Tomato & Eggplant Linguini

10 Roma tomatoes

1 large or 2 small eggplants

8 garlic cloves

1 red onion

¼ cup robust **extra virgin** olive oil (a **Manzanillo** or **Picual** is ideal)

¼ cup **Neapolitan Herb** dark balsamic vinegar

2 tsp cracked black pepper

1 tsp sea salt

1 tsp smoked paprika

8 oz linguini

½ cup grated Parmesan cheese

Here I've used **extra virgin** olive oil to allow the flavor of the **Neapolitan Herb** to claim the limelight, but if you're wanting to pump up the herbaceousness of this dish, feel free to use **Garlic**, **Rosemary**, **Tuscan Herb**, **Basil**, or **Wild Dill** instead.

Preheat the oven to 400°F. Line a rimmed baking tray with parchment paper.

Slice the tomatoes in half and lay them skin side down on the parchment. Slice the eggplant into 1-inch rounds, then slice each round into approximately 1-inch cubes. Scatter these across the parchment as well. Peel and crush the cloves of garlic, leaving them whole. Chop the onion into ½-inch chunks, and add the garlic and onion to the parchment.

Drizzle with the olive oil and balsamic and shake the pan gently to ensure that everything is evenly and well coated. Sprinkle with the pepper, salt, and paprika.

Bake for 35–40 minutes, until the tomatoes and eggplant are very soft and caramelized, and the juices have thickened.

Bring a pot of salted water to a rolling boil and cook the linguini according to the package directions until just al dente. Drain and place in a large serving bowl. Top the pasta with the vegetables, scraping all the drippings and juices from the pan onto the pasta as well. Toss to coat well. Divide between the serving plates and top each with Parmesan cheese. Serve immediately.

This will keep in the fridge (separately, or with the sauce mixed into the pasta) in an airtight container for up to 3 days.

One of the most heartwarming meals I can think of, this soup comes a close second to my favorite, chicken noodle—and it uses another of my all-time favorites, bone broth (page 119). If you have bone broth in the freezer, this soup comes together quickly without your having to turn to bouillon or store-bought stocks. Bone broth is richer and deeper in flavor than store-bought alternatives, and the balsamic enhances this richness more than words can convey to create the most delicious base with, of course, all the health benefits of bone broth to boot. **SERVES 4**

Beef Barley Soup

1 lb stewing beef
4 Tbsp **Garlic** infused olive oil, divided
1 red onion
2 garlic cloves
2 cups pearl barley
¼ cup **Neapolitan Herb** dark balsamic vinegar
6 cups bone broth (page 119)

If the garlic component is too intense for you, **Herbes de Provence**, **Basil**, or **Tuscan Herb** infused olive oil or a robust **extra virgin** are all delicious here.

Pat the stewing beef dry on all sides and set aside to come to room temperature. In a heavy-bottomed pot over medium-high heat, warm half the olive oil and brown the meat, searing well on all sides. Be careful not to crowd the pot. You might need to work in batches, transferring the browned meat to a bowl as you go.

Finely chop the onion and garlic. Add the remaining 2 Tbsp olive oil to the pan (there's no need to clean it first) and sauté the onions and garlic until just translucent. Add the barley and toss to coat in the onions, garlic, and olive oil. Deglaze the pot with the balsamic, scraping up any bits that may have stuck on the bottom. Pour in the broth and then the browned meat, cover, and bring to a boil. Turn down the heat to low and simmer, covered, for 45 minutes, until the barley is cooked and puffed. Serve with the Homemade Housewarming Loaf (page 33) for a hearty and delicious winter meal.

This is another summer favorite of mine, although it's lovely in the winter months as well. Tender flank steak has a long marinating time—in fact, sometimes I'll even freeze the steak in the marinade—but it's totally worth it, as it makes the meat so juicy and tender. Using the **Neapolitan Herb** balsamic allows the herb flavor to penetrate through the meat more fully than if the fresh herbs were added on their own. The sweetness of the lime and honey ginger vinaigrette is the perfect complement to the roasted veggies that complete this summer salad. **SERVES 4**

Marinated Flank Steak & Grilled Vegetable Salad

2 garlic cloves

¼ cup **Neapolitan Herb** dark balsamic vinegar

2 Tbsp Sriracha hot sauce

2 Tbsp lime juice

2 Tbsp robust **extra virgin** olive oil

2 Tbsp grainy Dijon mustard

2 tsp freshly grated ginger

1 lb flank steak

2 cobs of corn, husks intact

2 red onions

1 cup cherry tomatoes

1 zucchini

1 head leaf lettuce

¼ cup **Lime** fused olive oil

2 Tbsp **Honey Ginger** white balsamic vinegar

1 Tbsp honey

½ tsp chili flakes

½ cup crumbled feta cheese

If you're making this salad in winter, use 1½ cups frozen corn, thawed and drained in place of the cobs. Place vegetables on a parchment-lined rimmed baking tray and roast at 425°F for 30 minutes, until caramelized and golden. Fry the steak in a heavy-bottomed frying pan or place under the broiler if the weather won't let you use an outdoor grill.

Mince the garlic. Place it in a small bowl and whisk in the **Neapolitan Herb** balsamic, hot sauce, lime juice, **extra virgin** olive oil, 1½ Tbsp Dijon, and ginger. Place the flank steak in a resealable plastic bag and pour in the marinade. Seal the bag and remove as much air as possible. Rub the meat in the bag to ensure it is fully coated in marinade and place in the fridge for at least 12 hours, or up to 2 days.

When you're ready to serve, remove the steak from the fridge to allow it to come to room temperature in the marinade. Preheat the barbecue to 450°F.

Remove the hairs from the tops of the corn, leaving the husks intact, and soak the corn for 10 minutes in a saucepan of cold water. Remove the cobs from the water and place directly on the grill. Grill for 10–15 minutes, until the kernels are tender and the husks are charred. Remove from the grill and let rest, still wrapped in the husks.

Remove the flank steak from its marinade and place it on the grill. Grill for 5 minutes per side for rare, 7 for medium-rare, and 9 for medium. Remove the meat from the grill and let sit for 10 minutes before carving.

While the steak is cooking, roughly chop the onions, slice the tomatoes in half, and slice the zucchini into rounds. When the steak comes off the grill, place veggies in a grill basket and cook for 10–15 minutes, stirring often to prevent them from sticking, until they start to soften and char.

CONTINUED →

Wash and spin the lettuce dry and tear it into bite-sized pieces. Divide it evenly between the serving plates. Remove the kernels from the corn cobs with a sharp knife. Add to the salad and top with the grilled veggies.

Whisk together the **Lime** fused olive oil, **Honey Ginger** white balsamic, ½ Tbsp Dijon, honey, and chili flakes to make a fairly runny dressing that will seep into the cracks and crevasses of the salad. Drizzle it evenly over the veggies and salad on each plate.

Slice the flank steak against the grain into thin strips. Place on the side of the salad, top with feta, and serve.

All the components of this salad will keep in the fridge in individual airtight containers for up to 3 days.

Red Apple

This vinegar has an enticing aroma that is matched only by a delicate sweetness that comes from the apples. It adds a special something to salads, sauces, chutneys, and vegetables, and it is truly amazing drizzled over pork or chicken. You'll find **Red Apple** dark balsamic vinegar in the following recipes (and in several recipe variations throughout the book):

Baked apples were a favorite dessert in our home when I was growing up. They made the house smell incredible and were the best comfort food—and even better the next day for breakfast. This butter essentially gathers up all that flavor and keeps it fresh and ready to use in a jar. It's perfect slathered on toast or freshly baked biscuits, mixed into sauces, or spread over roasted meats. Cortland, Crispin, Golden Delicious, or Ida Red work best for this recipe. **MAKES 4 CUPS**

Baked Apple Butter

2 lb apples
Juice and grated zest of 1 lemon
2 Tbsp ground cinnamon, divided
2 cups brown sugar, packed
2 tsp ground nutmeg
1 cup **Red Apple** dark balsamic vinegar

If you're looking for something a little lighter in color, use **Apple** white balsamic instead of the **Red Apple** dark balsamic.

Baked Cranberry Apple Butter Use **Cranberry Pear** white balsamic vinegar in place of the **Red Apple** dark balsamic, add 1 cup of dried cranberries to the baking tray with the apples when roasting, and use orange juice and zest instead of lemon juice and zest.

Maple-Roasted Apple Butter Use **Maple** dark balsamic instead of the **Red Apple**.

Spice Baked Apple Butter Substitute the **Red Apple** dark balsamic with **Cinnamon Pear**.

Sweet Baked Apple Butter Substitute **Vanilla** white balsamic for the **Red Apple** dark balsamic.

Preheat the oven to 350°F. Line a rimmed baking tray with parchment paper.

Keeping their skins on, quarter the apples and remove the cores. Place them skin side down in one layer on the prepared baking tray.

Drizzle the lemon juice over the apples, sprinkle with half the cinnamon, and bake for 30–40 minutes, until the apples have softened and any moisture has evaporated. Remove from the oven and let cool on the pan for about 5 minutes.

Gently scrape the apples from the parchment paper and into a food mill or fine mesh sieve. Press them (with a spoon if you're using a sieve) into a large stockpot. The straining removes any skin and ensures all the apples get into the sauce.

Add the lemon zest, the remaining cinnamon, the brown sugar, and nutmeg with the balsamic. Mix well and bring to a boil over medium heat. Turn down the heat and simmer until you have a smooth paste thick enough to coat the back of a spoon.

Spoon the butter into hot, sterile 1-pint Mason jars, leaving ¼ inch headspace. Screw the lids on tightly and wait for them to seal; this could take 3–4 hours. To check if they've sealed, push each lid down in the center. If it makes a little popping noise, it hasn't sealed. If they don't seal, place them in the fridge for immediate use, or can them for longer storage.

To can the butter, prepare a hot water bath and canning rack in a canner or stock pot. Process the jars for 20 minutes (make any necessary elevation adjustments). Transfer to a cooling rack and wait for the lids to pop and seal.

A hearty beef stew is the epitome of comfort food. I love to make this on a rainy morning and then spend all day thinking about what a delightful dinner lies in store. This dish is perfect for a crowd, and if you're feeding a smaller group, it guarantees leftovers to enjoy with lunch the next day. If you're not a fan of mushrooms, you can omit them without spoiling the end result of this dish. **SERVES 6**

Red Apple Beef Bourguignon

½ lb extra-thick bacon
2 lb stewing beef, cut into cubes
2 Tbsp robust **extra virgin** olive oil
All-purpose flour for sprinkling
Sea salt and ground black pepper
5 large carrots
2 celery stalks
2 large onions
1½ cups full-bodied red wine
2 cups button mushrooms
3 large russet or Yukon gold potatoes
1 (28 oz) can diced tomatoes
¾ cup **Red Apple** dark balsamic vinegar
1 cup beef bone broth (page 119) or beef stock
4 unpeeled garlic cloves
2 thyme sprigs

Black Currant, Blackberry Ginger, and Neapolitan Herb dark balsamic all work well in this recipe—and if you want to really explore all your options, try Pomegranate, Fig, or Traditional.

Preheat the oven to 450°F.

Cut the bacon into ¼-inch pieces and fry until crispy in a large frying pan over medium-high heat. Remove the bacon and place it on a plate lined with paper towel to absorb the grease. Leave the bacon grease in the pan and turn down the heat to medium.

Rinse the beef well and pat it dry with paper towel (wet beef won't brown properly—I learned that from Julia Child!). Add the olive oil to the pan of bacon grease and add half the beef. Brown on all sides, and place on the plate with the bacon. Repeat with the remaining beef.

Place the beef and bacon in an ovenproof dish, sprinkle generously with flour, salt, and pepper. Toss to coat the beef and place in the oven for 5 minutes. Toss again and cook for an additional 3 minutes.

Meanwhile, peel and chop the carrots into ½-inch-thick rounds and roughly chop the celery. Place the carrots and celery in the same frying pan you used for the beef, and sauté in the residue oil for 2–3 minutes, until just brown. Transfer to a slow cooker (or Dutch oven). Roughly chop the onions, add to the frying pan, and sauté until soft.

Use a little of the red wine to deglaze the onions in the frying pan, then add the onions to the slow cooker (or Dutch oven). Slice the mushrooms in half, quarters if they are large, and sauté until brown and golden. The best way to ensure the mushrooms brown evenly is to not crowd them in the pan (another Julia Child trick!). Once the mushrooms are ready, add to the slow cooker (or Dutch oven). Remove the beef from the oven.

Wash and scrub the potatoes and chop them into 1-inch cubes. Place the beef, bacon, potatoes, and diced tomatoes with their juice in the slow cooker (or Dutch oven). Mix to combine, and then pour in the wine, vinegar, and just enough bone broth to cover the meat and vegetables.

Peel the cloves of garlic, leaving them whole, and scatter them over top, followed by the sprigs of thyme.

Cook on low for 6–8 hours in the slow cooker (or at 325°F for 2½ hours in the oven).

Ironically, it's faster to cook pulled pork in a slow cooker than by traditional methods. Crazy, right? This recipe is fast and easy, and all the work is done in the morning, so you can enjoy your day. The balsamic vinegar tenderizes and marinates the meat as it cooks, so it's juicy and caramelized right out of the slow cooker, and adds a new taste dimension, thanks to the apple. Try serving this pulled pork on a bun, Sloppy Joe–style—it's second to none. I like this with coleslaw (page 78) and more sauce on the side. **SERVES 6**

Slow-Cooker Pulled Pork

1 (5–6 lb) boneless pork shoulder
½ cup chicken broth
½ cup honey
½ cup **Red Apple** dark balsamic vinegar
¼ cup **Lime** fused olive oil or a fruity **extra virgin** olive oil
2 Tbsp Dijon mustard
3 garlic cloves, minced
½ cup diced onion
2 tsp chili powder
1 tsp fresh thyme or ½ tsp dried thyme
1 Tbsp cornstarch

Use **Chocolate** or **Espresso** dark balsamic for a richer sauce with a thicker, more luxurious mouth feel, or **Cherry** or **Pomegranate** for a sweeter sauce.

Feeling a little more adventurous? Try using your favorite fruity balsamic to switch up the flavor profile and make pulled pork tacos, topped with Roasted Tomato Salsa (page 117), Lime & Cilantro Guacamole (page 69), some shredded cabbage for a bit of crunch, and a few black beans if you're like me and have an undying love for black beans.

Trim the pork shoulder of excess fat and place it in a slow cooker.

Combine the chicken broth, honey, balsamic, olive oil, and Dijon with the garlic, onion, chili powder, and thyme. Pour over the pork. Cook on low for 8 hours.

Place the pork on a cutting board, shred it with two forks, and pile it into a large bowl.

Pour the cooking liquid from the slow cooker into a saucepan over medium-high heat. Combine the cornstarch with 2 Tbsp water and whisk it into the cooking liquid. Bring to a low boil, whisking until the sauce thickens, 3–5 minutes. Pour as much or as little sauce as you like over the shredded pork, then pile it on buns to your heart's content!

Slow and low is always the name of the game for ribs. When you finish these pork ribs on the grill, you can either keep the rack whole or cut it into individual ribs to prevent the whole thing falling apart, as it does get very tender. **Red Apple** balsamic vinegar pairs perfectly with pork. It's sweet and tangy, and it caramelizes the meat so well in this recipe. A match made in heaven. Serve with Summer Slaw (page 319). **SERVES 4–6**

Red Apple Ribs

1 large rack (about 5–7 lb) of pork ribs or 2 smaller ones
½ cup **Red Apple** dark balsamic, plus more for drizzling
2 garlic cloves, minced
½ small onion, grated
¼ cup dark brown sugar, packed
2 Tbsp soy sauce
2 Tbsp grainy Dijon mustard
1 tsp celery seed
Sea salt and ground black pepper

Honey Apple Ribs Substitute the **Red Apple** dark balsamic with **Apple** white balsamic and use honey instead of dark brown sugar.

Preheat the oven to 300°F.

Wash the ribs, pat them dry, and lay them on a parchment-covered rimmed baking tray.

In a small bowl, whisk together the balsamic, garlic, onion, sugar, soy sauce, Dijon, and celery seed until fully combined and the mixture is a saucy paste. Brush it on both sides of the ribs in a thin, even layer and sprinkle them with salt and pepper to taste. Cover with a layer of aluminum foil.

Place ribs in the oven, turn down heat to 225°F, and bake for 6 hours, basting every 2 hours with the juices. Remove from the oven and let rest 30 minutes, still covered.

Preheat the barbecue to high (at least 450°F).

Sear the ribs on both sides for about 5 minutes per side, drizzling any extra drippings and extra dark balsamic, if desired, over top to caramelize and crisp up the ribs. Serve immediately, and make sure to provide lots of napkins!

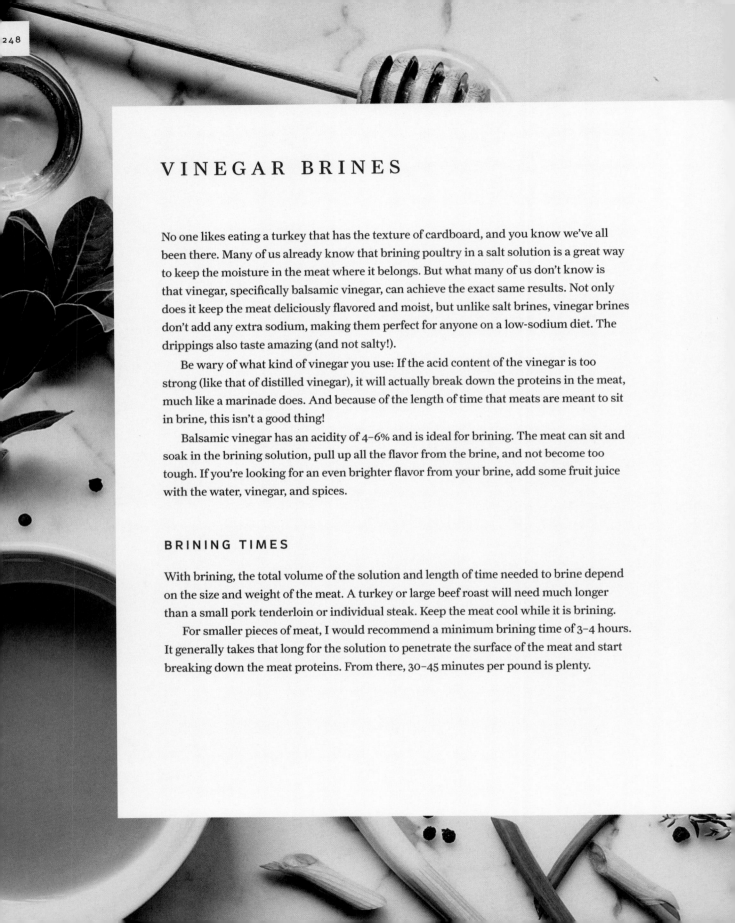

VINEGAR BRINES

No one likes eating a turkey that has the texture of cardboard, and you know we've all been there. Many of us already know that brining poultry in a salt solution is a great way to keep the moisture in the meat where it belongs. But what many of us don't know is that vinegar, specifically balsamic vinegar, can achieve the exact same results. Not only does it keep the meat deliciously flavored and moist, but unlike salt brines, vinegar brines don't add any extra sodium, making them perfect for anyone on a low-sodium diet. The drippings also taste amazing (and not salty!).

Be wary of what kind of vinegar you use: If the acid content of the vinegar is too strong (like that of distilled vinegar), it will actually break down the proteins in the meat, much like a marinade does. And because of the length of time that meats are meant to sit in brine, this isn't a good thing!

Balsamic vinegar has an acidity of 4–6% and is ideal for brining. The meat can sit and soak in the brining solution, pull up all the flavor from the brine, and not become too tough. If you're looking for an even brighter flavor from your brine, add some fruit juice with the water, vinegar, and spices.

BRINING TIMES

With brining, the total volume of the solution and length of time needed to brine depend on the size and weight of the meat. A turkey or large beef roast will need much longer than a small pork tenderloin or individual steak. Keep the meat cool while it is brining.

For smaller pieces of meat, I would recommend a minimum brining time of 3–4 hours. It generally takes that long for the solution to penetrate the surface of the meat and start breaking down the meat proteins. From there, 30–45 minutes per pound is plenty.

MEAT	BASIC MINIMUM BRINING TIME	PLUS TIME PER POUND
Beef — Steak	4–5 hours	30–45 minutes
Beef — Roast (3–4 lb)	12 hours	45–60 minutes
Pork	3–4 hours	30–45 minutes
Poultry — Whole chicken	4–5 hours	25–30 minutes
Poultry — Breasts, thighs	3–4 hours	25–30 minutes
Fish and Other Seafood	Not recommended	

SIMPLE VINEGAR BRINES

To make these brines, make sure you start with a container large enough to completely submerge the meat in the liquid. If it's a turkey, you might need a bucket or tub made out of food-grade plastic; sometimes a really large stock pot will work too. You can also buy bags that are made for brining turkeys, which are handy, and you don't need a ton of brine to fill them up either.

Then, simply pick your meat and your vinegar, and combine all the brine ingredients. Again, make sure you'll have enough brine to cover the meat; that could depend on the size of your container. Double the recipe if necessary.

Put your meat in the container and pour the brine overtop. (Sometimes I put a heavy mixing bowl on top of a brining turkey to make sure it stays submerged.) Leave the container in a cool spot for the time specified (see above chart). The fridge is ideal, but if the container is too big and the temperature outside is under 40°F, you can keep it outside, too. Another good place to brine is the root cellar or the beer fridge (a great excuse to drink all the beer).

After you've removed the meat from the brine, remember to pat it dry and season well with salt and pepper before putting it in the oven. This will keep all the juices that have been absorbed in the meat, which means the flavors will stay there as well.

MANGO BRINE
FOR CHICKEN

1 cup **Mango** white balsamic vinegar
1 cup orange juice
3 cups water
2 star anise
1–2 cinnamon sticks
5–6 whole cloves
4–5 whole cardamom pods

LEMON BRINE
FOR CHICKEN

1 cup **Sicilian Lemon** white balsamic
   vinegar
4 cups water
4 sprigs thyme
1 sprig rosemary
Ground black pepper

HONEY GINGER BRINE
FOR TURKEY

(If your turkey is smaller—say, 8–10 lb—
   you can halve this recipe.)
6 cups **Honey Ginger** white balsamic
   vinegar
3 cups apple juice
12 cups water
10 bay leaves
3 oranges, quartered and placed in the
   cavity
3 small onions, halved and placed in the
   cavity

GRAPEFRUIT BRINE
FOR TURKEY

2 cups **Grapefruit** white balsamic vinegar
1 cup orange juice
4 cups water
4 sprigs fresh tarragon
Ground black pepper
2 shallots, halved and placed in the cavity
2 lemons, quartered and placed in the
   cavity

MAPLE BRINE FOR PORK

1 cup **Maple** dark balsamic vinegar
1 cup cranberry juice
3 cups water
2 sprigs thyme
2 garlic cloves, crushed

RED APPLE BRINE FOR PORK

1 cup **Red Apple** dark balsamic vinegar
3 cups water
2 Tbsp soy sauce
¼ cup brown sugar, packed
2 Tbsp grated ginger

CHOCOLATE BRINE FOR BEEF

1 cup **Chocolate** dark balsamic vinegar
1 cup brewed coffee
2 cups water
2 oranges, quartered
1 onion, roughly chopped
Ground black pepper
Ground cumin

OREGANO BRINE FOR BEEF

1 cup **Oregano** white balsamic vinegar
2 cups water, or enough water to cover
   the meat
1 tomato, roughly chopped
2 sprigs rosemary
2 sprigs thyme

White Balsamic Vinegars

White balsamic is fresh, delicious, and complex, and uses a relatively new way of creating a balsamic-like vinegar. The traditional grapes—Trebbiano and Lambrusco—are still used as the base for this balsamic, but the traditional production methods have been slightly modified to create a vinegar that is as complex and rich as balsamic but white in color. White balsamic can't hold any of the designations that **Traditional** dark balsamic does, isn't graded in the same way, and isn't aged for hundreds of years, but it adds an incredible depth and freshness to dishes. The idea of creating it came from chefs in the region of Modena who had grown tired of the way balsamic turned their food brown. With white balsamic, instead of squishing and then caramelizing the grapes to make the traditional must, the grapes are crushed, reduced in a double boiler so they don't gain any color, and aged in stainless steel rather than wood containers. Its acidity is 4–5%, so it's less acidic than traditional white wine vinegars and has a healthy balance between sweetness and acidity. One of my favorite ways to use the flavored white balsamics is in soda water for a healthy flavor twist. When you use them in salad dressings, you won't need to add any honey or maple syrup and you can rest easy that they won't change the color of any of the ingredients!

This is the white balsamic version of dark balsamic crème (page 159). The process is the same: Reduce the balsamic to make a thick, concentrated syrup. It takes a minute or two to make, and you can put it on absolutely anything. Ice cream is my favorite. **MAKES ⅓ CUP**

White Balsamic Crème

½ cup any white balsamic vinegar

Coconut, **Peach**, and **Pineapple** are my favorite white balsamic reduction flavors. Stick to fruity flavors if you're drizzling it on top of desserts. Or try reducing **Oregano** or **Lemongrass Mint** white balsamic to drizzle over feta or goat cheese.

In a shallow saucepan or 8-inch frying pan, bring the vinegar to a simmer over medium heat. Bring just to a boil and gently swirl the balsamic over the bottom of the pan a few times—three swirls should do the trick. As you gently swirl the vinegar you'll notice it going from moving around the pan quickly to leaving a trail behind. As soon as you see an even trail being left behind, remove the pan from the heat and let cool to room temperature. You'll have a thick crème. This process will take 20–30 seconds at most. Don't take your eyes off it for a second! You might find—as I have on occasion—that you have balsamic pull taffy on the stove rather than the glaze you were planning for. If it's too thick, warm it again and add a little more balsamic, but don't let it boil. If you pull it off the heat too soon, just warm it for a little longer to thicken.

This is best used at room temperature. If it's stored in the fridge, it will thicken to the consistency of molasses—and it moves as slowly as molasses when it comes to returning to a room-temperature consistency. I prefer to drizzle it warm or just above room temperature if I'm using it on a warm salad, roasted vegetables, or a meat dish, so it drizzles smoothly and easily and doesn't cool down the rest of the dish. When I'm drizzling it over ice cream, cheese, or any other cold dish, I use it at room temperature, so it doesn't warm up the dish too much but is still of drizzling consistency.

This reduction will last basically indefinitely at room temperature. Store it in a cupboard in an airtight container, such as a Mason jar. I tend to keep a jar of it beside my honey pot and quadruple this recipe to make 2 cups at a time.

Cranberry Pear

Tart, sweet, and crisp this balsamic makes me think about the holiday season, although I actually use it all year long. Boasting a stunning blush rosé color, it is as beautiful as it is delicious. A favorite for simple, everyday salads or reduced and drizzled over cheese, this combines all the best parts of tart fresh cranberries with the sweetness of fresh pears. This is one of my favorites to add to soda water, sweet tea, or even hot tea, and it also pairs well with cocktails (see chart on page 341). You'll find **Cranberry Pear** white balsamic vinegar in the following recipes (and in several recipe variations throughout the book):

Bright and colorful, this quick and easy chutney is delicious with Brie, tucked into
puffed pastry, or just slathered on toast for the mango lovers of the world! I also like to
serve it with pork or chicken. **MAKES 1 ¹/₂ CUPS**

Cranberry Pear Mango Chutney

6 green onions

2 Tbsp **Lemon** fused olive oil

1 large mango, peeled and coarsely chopped

¹/₃ cup dried cranberries

2 Tbsp granulated sugar

¹/₄ cup **Cranberry Pear** white balsamic
vinegar

Herbaceous Apricot Chutney Substitute
apricots for the mango, **Apricot** white
balsamic for the **Cranberry Pear**, and
Herbes de Provence infused olive oil for the
Lemon fused olive oil.

Savory Plum Chutney Substitute plums for
the mango, **Plum** white balsamic for the
Cranberry Pear, and **Rosemary** infused olive
oil for the **Lemon** fused olive oil.

Chop the green onions and separate the white parts from
the green. Sauté the white parts in the olive oil in a frying
pan over medium heat until tender and soft. Add the
mango, cranberries, and sugar, and then the balsamic.
Bring to a gentle boil, turn down the heat, and simmer,
uncovered, until the mango has softened, the dried
cranberries have plumped, and the entire mixture has
thickened, 7–10 minutes. Use the green parts of the green
onions as a garnish if desired.

This will keep in the fridge in an airtight jar for up to
1 week.

These cookies are festive and delicious, although they can be enjoyed any time of the year. The **Cranberry Pear** white balsamic vinegar adds a lovely zip to the sweetness of the cookies and ensures the cranberry flavor is a part of every bite. The **Blood Orange** olive oil keeps the cookies fruity and moist, and offers a unique and delicious spin on a classic recipe. **MAKES 36 COOKIES**

Oatmeal Cookies with Cranberries & White Chocolate Chips

1/2 cup **Blood Orange** fused olive oil
3/4 cup light brown sugar, packed
1 egg
2 Tbsp **Cranberry Pear** white balsamic vinegar
1 cup all-purpose flour
1 tsp baking powder
1/2 tsp sea salt
1 cup rolled oats
1/2 cup dried cranberries
1/2 cup white chocolate chips

Oatmeal Chocolate Chip Cookies For a more classic option, use **Chocolate** dark balsamic vinegar instead of the **Cranberry Pear** white balsamic and 1 cup of dark chocolate chips instead of the cranberries and white chocolate chips.

Oatmeal Raisin Cookies Substitute an **extra virgin** olive oil, such as **Arbequina**, in place of the **Blood Orange** fused olive oil and 1 cup of raisins in place of the dried cranberries and white chocolate chips.

Preheat the oven to 350°F. Line a baking sheet with parchment paper.

In a large bowl, whisk the olive oil with the sugar until well combined. Add the egg and vinegar and continue to beat until the batter is light and frothy.

Sift the flour and baking powder over top of the wet ingredients and then add the salt. Mix everything two or three times to just combine, then add the oats and continue to mix until fully combined. Add the cranberries and chocolate chips and mix to incorporate evenly.

Drop 1–2 tablespoons of batter onto the prepared cookie sheet, spacing the drops at least 2 inches apart. I usually get 12 or 16 on a standard cookie sheet. Using your fingers gently press the cookies to flatten them to about 1/2-inch thick and about 2 inches in diameter.

Bake for 8–10 minutes for soft chewy cookies and 10–12 minutes for crunchier cookies.

Transfer the baked cookies to a wire rack to cool completely. Repeat with the remaining cookie dough. (You can bake these on two sheets at the same time, if you prefer. Simply swap their positions halfway through baking time.)

You can store these in an airtight container on the counter for up to 1 week—although I've never had them last that long!

This caramelized, robust jam is great with pork or chicken, but my favorite way
to eat it is with blue cheese or goat cheese on top of crostini or Easy Flatbread
(page 22). **MAKES 2 CUPS**

Cranberry Apple Onion Balsamic Jam

1 large onion
1 tart crisp apple (Granny Smith is perfect)
3 Tbsp **Lemon** fused olive oil
1 cup granulated sugar
¾ cup **Cranberry Pear** white balsamic
    vinegar
1 cup cranberries, fresh or frozen (no need
    to thaw first)

Apple Onion Jam Use 2 apples, omit the
cranberries, and use **Apple** white balsamic
in place of the **Cranberry Pear** for a more
apple-forward flavor.

Plum Apple Onion Balsamic Jam Substitute
1 cup sliced plums for the cranberries and
use **Plum** white balsamic instead of the
Cranberry Pear.

Slice the onion into rounds. Peel and thinly slice the apple.

In a frying pan, warm the olive oil over medium heat
and sauté the onion and apple until soft, 5–7 minutes.
Sprinkle with the sugar and continue to cook, stirring
to coat the onion and apple well with the sugar. Add the
balsamic and use it to deglaze the pan, scraping up any
bits of onion or apple that may have stuck to the pan.
Add the cranberries, bring to a gentle boil, then turn
down the heat and allow to simmer, covered, for about
20 minutes, until the cranberries have split and are soft
and the sauce has thickened. If it appears really watery
(which can happen if frozen cranberries were extra juicy
when they went in the freezer), stir constantly for a few
minutes with the lid off to encourage some of the juice to
evaporate. Once thick, remove it from the heat and let cool
to room temperature.

This will keep in the fridge in an airtight container for
up to 1 week.

Sicilian Lemon

If you like to squeeze fresh lemon juice over your favorite dishes, this balsamic will be your new best friend. And talk about versatile! This will enhance the flavor of roasted meats, fish, fruit salads, ice cream, desserts, and cocktails. You'll find **Sicilian Lemon** white balsamic in the following recipes (and in several recipe variations throughout the book):

This easy dip is a perfect summer appetizer. You can use any leftover dip to dollop onto burgers or to fill mushroom caps. You don't need to stick with rosemary—the recipe is adaptable enough that you can use your favorite herbs or spices and match this to the rest of your menu. **MAKES ABOUT 1 CUP**

Whipped Feta Dip

1 cup crumbled feta cheese

3 Tbsp robust **extra virgin** olive oil, plus more for drizzling

2 Tbsp **Sicilian Lemon** white balsamic vinegar

1 tsp fresh rosemary leaves, divided

½ tsp ground black pepper

Sea salt

Tuscan Herb, **Rosemary**, **Garlic**, or **Chipotle** infused olive oil or **Cayenne** fused olive oil are all good alternatives for drizzling over top and adding another flavor component.

Place the cheese, olive oil, balsamic, ½ tsp of the rosemary, and the pepper in a food processor or blender (a small one is ideal) and blend until well combined. You may need to use a spatula to scrape it down and pulse until it's fairly smooth. Don't try to get all the lumps out; the feta tends to remain a bit chunky. Place the dip in a serving dish, either a bowl or a plate for this one, and use the back of a spoon or spatula to smooth the top. Drizzle with some more olive oil for garnish, season to taste with salt and pepper, and sprinkle with the remaining ½ tsp rosemary for a decorative touch.

Salty and sweet, scallops are truly delicious. The freshness of the **Sicilian Lemon** white balsamic in this recipe lets the flavor of the scallops shine through. The salad is one of my favorites, with creamy avocado, plenty of herbs, crispy bacon, salty capers, and tangy pomegranate seeds. The **Pomegranate** dark balsamic and **Blood Orange** fused olive oil in the dressing meld all the flavors together. In fact, you can serve the salad without the scallops and still have a very tasty meal—especially if you top it with some crumbly blue cheese and some orange wedges rather than lemon for a sweeter note. If you're feeling more like fish than shellfish, the salmon from the salmon tacos (page 77) is a delicious protein to top this salad. **SERVES 4 AS A SIDE OR LUNCH**

Lemon Pomegranate Scallops on Greens

4 strips bacon
¼ cup **Blood Orange** fused olive oil
2 Tbsp **Pomegranate** dark balsamic vinegar
2 tsp grainy Dijon mustard
2 tsp honey
2 sprigs thyme
1 shallot, minced
Sea salt and ground black pepper
3 cups green leaf lettuce
3 sprigs fresh flat-leaf parsley, chopped
1 Tbsp fresh chives
1 avocado, sliced
⅓ cup fresh pomegranate arils, plus more
    for garnish
1 Tbsp capers
3 Tbsp **Sicilian Lemon** white balsamic
    vinegar
16 large sea scallops
Lemon wedges for garnish

In medium-sized frying pan over medium heat, fry the bacon until crisp. Set it on some paper towel to soak up any grease.

In a small bowl, whisk together the olive oil, **Pomegranate** balsamic, Dijon, honey, thyme, and shallot for the dressing. Add salt and pepper to taste.

In a large serving bowl, place the lettuce, parsley, and chives. Drizzle with half the dressing and toss to combine. Chop the bacon into small pieces. Top the tossed lettuce with the bacon, avocado, pomegranate arils, and capers and drizzle with the remaining dressing.

Pour out any residual bacon grease from the frying pan, add the **Sicilian Lemon** balsamic, and bring to a boil over medium-high heat. Place the scallops in a single layer in the pan, with at least 1 inch between them. You may need to do this in batches. Every 15–20 seconds, shake the pan to ensure the scallops are not sticking, turning after 1–2 minutes when golden and caramelized. Keep shaking the pan to avoid sticking and remove from the heat when the scallop centers are just translucent, about 1 minute more.

Arrange the scallops on the salad, season with salt and pepper, and garnish with lemon wedges and a few more pomegranate arils.

Serve immediately. The lettuce salad will keep in the fridge overnight (although it keeps better without the dressing), but the scallops should be enjoyed the day they are made.

You can prep this bright, colorful salad the day before you plan to eat it. The veggies will soak up the flavorful dressing if it sits in the fridge for a day. The **Sicilian Lemon** white balsamic adds such a freshness that I can describe it only as the perfect match for the veggies. **SERVES 4 AS A SIDE**

Summer Fresh Veggie Salad

2 cups blanched broccoli florets
1 cup blanched cauliflower florets
1 cup blanched chopped carrots
½ cup **Milanese Gremolata** infused olive oil
¼ cup **Sicilian Lemon** white balsamic vinegar
Sea salt and ground black pepper
1 Tbsp chopped fresh curly-leaf parsley
Lemon zest, for garnish

Tuscan Herb, Garlic, Rosemary, or **Wild Dill** infused olive oil, or even a lovely robust single varietal **extra virgin** olive oil, can be used in place of the **Milanese Gremolata**.

For more herbaceous options, **Lemongrass Mint** or **Oregano** white balsamic are also delicious in place of the **Sicilian Lemon** white balsamic.

In a large bowl, toss the veggies with the oil and balsamic, making sure they are evenly coated. Season to taste with salt and pepper. Place in the fridge to allow the flavors to develop, at least 2–3 hours, or overnight. Garnish with parsley and lemon zest before serving.

When I offered cooking classes through our retail store to help teach customers how to cook with olive oil, our Night in Syria class was the most popular and requested class. We were lucky enough to have an employee whose father was Syrian, and he taught us countless useful tricks. These kebabs were the key recipe for the class; they are easy to prepare and super delicious. Incorporating the **Sicilian Lemon** white balsamic in the marinade for the chicken creates a lovely balance, as it tenderizes the chicken and freshens the flavor. It's crisp and bright on the palate and complements the za'tar beautifully without overpowering the tomato flavor. **SERVES 4**

Syrian-Style Chicken Kebabs

4 garlic cloves, finely crushed

1 Tbsp tomato paste

½ cup robust **extra virgin** olive oil

5 Tbsp **Sicilian Lemon** white balsamic vinegar, divided

1½ tsp za'tar (see sidebar)

¼ tsp smoked paprika

1½ lb boneless skinless chicken thighs, cut into 1-inch pieces

½ tsp sea salt

½ tsp cracked black pepper

For a spicier version, use **Harissa** infused olive oil in place of the **extra virgin** olive oil.

If you're looking for a sweet tangy version, **Mango** white balsamic is a lovely substitution in place of the **Sicilian Lemon**.

To enhance the za'tar flavor, substitute **Oregano** white balsamic for the **Sicilian Lemon**.

Za'tar is a spice blend used in many Middle Eastern and eastern Mediterranean cuisines. You should be able to find it in the grocery store or in Mediterranean or Middle Eastern markets. If you can't source it, you can make your own version, but the secret ingredient is sumac, and that can also be hard to find. If you do manage to find sumac, make your own za'atar with the following ingredients: 1 tsp dried oregano, ½ tsp dried thyme, ½ tsp toasted sesame seeds, ½ tsp sumac, and salt to taste.

Soak eight wooden skewers for an hour in cold water.

In a large mixing bowl, stir together the garlic and tomato paste until smooth and well combined. Add the olive oil, 3 Tbsp of the balsamic, the za'tar, and paprika, mixing well. Add the chicken thighs and toss to coat well. Marinate for 20 minutes, or up to overnight, in the fridge.

Preheat the barbecue to high. Thread the meat onto the skewers; cook the chicken on the hot grill for 4–5 minutes per side, turning frequently and brushing with the remaining 2 Tbsp balsamic after each turn, until cooked through and no longer pink inside.

If a hot grill isn't within reach, you can remove the chicken from the marinade and sear it (on the skewers) in a hot frying pan for 4–5 minutes per side (remember to add a little oil if your pan isn't nonstick). Deglaze the pan with the 2 Tbsp balsamic. Pour the resulting sauce over the chicken.

Serve on warm flatbread (page 22) or with rice and roasted root vegetables as a main dish.

Grapefruit

Both the aroma and the flavor of sweet, tart grapefruit are captured perfectly in this balsamic. Pair it with a robust **extra virgin** olive oil for a delightful dressing on a spinach salad with fresh grapefruit segments, roasted nuts, and dried cherries, or add a few drops to sparkling water for a refreshing drink on a hot day. You'll find **Grapefruit** white balsamic vinegar in the following recipes (and in several recipe variations throughout the book):

Who doesn't love a simple salad? This one is balanced thanks to the freshness of the grapefruit, the crunch of the walnuts, and the tangy sweetness of the cranberries.

SERVES 4 AS A SIDE

Arugula Salad with Grapefruit Vinaigrette

SALAD

2 cups arugula

¼ cup toasted whole walnuts

¼ cup dried cranberries

Grapefruit segments for garnish

Shaved Parmesan

GRAPEFRUIT VINAIGRETTE

3 Tbsp **Grapefruit** white balsamic vinegar

2 Tbsp creamy **extra virgin** olive oil

1 tsp Dijon mustard

1 minced shallot

To make the salad, on a serving plate, arrange the arugula in a pretty pile, sprinkle with the walnuts and cranberries, and arrange the grapefruit segments on top.

To make the vinaigrette, mix the balsamic, olive oil, Dijon, and shallot together in a small bowl or glass. Pour the dressing over the salad, top with Parmesan shavings, and serve.

You can also use this simple olive oil and balsamic marinade on scallops, shrimp, and even chicken (marinate the chicken for at least 30 minutes). Try drizzling it over open, grilled oysters to glaze them. **SERVES 4**

Halibut in Summer Citrus Seafood Marinade

¼ cup **Blood Orange** fused olive oil
2 Tbsp **Grapefruit** white balsamic vinegar
4 pieces (4 oz each) of halibut
2 sprigs fresh thyme, leaves only

For a slightly savory option, substitute **Herbes de Provence** or **Milanese Gremolata** infused olive oil in place of the **Blood Orange** fused olive oil.

In a shallow dish, whisk together the olive oil and balsamic to emulsify. Coat each piece of fish in marinade and then place it in an 8- × 8-inch baking pan. The fish should be crowded in the dish. Drizzle the remaining marinade over top and place in the fridge for 20 minutes.

Preheat the oven to 375°F or the barbecue to high.

Let the halibut rest on the counter for 2 minutes before you are ready to cook it, then place it on a rimmed baking tray in the oven or directly on the barbecue.

Cook until flaky and cooked through, ensuring the edges are crisp, 10–15 minutes in the oven and around 7–10 minutes on the barbecue. Sprinkle the thyme leaves over the cooked halibut.

Serve with a citrus chutney (the Cranberry Pear Mango Chutney on page 257 is delicious with this!) on a bed of rice or with grilled potatoes.

I love to serve grilled fruit in the summer. Grilling caramelizes the natural sugars and makes it extra sweet. The fruit stays firm and is equally delicious on its own or topped with a dollop of whipped cream. **SERVES 4**

Grilled Pineapple with Coconut

8 fresh pineapple rings
¼ cup **Grapefruit** white balsamic vinegar
Vanilla ice cream to serve
¼ cup shredded coconut (sweetened or unsweetened)

For a less citrus-forward variation, substitute **Apple**, **Plum**, or **Mango** white balsamic for the **Grapefruit**.

For coconut lovers, use **Coconut** white balsamic in place of the **Grapefruit**.

In a large shallow bowl, soak the pineapple rings in the balsamic for at least half an hour, or up to 12 hours.

Heat the barbecue to high, lightly grease the grill (**Lemon** fused olive oil works well for this), and remove the pineapple rings from the balsamic, shaking off any excess. Place the pineapple rings on the grill. Flip every minute until the outsides are caramelized and grill marks are evident. Drizzle with the remaining balsamic marinade, let grill for 30 more seconds, and remove from the heat.

Put ice cream in four bowls, top with two pineapple rings each, and sprinkle with coconut.

This is my twist on a classic cocktail. The flavor of the **Grapefruit** white balsamic vinegar works well with the botanicals in the gin and makes the soda tart and sweet; the acid from the vinegar melds them together and brings them to life. If you've ever had the chance to try a peabody flower gin, you'll be familiar with its deep blue-purple color. When mixed with an acid, it turns to a beautiful opal color. When I'm making G&Ts for a crowd or special occasion, peabody flower is my favorite gin to use with the **Grapefruit** white balsamic. If you're making these for a crowd, add some **Grapefruit** white balsamic to the water in your ice cube tray, quadruple this recipe, and serve it in a pitcher along with the grapefruit infused ice cubes so the flavor doesn't dilute as they melt. **SERVES 2**

Grapefruit Gin & Soda

4 oz gin of choice
8 oz soda water
2 Tbsp **Grapefruit** white balsamic vinegar
2 wedges fresh ruby grapefruit

Divide the gin, soda water, and balsamic equally between two tumbler-style glasses. Add enough ice cubes to fill each glass, bringing the liquid level to ¼ inch from the top. Garnish with a wedge of grapefruit on the rim.

Serve immediately and enjoy.

Coconut

Sweet, refreshing, tart, and utterly tropical, this balsamic makes a great salad dressing when paired with **Lime** fused olive oil or **Blood Orange** fused olive oil. It's incredible drizzled over shrimp and prawns, of course, but also lovely in simple cocktails—think mojitos, margaritas, and even mocktails. For a simple dessert, reduce it and drizzle it over ice cream (see the white balsamic crème recipe on page 255). You'll find **Coconut** white balsamic vinegar in the following recipes (and in several recipe variations throughout the book):

The coconut balsamic in this simple fruit salad adds to the tropical flavor. The dressing not only flavors but also tenderizes the fruit, so prep this a few hours before you plan to serve it. I like to use a fruit-based balsamic that introduces the flavor of a fruit I haven't used in the salad. If mangos aren't available, for example, I like to use **Mango** white balsamic. Top the salad with thick Greek yogurt for a creamy dessert or chop the fruit very finely and serve alongside grilled shrimp. **SERVES 2–4**

Sweet Citrus Coconut Salad

4 cups chopped assorted tropical fruit
   (dragon fruit, kiwi, bananas, mango, etc.)
¼ cup **Coconut** white balsamic vinegar

In a large bowl, toss the fruit with the white balsamic to coat. Allow to sit for about 2 hours to let the flavors develop. Stir well before serving.

This salad is equally delicious with **Apple**, **Grapefruit**, **Sicilian Lemon**, **Plum**, **Vanilla**, **Peach**, or **Mango** white balsamic vinegar.

This has all the flavor of traditional deep-fried coconut shrimp with none of the work (or the fat). You can also omit all the veggies and just bring the **Coconut** balsamic to a rolling boil, toss in your shrimp, and let the balsamic reduce and glaze them. **SERVES 4**

Tropical Coconut Lime Shrimp

¾ lb large shrimp or prawns (about 15), shelled and deveined
1 Tbsp **Lime** fused olive oil
¼ tsp sea salt
Pinch chili flakes
¼ cup **Coconut** white balsamic vinegar
½ red bell pepper, thinly sliced
¼ cup diced red onion
¼ cup chopped mango
1 Tbsp chopped fresh cilantro

In a mixing bowl, toss the shrimp or prawns in the olive oil, salt, and chili flakes.

Heat a nonstick frying pan over medium-high heat and add the balsamic. Bring to a boil. Add the prawns, bell pepper, and red onion immediately. Sauté for 2 minutes, or until the shrimp or prawns are just pink and have curled.

Add the mango and stir to combine. Remove from the heat, sprinkle with chopped cilantro, and serve over jasmine rice.

I use frozen fruit rather than juice to make these ice pops because it helps them keep their integrity and not turn into a dry ice cube after a few licks. I keep these in the freezer all year for a refreshing, quick treat. Experiment with your favorite fruits and white balsamic to come up with your own flavor combinations. For more ice pop recipes, see page 205. **MAKES 10 ICE POPS**

Mango Coconut Lime Ice Pops

1 large or 2 small mangos
½ cup granulated sugar
¼ cup **Coconut** white balsamic vinegar
¼ cup lime juice (2–3 limes)

Peel and roughly chop the mango. Place it in a saucepan over medium heat with the sugar and balsamic. Bring to a simmer and allow the mango to soften, 5–7 minutes, stirring to ensure even cooking. Remove from the heat and allow to cool to room temperature.

Place the mango mixture and lime juice in a food processor or blender and blend until smooth. Pour into molds or small paper cups, and place ice pop sticks in the middle of each mold or cup.

Freeze for at least 6 hours. To remove the ice pops from the molds, dip the molds/cups in near-boiling water for 5 seconds, remove, and then slowly remove the ice pops. Enjoy immediately, or wrap any leftovers in parchment paper, place them in resealable plastic bags, and return to the freezer.

Believe it or not, I like to use Ritz crackers in this pie. Their taste and texture work so
well with the tart white balsamic. The lime juice helps to cut some of the sweetness from
the condensed milk and make this utterly moreish. MAKES ONE (9-INCH) PIE

Pomegranate-Glazed Coconut Key Lime Pie

1 cup (8 oz) Ritz crackers
¼ cup **Lime** fused olive oil
2 Tbsp granulated sugar
1 (14 oz) can sweetened condensed milk
3 egg yolks
¼ cup **Coconut** white balsamic vinegar
¼ cup lime juice (2–3 limes)
1 Tbsp grated lime zest
1 cup pomegranate juice (store-bought)
1 Tbsp cornstarch
Pomegranate arils for garnish

Preheat the oven to 350°F.

Using a rolling pin, smash the crackers in a resealable bag until most pieces are smaller than a dime, but not powdered. Pour them into a mixing bowl and add the olive oil, followed by the sugar. Mix well to combine, breaking up any larger pieces of cracker. Press the crumble into a 9-inch pie dish and bake until golden brown, 8–10 minutes. Leave the oven on.

While the crust is baking, in a large mixing bowl, beat the condensed milk with the egg yolks, balsamic, lime juice, and lime zest until completely combined and frothy.

Pour the mixture into the pie crust and return to the oven until just set, about 15 minutes. The middle will still jiggle, and the top will be just golden.

Remove from the oven and allow to cool.

In a saucepan, whisk the pomegranate juice with the cornstarch until the cornstarch is completely lump-free. Place over medium heat and bring just to a boil, stirring constantly. The juice will turn milky and then deep red. Remove from the heat and pour over the pie. Shake slightly, allowing the glaze to level out and any air bubbles to come to the surface. Allow the glaze to cool and set before serving.

Serve with a dollop of whipped cream or ice cream with some pomegranate arils for garnish.

Peach

This white balsamic is crisp, sweet, and clean and sparkles with flavor. It's versatile enough to use with any of the **extra virgin** olive oils or infused olive oils. It actually tastes more like peach juice than vinegar! I like to drizzle it over fresh, creamy goat cheese. You'll find **Peach** white balsamic vinegar in the following recipes (and in several recipe variations throughout the book):

In this recipe, you let the sun make your tea. When I first heard about it, I thought the idea was ludicrous. There could be no difference between brewing tea with hot water and brewing tea with cold water, I thought. Oh, I was wrong! The white balsamic makes this drink refreshing, not too sweet, not too tart, and adds character and complexity. I find Red Rose or Earl Grey tea bags are best for this. **SERVES 6**

Peach Sweet Sun Tea

½ cup granulated sugar or honey
¼ cup **Peach** white balsamic vinegar
8 cups cold water
4 black tea bags
1 peach, sliced (skin on or off)

Apricot Sweet Sun Tea Substitute **Apricot** white balsamic vinegar for the **Peach** and 2 apricots in place of the peach for garnish.

Mango Sweet Sun Tea Substitute **Mango** white balsamic vinegar for the **Peach** and a mango for the peach garnish, or use ¾ cup chopped frozen mango as ice cubes when serving.

Plum Sweet Sun Tea Substitute **Plum** white balsamic vinegar for the **Peach** white balsamic and use 2 plums in place of the peach for garnish.

Place the sugar and balsamic in a small saucepan over medium heat and stir until the sugar is completely dissolved. Add 8 cups of cold water to a large glass pitcher, then pour in the balsamic simple syrup mixture, and stir. Place the tea bags in the water, cover the pitcher lightly with plastic wrap so the bugs can't get to it, and set the pitcher out in the sun.

Let it sit for 4 hours, giving the sun the chance to pull the tea from the bags. You'll notice some condensation develop, but that's nothing to worry about. Stir and taste, and then let the tea sit for another 2 hours at most, if you like.

Remove the tea bags, trying not to squeeze the extra tea from them (this makes the tea bitter). Put 2–3 ice cubes in a glass and fill with tea. Add fresh peach slices to the glass for garnish.

This will keep in the fridge for 2–3 days after you remove the tea bags.

This sauce is both sweet and savory, making it lovely on chicken or pork ribs. The **Chipotle** infused olive oil adds a hint of heat and a lovely smokiness. For a spicier sauce, add a diced jalapeño or two while you sauté the onion and garlic. MAKES 4 CUPS

Peach Barbecue Sauce

5 medium-sized ripe peaches
3 large garlic cloves
2 shallots
2 Tbsp **Chipotle** infused olive oil
¾ cup **Peach** white balsamic vinegar
½ cup brown sugar, packed
¼ cup tomato paste
2 Tbsp grainy Dijon mustard
1 Tbsp Worcestershire sauce
2 tsp smoked paprika
½ tsp ground nutmeg
1 tsp sea salt
½ tsp ground black pepper

Peel the peaches. The easiest way to do this is to gently drop each peach in boiling water for 10–15 seconds. Then, using tongs, hold it under cold, running water until it is cold enough to handle. Pressing gently, run your thumb over the surface. The peel should just slip off. If the skins are being stubborn, place the peach back in the boiling water for an additional 5–8 seconds and try again. This works best with ripe peaches. Chop the peeled peaches into ½-inch pieces and set aside.

Mince the garlic and shallots and place them in a large, heavy-bottomed saucepan with the oil. Sauté over medium heat until the shallots are soft and just browned, 3–5 minutes. Pour in the balsamic, scraping off any bits that are sticking to the pan, then add the sugar, tomato paste, Dijon, Worcestershire sauce, paprika, and nutmeg. Season to taste with the salt and pepper. Mix well to combine. Add the peaches and bring everything just to a boil. Turn down the heat and simmer, uncovered, for 30 minutes, until the sauce is thick and the peaches are soft.

Remove from the heat and allow to cool to room temperature. Purée with an immersion blender, or in batches in a traditional blender, until smooth and creamy.

This will keep in the fridge in an airtight container for up to 2 weeks.

As sweet and delicious as this pie might be, it's also a bittersweet dessert for me. I am originally from Ontario, Canada, where peaches signal the beginning of summer's end. When peaches are in season, I try to savor every bite, knowing that neither they nor summertime are going to last forever. **MAKES ONE (9-INCH) PIE**

Fresh Peach Pie

PASTRY

4 cups cake and pastry flour

2 tsp baking powder

1 cup mild and fruity **extra virgin** olive oil

1 egg

2 Tbsp **Peach** white balsamic vinegar

FILLING

6 large ripe peaches, peeled and sliced (see page 282)

½ cup **Peach** white balsamic vinegar

½ cup granulated sugar

3 Tbsp cornstarch, plus more for dusting

1 tsp ground nutmeg

Apricot Pie Substitute the peaches with an equal volume of halved apricots (18–20 large apricots) and use **Apricot** white balsamic instead of the Peach.

Plum Pie Substitute the peaches with an equal volume of plums (8–10 large plums) and use **Plum** white balsamic vinegar in place of the **Peach**.

To make the pastry, sift the flour and baking powder together in a large bowl.

Make a well in the center and pour in the olive oil. Using two knives or a pastry blender, mix the flour and oil until the mixture resembles a coarse oatmeal.

Crack the egg into a 1 cup measure, add the balsamic, and beat carefully. Fill the 1 cup measure to the top with ice-cold water. Slowly pour the egg mixture into the flour and mix very gently with the forks, pressing the mixture into a ball.

Divide the pastry in half, wrap each half in plastic wrap, and chill in the fridge for at least 30 minutes, or until you're ready to roll out each crust.

To make the filling, place the sliced peaches in a large bowl.

Warm the balsamic in a small saucepan over medium heat with ¼ cup water.

In a small dish or glass, mix together the sugar and cornstarch. Pour this into the water and balsamic. Stirring constantly, bring the mixture to a boil. Allow to boil for 30 seconds and then remove from the heat. Pour the syrup over the peaches and toss to coat.

Preheat the oven to 400°F.

Roll out half the pastry and place it in the bottom of a 9-inch pie dish, allowing the extra pastry to fall over the side of the dish. Dust the bottom of the crust with cornstarch.

Place the peaches in the crust, scraping out all the sauce to cover them. Sprinkle the peaches with the nutmeg. Roll out the remaining pastry and cover the pie.

CONTINUED →

Using your thumb and index finger, press the crusts together around the edge of the plate. Use a sharp knife to cut off any excess pastry from around the shell. Pierce the top crust several times with a knife to allow the steam to escape.

Bake at 400°F for 15 minutes, then turn down the heat to 325°F for 45 minutes. Allow the pie to cool completely before serving so that the cornstarch can set properly. If you prefer to eat warm pie, you can reheat it before serving.

Honey Ginger

Honey and ginger generally play well together, and their partnership shines in this slightly spicy balsamic. If you feel a bug coming on, add a little of this balsamic to a mug of hot water and you'll be feeling right as rain in no time. You'll find **Honey Ginger** white balsamic vinegar in the following recipes (and in several recipe variations throughout the book):

Years ago, I spent a few months in China. While I was there, I lived on fried rice. I couldn't get enough of the pillowy eggs and tasty grains of rice. In this version, the Honey Ginger white balsamic vinegar brings out the best in the soy sauce and sesame oil, creating a delicious, bright, and flavorful sauce to fry the rice in. There are two tricks worth knowing for this recipe: Make sure you use cold, cooked rice (hot and steamy rice doesn't allow the individual grains to combine with the egg and sauce properly) and add the eggs to the pan first. This prevents the eggs from drying out or making the rice oddly gummy. **SERVES 4**

Ginger Fried Rice

3 eggs
¼ cup **extra virgin** olive oil
4 cups cold cooked long-grain rice
2 Tbsp **Honey Ginger** white balsamic
    vinegar
2 tsp soy sauce
2 tsp toasted sesame oil
½ tsp sea salt
2 green onions
2 Tbsp fresh chopped curly-leaf parsley

To make this more of a main course, add 1 cup of diced cooked chicken or ham to the rice. This is a great way to use up leftover Apricot & Lemon Pulled Chicken (page 307) or Overnight Pomegranate-Glazed Ham (page 203)

Whisk together the eggs, olive oil, and 2 Tbsp of cold water, until fully combined and the eggs are light and fluffy.

Place a large frying pan or wok over medium-high heat. Add the eggs and rotate the pan so the eggs coat it evenly. Allow to cook for 1–2 minutes, just until the eggs start to puff up and cook through. While the eggs are cooking, separate out the grains of the cooked rice. Gently place the rice on top of the eggs. Using a fork, gently mix the eggs and rice together. Be careful not to press down; the idea is to keep the rice fluffy and break up the eggs gently as you mix. When the rice is warmed through, about 3–4 minutes, pour in the balsamic, soy sauce, and sesame oil. Season with the salt and continue to mix thoroughly. The rice should be an even toasty brown color.

Remove from the heat. Slice the green onions finely and on a sharp bias. Mix in the onions and parsley right before serving in individual bowls.

This will keep in the fridge in an airtight container for up to 2 days.

This vinaigrette is not only a great spinach salad dressing but is also tangy enough to use as a veggie dip at a party. It's also good with goat cheese, toasted nuts, and fresh fruit, and as a chicken marinade. Versatile? I should say so. **MAKES 2 CUPS**

Honey Ginger Dijon Vinaigrette

½ cup **Honey Ginger** white balsamic vinegar
¼ cup Dijon mustard
2 Tbsp finely minced shallot
2 tsp tarragon leaves (optional)
Sea salt and ground black pepper
1 cup fruity **extra virgin** olive oil

Place the balsamic and Dijon in a food processor or blender and add the shallot, tarragon, if using, and salt and pepper to taste. Pulse a few times to mix. Slowly pour in the olive oil while the machine is running to emulsify the mixture.

This will keep in the fridge in an airtight container for up to 1 week.

I love tuna's rich texture and flavor, and fresh tuna really doesn't need much to be at its best. The sesame seeds, sesame oil, and spicy wasabi create a great crust just after the tuna is seared. Use this to top a soba noodle salad, to serve alongside hot soup, or even as an appetizer. It's particularly good on a bed of rice with a fresh green salad. **SERVES 2**

Japanese Seared Ahi Tuna Steak

2 Tbsp Japanese toasted sesame oil

2 Tbsp **Honey Ginger** white balsamic vinegar

1 tsp wasabi paste

2 (4–5 oz each) ahi tuna steaks

1 Tbsp sesame seeds (mix of black and white is best)

If tuna isn't your thing, feel free to use boneless, skinless chicken breasts (one per person) or extra-firm tofu (½–¾ cup per person) instead.

If wasabi is too spicy for your taste, feel free to substitute tahini or mustard.

In a shallow bowl, whisk together the sesame oil, white balsamic, and wasabi paste. Place the tuna steaks in the bowl, turning to coat, and then transfer to the fridge for 25 minutes.

Preheat the barbecue to at least 500°F.

Sprinkle the sesame seeds on a separate plate. Turn the tuna in the marinade once last time, then place the steaks on the hot grill. Sear for 35–40 seconds per side, remove from the grill, and place on the sesame seeds. Press each piece of tuna onto the seeds, turning so both sides are lightly coated.

If a grill isn't available, heat a frying pan with a few tablespoons of olive oil on medium-high heat until very hot, sear the tuna as if on the grill, and complete the recipe as detailed above.

Serve immediately.

Mango

Mango, mango, mango! This balsamic is incredible in salsas and atop chicken and all kinds of seafood. It pairs perfectly with a mild **extra virgin** or **Blood Orange** fused olive oil as a great addition to salads, grilled fruit, and glazed donuts. Sweet and tangy, refreshing and delicious, try some in soda water for a delicious drink. You'll find **Mango** white balsamic vinegar in the following recipes (and in several recipe variations throughout the book):

This smoothie gives you a great start on busy days. It's not too sweet, and it's full of nutrients—greens, fruit, healthy fats, everything you need to start your day on the right foot. If you prep the fresh ingredients at night, all you have to do is add the olive oil and balsamic and pop it in the blender in the morning. **MAKES ABOUT 3 CUPS**

Favorite Breakfast Green Smoothie

2 cups spinach
1 banana
1 cup cubed mango
1 cup plain yogurt
2 Tbsp **Mango** white balsamic vinegar
1/4 cup **extra virgin** olive oil
1 cup ice cubes

Instead of the **Mango** white balsamic, try **Apple**, **Grapefruit**, **Cranberry Pear**, **Peach**, **Apricot**, or **Plum** for a different variation each day of the week!

Use a peeled, cubed apple in place of the cubed mango.

Place the spinach and 1/4 cup of water in the blender and blend until the spinach is fully liquefied, 15–20 seconds. Add the remaining ingredients in the order listed into a blender. Blend until creamy and smooth. And that's it!

If you're using frozen fruit, only use 1/2 cup ice and add 1/2 cup of water to help everything mix evenly.

Mango salsa can be the best of salsas or the worst of salsas. Sometimes it is just too sweet, in which case it becomes more of a dessert than a salsa; sometimes the mango is noticeable only because of its absence. This salsa, however, hits the mark. It is bright and mango-filled, but also balanced between sweet and sour. The balsamic contrasts with the sweetness of the mango and creates a balanced flavor with just a touch of heat. It's perfect with Salmon Tacos (page 77). **MAKES ABOUT 3 CUPS**

Mango Jalapeño Salsa

3 Roma tomatoes
1 large ripe mango
½ small red onion
1 serrano chili pepper
3 Tbsp **Lime** fused olive oil
2 Tbsp lime juice
1 Tbsp **Mango** white balsamic vinegar
½ cup chopped cilantro
Sea salt and ground black pepper

Roughly chop the tomatoes (discarding the seeds) and the mango and place them in a serving bowl. Dice the onion and add it to the bowl. Slice the chili in half, remove and discard the membrane and seeds, dice the chili finely, and add to the bowl.

Drizzle the olive oil, lime juice, and balsamic over the veggies and toss to coat. Mix in the cilantro and season to taste with salt and pepper. Cover, place in the fridge, and allow the flavors to meld for at least 1 hour before eating.

You can store this in the fridge in an airtight container for up to 1 week.

Easy desserts that bake while you eat your main meal are my absolute favorites! This rice pudding is super creamy and can be adapted according to what's in the cupboard and who's coming for dinner. **SERVES 4**

Creamy Coconut Rice Pudding

½ cup plus 2 Tbsp sweetened shredded coconut

½ cup short-grain rice

¼ cup **Lime** fused olive oil

2 cups coconut milk

¼ cup **Mango** white balsamic vinegar

1 cup chopped mango

> **Vanilla**, **Pineapple**, **Peach**, **Plum**, or **Coconut** white balsamic are delicious options for the balsamic component, especially if you use their respective fruits in place of the mango in the pudding as well.

Preheat the oven to 350°F.

Place the coconut in a dry frying pan over medium heat. Toast until it is just golden and smells delightful. Remove from the heat and set aside.

In an 8- × 8-inch baking dish, combine the rice with the olive oil and stir until fully coated. Pour in the coconut milk and balsamic and ½ cup of the toasted coconut.

Mix well and bake, uncovered, for 45 minutes, until the rice is cooked and all the coconut milk has been absorbed. If a skin forms on the top of the pudding, peel it off and discard it.

Serve the pudding warm with a garnish of chopped mango and the remaining toasted coconut.

Vanilla

Sultry, pure Madagascar vanilla delights the senses in this tasty white balsamic. Drizzle it over fruit salad or yogurt or add a few drops to sparkling water. It's also tasty over oatmeal, in cooked whole grain cereals, and in pancakes. It pairs particularly well with light fruity **extra virgin** oils and **Blood Orange** infused olive oil. You'll find **Vanilla** white balsamic vinegar in the following recipes (and in several recipe variations throughout the book):

Strawberries are by far one of my favorite fruits and drizzling them with a touch of **Vanilla** white balsamic vinegar takes them to the next level. This recipe is simple and allows the strawberries to just hang out with the balsamic while the magic happens. Enjoy often! **MAKES 2 CUPS**

Macerated Strawberries

2 cups fresh strawberries
¼ cup **Vanilla** white balsamic vinegar
2 Tbsp granulated sugar or maple syrup

Slice the strawberries in half or quarters, depending on their size, and place them in a serving bowl. Drizzle with the balsamic and toss to coat. Sprinkle the sugar evenly over the berries. Cover and place in the fridge for 2–3 hours, or up to overnight. The longer you let the berries sit the juicer they will be.

Remove from the fridge and stir a few times before serving. Spoon over ice cream or pudding, or serve on their own with a dollop of whipped cream for a simple spring dessert.

These also make lovely strawberries to pair with shortcake (see the sweet version of the savory scones on page 29).

Why is hot chocolate the only drink considered special enough to be topped with decadent marshmallows? I think that a hot beverage as regal as Earl Grey tea or Irish Breakfast also deserves this treatment. This recipe is the result of much marshmallow recipe research. The olive oil makes the mallows less goopy and hard to deal with but also keeps them extra moist, and the flavors of the **Blood Orange** fused olive oil and **Vanilla** white balsamic vinegar combine to make a subtle yet present taste that is delicious alongside tannic, tart British-style teas. **MAKES 20–30 MARSHMALLOWS**

Mallows for Tea

3 Tbsp unflavored gelatin
1 cup icing sugar
¼ cup cornstarch
¼ cup **Vanilla** white balsamic vinegar
¼ cup light corn syrup
2 cups granulated sugar
2 egg whites
⅓ cup **Blood Orange** fused olive oil

If you don't have **Blood Orange**, use **Lemon** fused olive oil—so good on hot chocolate!

Line a 7- × 11-inch baking pan with parchment paper so there is plenty of paper coming over the sides; this way you can grab and easily lift out the marshmallows once they are ready.

Pour ¾ cup water into a large mixing bowl or stand mixer bowl. Sprinkle the gelatin on top and allow to bloom, about 5–6 minutes.

In a small bowl, mix together the icing sugar and corn-starch. Using a sifter or small strainer, dust the prepared pan with half of the cornstarch–icing sugar mixture and set the rest aside.

In a deep, heavy-bottomed pot (the candy mixture will bubble up quite high), place the balsamic and corn syrup. Add the granulated sugar and 2 Tbsp water. Using a wooden spoon, slowly stir over medium heat until the sugar is dissolved. Turn up the heat to medium-high and stop stirring. Bring to a boil and continue to boil until the temperature reaches 240°F on a candy thermometer, about 10–12 minutes.

Meanwhile, with a stand or handheld mixer beat the egg whites to stiff peaks and set aside.

As soon as the sugar candy mixture has reached 240°F, pour it over the gelatin. Stir gently to ensure all the gelatin is dissolved and then mix on high speed. Beat until the brown caramel mixture has developed a creamy, fluffy texture and has at least tripled in volume, 5–10 minutes, depending on your mixer.

Add the beaten egg whites in one addition and then begin to mix slowly on low speed. While the machine is running, drizzle in the olive oil. Beat for 1 more minute then quickly remove the beaters and use a spatula to scrape as much of the marshmallow as you can out of the bowl and into the prepared pan, smoothing the top as much as possible. Work quickly, because the longer it sits, the goopier it will become.

Dust the top of the marshmallow with the remaining cornstarch–icing sugar mixture. Place in the fridge, uncovered, for 5 hours, or overnight, to set.

Once set, lift out the marshmallow with the parchment paper and peel back the sides. Put a few drops of oil on the blade of a long knife or bench scraper and gently and carefully oil the surface the marshmallows are on to help prevent sticking. Cut the mallows into 20–30 squares, according to how large you like them, rolling the sides against the parchment to pick up any remaining sugar, which helps to keep them from sticking together.

Store in an airtight container for up to 2 weeks.

Simple and so easy, this fruit dip means I don't need to keep both vanilla yogurt and plain yogurt in the fridge. I love using plain yogurt in curries and sauces, but I don't always want to be adding sugar and jams and things to it for breakfast. This is the ideal compromise. The **Vanilla** white balsamic, or any fruity white balsamic really creates a perfect topping for Harvest Granola (page 74), Baked Oatmeal (page 229), or a dish of fresh fruit. MAKES 1 CUP

Vanilla Yogurt Fruit Dip

1 cup Greek yogurt
2 Tbsp Vanilla white balsamic vinegar

* **Apricot Yogurt Fruit Dip** Substitute Apricot white balsamic for the Vanilla

* **Coconut Yogurt Fruit Dip** Substitute Coconut white balsamic for the Vanilla

* **Mango Yogurt Fruit Dip** Substitute Mango white balsamic for the Vanilla

* **Peach Yogurt Fruit Dip** Substitute Peach white balsamic for the Vanilla

* **Pineapple Yogurt Fruit Dip** Substitute Pineapple white balsamic for the Vanilla

* **Plum Yogurt Fruit Dip** Substitute Plum white balsamic for the Vanilla.

Whisk together the yogurt and balsamic until fully combined and lump free. Serve with fresh fruit, berries, and ginger cookies for a simple dessert.

Don't try to make this ahead or store it. The vinegar will make the yogurt curdle after a few hours, so whisk together right before enjoying and eat it all up.

Apricot

Tangy and sweet, just like apricots themselves, **Apricot** white balsamic vinegar is invaluable in the kitchen. Use it to inject new life into your faithful standby recipes. Add it to glazed pork roasts and shoulders, and even your favorite barbecue sauces. Reduce it and drizzle it over aged white cheddar, goat cheese, or Camembert as an appetizer, or over ice cream and fresh fruit for dessert. You'll find **Apricot** white balsamic vinegar in the following recipes (and in several recipe variations throughout the book):

This Middle Eastern drink is beautifully refreshing on a hot summer day. For a more intense flavor, let it sit to allow the mint leaves to infuse their magic into it. For just a hint of mint, add the sprigs without chopping the leaves. **MAKES 6 CUPS**

Summer Polo Spritzer

½ cup orange juice (1–2 oranges)
¼ cup lemon juice (about 2 lemons)
½ cup mint leaves
¼ cup granulated sugar
2 Tbsp **Apricot** white balsamic vinegar
4–5 cups sparkling water

Peach, **Sicilian Lemon**, or **Pineapple** white balsamic vinegars are all lovely here in place of the **Apricot**.

Pour the orange and lemon juices into a blender.

Tear the mint leaves roughly, removing the stems, and add to the blender with the sugar and balsamic. Blend until smooth and well combined, but still with some pulp for texture.

Pour the sparkling water into a serving jug and add the minty lemon mixture. Stir well and serve with lots of ice.

The combination of apricots and pork is wonderful, but it's not one that always springs to mind when you're planning dinners. In this recipe, I sear the meat first in the oven to create a crust. This seals in the juices and spreads flavor all the way through, but it doesn't dry out the meat in the process. Leftovers are perfect for lunches or diced and added to a salad. **SERVES 8**

Apricot Roasted Ham

1 bone-in ham, about 4 lb
¼ cup **Apricot** white balsamic vinegar
2 Tbsp honey
1 Tbsp robust **extra virgin** olive oil
1 Tbsp cornstarch
1 tsp Dijon mustard
1 sprig rosemary, or 1 tsp dried rosemary
½ tsp ground black pepper

Pineapple Roasted Ham Substitute the **Apricot** white balsamic for **Pineapple**.

Apple Roasted Ham Try **Apple** white balsamic in place of the **Apricot**.

Preheat the oven to 425°F.

Rinse the ham in hot water and pat dry. Place it in a roasting pan just large enough to hold it snugly. With a sharp knife, pierce the ham several times, at least 2 inches deep.

In a small bowl, combine the balsamic, honey, olive oil, cornstarch, and Dijon, and mix them into a paste. Brush or spoon this over the ham and sprinkle the rosemary and pepper over top. Bake, uncovered, for 10 minutes to seal in the juices and create a crust. Turn the oven temperature down to 325°F and roast the ham for an additional 45 minutes, or until its internal temperature is 165°F.

Remove the ham from the oven, baste it with its cooking juices, and let stand for 10 minutes before carving. Use the pan drippings for gravy.

This dish was one of the first Valentine's Day dinners that my husband, Steve, and I made together. It has since become one of our favorite "cooking together" meals—I make the sauce while he makes the pasta, and presto, dinner's ready! The balsamic here livens up the seafood and takes the creamy sauce to the next level by adding a fresh zestiness to it while also leaving a refreshing sweetness that complements the seafood perfectly. **SERVES 4 AS A SIDE, 2 AS A MAIN DISH**

Seafood Pasta

3 Tbsp **Apricot** white balsamic vinegar
1 cup shrimp, cleaned and deveined
½ cup scallops, cleaned and trimmed
2 cups whole milk
¼ cup robust **extra virgin** olive oil
2 Tbsp all-purpose flour
3 cups farfalle (bowtie pasta)
¼ dry white wine (Riesling or Pinot Grigio)
Sea salt and ground black pepper
½ cup shredded lox

If **Apricot** white balsamic isn't in your cupboard, **Peach**, **Pineapple**, or **Plum** would work just as well.

In a nonstick frying pan, bring the balsamic to a simmer over medium heat. Toss in the shrimp and cook for 2–3 minutes, stirring. Add the scallops and cook for an additional 2 minutes. Remove from the heat and set aside the pan.

In a saucepan over medium heat, warm the milk. In a separate saucepan over medium heat, mix the olive oil and flour together to form a smooth paste. Cook until bubbly and creamy, 2 minutes. Slowly begin to add the warm milk, ¼ cup at a time, whisking after each addition. Once all the milk has been added, simmer until the sauce is creamy and thick. Be careful not to let the sauce come to a boil.

Cook the pasta in a large saucepan of salted boiling water until al dente, about 10 minutes, then drain and rinse.

Warm the seafood in the frying pan it's sitting in, adding wine to deglaze the pan. Once the wine has reduced by half, 3–5 minutes, add the sauce and stir to combine, making sure everything is warmed through. Season lightly with salt and pepper.

Arrange the pasta on serving plates, pour the sauce over top, and top with the lox.

The **Apricot** white balsamic and **Lemon** fused olive oil add so much flavor that extra seasonings aren't really needed. Everything can go in the slow cooker in the morning, and the house smells amazing when you walk in the door ready to eat.

Serve with Wild Mushroom Risotto with Roasted Butternut Squash (page 25), or Roasted Beet Salad with Cinnamon Pear Balsamic & Goat Cheese Crumble (page 232) for a delicious hearty dinner. **SERVES 4**

Apricot & Lemon Pulled Chicken

6–8 boneless, skinless chicken thighs
4 garlic cloves
3 Tbsp **Apricot** white balsamic vinegar
3 Tbsp **Lemon** fused olive oil, divided
2 Tbsp Dijon mustard
1 tsp sea salt
½ tsp ground black pepper
2 tsp fresh thyme leaves

Pat dry the chicken with a paper towel. Place on a plate or in a shallow bowl.

Smash the garlic cloves and then mince them. Place them in a small bowl and whisk in the balsamic, 1 Tbsp of the olive oil, and the Dijon. Pour this over the chicken and massage it into the meat, covering it completely. Let it sit for 30 minutes, or for a maximum of 8 hours, in the fridge.

OVEN METHOD Preheat the oven to 350°F.

In an ovenproof frying pan (a cast iron frying pan is great here) over high heat, heat the remaining 2 Tbsp olive oil. Add the chicken and sear it on all sides to create a good crust, 2–3 minutes per side. Season with the salt and pepper.

Place the pan in the oven and roast for 35 minutes, until the internal temperature is at least 150°F. If you cover it while roasting, it will be juicier; if you roast it uncovered, it will be deliciously crispy. Use whichever method you prefer.

Remove from the oven and let rest 5 minutes. Using two forks, pull the chicken apart into strips. Place on a serving plate and sprinkle with thyme. (I usually pull it apart in the drippings/sauce, then toss it in the sauce before serving to make sure it's super juicy.)

SLOW COOKER METHOD Place the dried chicken (without marinating) in a slow cooker. Smash and then mince the garlic. Place it in a small bowl and whisk in the balsamic, olive oil, and Dijon. Rub this into the chicken. Sprinkle with the salt, pepper, and thyme. Cook on low for 6–8 hours, and then pull apart as described in oven method.

Standard olive oil cake recipes are a dime a dozen, but this isn't your standard olive oil cake. Spiced with cinnamon, nutmeg, and cloves, it is similar to a coffee cake but has a fine velvety crumb because of the brown sugar, olive oil, and buttermilk. The balsamic in the buttercream is perfect for those who don't enjoy terribly sweet frostings (the ones that make your cheeks tingle). **MAKES ONE (10-INCH) BUNDT CAKE, OR ONE (8-INCH) ROUND TWO-LAYER CAKE**

Velvet Spice Bundt with Apricot Buttercream

CAKE

2½ cups sifted cake and pastry flour

2 tsp baking powder

1 tsp baking soda

2 tsp ground cinnamon

1 tsp ground nutmeg

½ tsp ground cloves

½ tsp sea salt

3 eggs

½ cup fruity **extra virgin** olive oil or
    Blood Orange fused olive oil

1 cup brown sugar, packed

1½ cups buttermilk (see page 43)

BUTTERCREAM

2 Tbsp fruity **extra virgin** olive oil

3½ cups icing sugar, divided

¼ cup **Apricot** white balsamic vinegar

1–2 Tbsp whipping (35%) cream

Preheat the oven to 350°F. Grease a 10-inch Bundt pan (or two 8-inch round pans).

To make the cake, sift the flour with the baking powder, baking soda, cinnamon, nutmeg, cloves, and salt onto a piece of parchment paper. In a large bowl, beat the eggs and olive oil with the brown sugar until creamy and frothy.

Pour in 1/3 of the flour mixture, fold in with a wooden spoon, and then add half the buttermilk. Mix well. Add half of the remaining flour, mixing well, and then add the remaining buttermilk, also mixing well. End with the rest of the flour mixture. Whip until smooth. Pour the batter evenly into the cake pan and tap it gently on the counter to remove any extra air bubbles and level the batter. Bake for 45–50 minutes (30–35 minutes for the 8-inch pans) or until a toothpick inserted in the center comes out with just a few light crumbs stuck to it.

Remove the cake from the oven. Let cool for 5 minutes and then turn onto a wire rack to cool completely.

To make the buttercream, in a small bowl, whisk together the olive oil with about half of the icing sugar to form a smooth paste. Whisk in the balsamic and then the remaining icing sugar. If the frosting is too thick, add the whipping cream 1 Tbsp at a time and whip until the frosting is thick and creamy but still pourable enough to leave lovely long drips down the side of the cake. (You're looking for something between the consistency of a loose icing sugar glaze and thick spreadable frosting.)

Place the cake on a serving platter or cake plate and generously pour the buttercream over the top of the cake, allowing it to drip down the sides.

Plum

This jewel-toned white balsamic owes its tart, crisp flavor to juicy fresh plums. It pairs beautifully with **Blood Orange** fused olive oil, **Lime** fused olive oil, and fruitier **extra virgin** olive oils such as **Hojiblanca** and **Picual**. Use this in dressings, in marinades, as a glaze for chicken or pork, in sparkling water or mixed drinks, over fresh fruit, or reduced (see page 255) and drizzled over salty aged cheese. You'll find **Plum** white balsamic vinegar in the following recipes (and in several recipe variations throughout the book):

These simple muffins are a staple in our house at the end of summer when backyard plums are in abundance. The sweetness of the plums, combined with the fresh tartness of the lemon and spicy ginger, reminds me that fall is coming, but it's not quite here yet. Allowing the plums to macerate in the vinegar keeps them fresh and moist and makes the muffins a beautiful pink color. **MAKES 12 MUFFINS**

Plum Lemon Muffins with Ginger Glaze

1 cup sliced plums
⅓ cup granulated sugar
2 Tbsp **Plum** white balsamic vinegar
2 eggs
¼ cup **Lemon** fused olive oil
2 cups all-purpose flour
2 tsp baking powder
1½ tsp ground ginger, divided
½ tsp sea salt
½ cup plain yogurt
¼ cup icing sugar

In a small bowl, place the sliced plums. Sprinkle with the sugar, toss to coat evenly, and then drizzle with the balsamic.

Preheat the oven to 400°F. Line a muffin tin with paper liners.

In a large bowl, whisk together the eggs and olive oil until light and fluffy and fully combined, 1–2 minutes. Sift the flour, baking powder, 1 tsp of the ginger, and salt over top of the egg mixture. Using a wooden spoon or spatula, fold the wet and dry ingredients together until just combined. Add the plums and the yogurt and fold a few more times to combine.

Spoon the batter into the prepared muffin tins, filling them two-thirds of the way.

Bake for 20–22 minutes, until the muffins have risen and a toothpick inserted in the center of a muffin comes out clean. Remove from oven and, using a knife to help if necessary, carefully take the warm muffins out of the tin and place them on a wire rack.

In a small bowl whisk together the remaining ginger, icing sugar, and 1 Tbsp of water to make a glaze. Using a pastry brush, brush the warm muffins evenly with the glaze. Allow the muffins to cool completely before serving.

You can store these in an airtight container for up to 3 days on the counter.

A twist on an old favorite, this cocktail is the one that started them all. Using **Plum**
white balsamic vinegar instead of the traditional bitters adds a new complexity that
pairs perfectly with bourbon. **SERVES 1**

Bourbon Old Fashioned

1 orange
½ tsp brown sugar
1 tsp **Plum** white balsamic vinegar
One large ice cube
2 oz bourbon

If **Plum** white balsamic isn't in the cupboard,
Apricot or **Peach** are also great options for
this classic drink.

Using a vegetable peeler, peel off a long slice of orange
rind and place it in the bottom of a heavy-bottomed glass.
Add the sugar and balsamic. Using the back of a wooden
spoon, gently smash and squish the sugar into the orange
rind, until the sugar is almost dissolved and the rind has
turned bright orange. Place a large ice cube in the glass
and pour the bourbon over top.

Enjoy immediately.

I love plums. They are so juicy and sweet yet tart all at the same time. Adding the balsamic to the base and the topping makes for a rich, complex, tart flavor throughout. The cardamom in the crumble topping makes the kitchen smell heavenly while it's cooking. **SERVES 6**

Plum Crisp

12 large purple plums
½ cup cranberry juice
½ cup **Plum** white balsamic vinegar
½ cup granulated sugar
2 Tbsp cornstarch
½ tsp sea salt
1½ cups rolled oats
¾ cup all-purpose flour
¼ cup brown sugar, packed
½ cup **Blood Orange** fused olive oil
2 tsp ground cardamom
1 tsp ground nutmeg
1 tsp ground cinnamon
Pinch of cloves

If **Plum** white balsamic isn't in the cupboard, feel free to substitute with **Apricot**, **Ginger Honey**, or **Peach**.

Preheat the oven to 400°F.

Wash the plums, pit them, slice them into quarters, and place in a 14- × 10-inch baking dish.

In a small saucepan, whisk together the cranberry juice, balsamic, sugar, cornstarch, and salt, until no lumps remain. Place over medium heat and bring to a boil. Boil for 1 minute, or until the sauce is fully opaque. Drizzle the sauce over the plums.

In a small bowl, mix together the oats, flour, and sugar. Toss to combine. Drizzle in the olive oil and mix to form a soft, moist crumble. Add the spices and mix until fully incorporated. Spread the oat mixture evenly over the plums.

Bake for 35–40 minutes, until bubbling and the crumble is toasted golden.

This will keep in the fridge for up to 3 days in an airtight container.

Pineapple

The unique taste of pineapple will enhance a huge variety of meals. Pair this balsamic with soy sauce and sesame seeds to create an amazing marinade for chicken or a tangy dressing for coleslaw. Combine it with **Lime** fused olive oil and fresh thyme for the perfect finish to grilled shrimp. A few drops of it add pizzazz to sparkling drinks when you're looking for an extra-special something for your designated driver. You'll find **Pineapple** white balsamic vinegar in the following recipes (and in several recipe variations throughout the book):

A word of warning: The longer this mustard sits, the spicier it will become. Feel free to add some extra honey to the mix if you forget about it for a while to tame the heat a bit. This is perfect with pork, and it's delicious in a simple baguette sandwich with leftover Overnight Pomegranate-Glazed Ham (page 203) or Apricot & Lemon Pulled Chicken (page 307) and a simple Summer Slaw (page 319) in a pita for a quick and easy lunch. **MAKES ABOUT 2 CUPS**

Pineapple Balsamic–Infused Grainy Hot Mustard

³/₄ cup yellow mustard seeds

¹/₄ cup dry mustard

1 tsp sea salt

¹/₂ cup **Pineapple** white balsamic vinegar

¹/₄ cup herbal tea (your choice of flavor)

¹/₄ cup orange zest honey (optional, for extra sweetness)

¹/₄ cup fresh herbs of your choice (optional, for more complexity)

Cranberry Mustard Substitute **Cranberry Pear** white balsamic for the **Pineapple** and use on turkey sandwiches during the holidays, or any time of year for that matter.

Coarsely grind the whole mustard seeds for a few seconds in a spice or coffee grinder, or by hand with a mortar and pestle. Because you are adding dry mustard too, you want the seeds to be mostly whole so they're broken rather than ground up completely.

Pour the coarsely ground seeds into a medium-sized mixing bowl and mix in the dry mustard and salt to combine.

Gently pour in the balsamic and tea, mixing to form a creamy paste. Mix in the honey and herbs, if using. Transfer the mustard to an airtight container (a Mason jar is perfect) and let it sit in the fridge for at least a day before using. It will keep for a few months in the fridge.

This simple slaw is a perfect snack on a warm day. It's crisp, crunchy, slightly sweet, and tangy. Eat it with chicken or leftover ham for a quick lunch. **SERVES 6**

Summer Slaw

2 carrots
1 small green cabbage
1 small sweet onion
¼ cup **Pineapple** white balsamic vinegar
1 tsp celery seed

For a more refreshing version, try **Grapefruit** white balsamic. **Mango** is a great option for another fruity version. For a more savory option, use **Lemongrass Mint** or **Oregano** white balsamic.

Roughly grate the carrots, chop the cabbage, and slice the onion very thinly. Place them in a serving bowl. Drizzle with the balsamic and mix to coat evenly. Let the slaw sit for a few hours to allow the flavors to develop, mixing again and scattering the celery seeds over top just before serving.

This lovely summer drink is a tasty combination of the refreshing notes of the Pineapple white balsamic and the creamy part of the coconut milk. It's the perfect drink—or pitcher!—for a summer party. **SERVES 2**

Pineapple Piña Colada

¼ cup coconut cream (the thick stuff at the top of the can)
2 Tbsp **Pineapple** white balsamic vinegar
4 oz white rum
Ice cubes
Soda water
2 slices fresh pineapple

In a cocktail shaker, place the coconut cream, balsamic, and rum. Add a few ice cubes and shake well to blend and combine. Strain into a cocktail glass filled with ice and top with soda water. Garnish each glass with a slice of fresh pineapple.

This doesn't keep, so enjoy it the day it's made.

Lemongrass Mint

A wonderful base for marinades, this balsamic explodes with flavor when fresh Thai chilies and cilantro are added (read more about marinades on pages 152–154). It also pairs beautifully with the **Milanese Gremolata** and **Basil** infused olive oils and **Lime** fused olive oils to make dressings (read more about dressings on pages 40–41). Try using it in rice dishes to pair with a spicy curry or in noodle salads, on seafood, or in dipping sauces. You'll find **Lemongrass Mint** white balsamic vinegar in the following recipes (and in several recipe variations throughout the book):

Cool, creamy, and fresh, this tzatziki is perfect on sandwiches in place of mayo. Try a dollop on lamb burgers or a slice of roast beef, or use it as a dip for roasted potatoes. **MAKES 3 CUPS**

Lemongrass Mint Tzatziki

1 English cucumber

2 tsp sea salt

2 garlic cloves

¼ cup chopped fresh dill, plus a sprig of dill for garnish

1 Tbsp chopped mint leaves

2 Tbsp fruity, creamy **extra virgin** olive oil

1½ cups Greek yogurt

2 Tbsp **Lemongrass Mint** white balsamic vinegar

2 Tbsp lemon juice

> If you really love dill, use **Wild Dill** infused olive oil in place of the **extra virgin**.
>
> If you're a garlic lover, use **Garlic** infused olive oil in place of the **extra virgin**.

Peel the cucumber, slice it lengthwise, and scrape out the seeds. Grate it into a fine mesh sieve lined with cheesecloth and set over a bowl.

Add the sea salt, toss well, and let drain at room temperature for at least 1 hour, or overnight in the fridge. Squeeze the cucumber really well to get out as much water as possible. (You can pop a weigh on top of the cucumber, if you like.)

Mince the garlic, then use a mortar and pestle to mash it to a fine paste. Mix the dill and mint with the garlic, gently mashing them together.

Scoop this mixture into a mixing bowl. Add the drained cucumber and olive oil and mix to combine. Stir in the yogurt, balsamic, and lemon juice. Season to taste with salt. Garnish with a sprig of dill before serving.

This will keep for 2 days in the fridge in an airtight container.

This lamb recipe is so simple and delicious, there's no reason to save it for Easter Sunday dinner. The combination of the **Lemongrass Mint** white balsamic and **Milanese Gremolata** infused olive oil will have your taste buds thinking it's spring, no matter what the calendar tells you. **SERVES 4**

Mint Marinated Lamb Chops

2 garlic cloves, minced
2 Tbsp **Milanese Gremolata** infused olive oil
2 Tbsp **Lemongrass Mint** white balsamic vinegar
1 tsp grainy Dijon mustard
4 (½–¾ lb each) frenched lamb chops
2 Tbsp finely chopped mint leaves, divided

If Mint isn't your favorite, **Wild Dill** infused olive oil or a robust **extra virgin** paired with the **Sicilian Lemon**, **Oregano**, or **Apricot** white balsamic are lovely substitutes.

In a small bowl, whisk together the garlic, olive oil, balsamic, and Dijon.

Place the lamb in a shallow dish and drizzle with the marinade, turning to coat both sides. Place 1 Tbsp of the mint leaves on top. Cover with plastic wrap and place in the fridge for 4 hours, or up to overnight.

Preheat the oven to 350°F.

Bake the chops, uncovered, for about 20 minutes, turning halfway through cooking time.

Sprinkle with the remaining mint before serving.

Every other week, the retail store staff used to gather in our apartment for a meeting. We would connect, talk about work and life, and eat dinner, which we would often cook together. This dish was a big favorite on those nights—and still is. It is easily doubled or tripled to serve a crowd and takes about 15 minutes to put together from start to finish, which is ideal when you're walking in the door at the same time your guests arrive. Luckily, our staff never thought of themselves as guests; they were more like family. I like to serve this on a bed of rice, and sometimes I use 2 cups of baby spinach instead of the bell pepper. **SERVES 4**

Staff Meeting Stewed Chickpeas

2 Tbsp robust **extra virgin** olive oil
1 large onion, chopped
Sea salt
2 Tbsp **Lemongrass Mint** white balsamic vinegar
1 (28 oz) can diced tomatoes
1 (19 oz) can chickpeas, drained and rinsed
1 green bell pepper, chopped
½ cup sliced garlic-stuffed olives
2 Tbsp finely chopped fresh flat-leaf parsley

Oregano white balsamic vinegar is delicious in this recipe instead of the **Lemongrass Mint**.

Wild Dill, **Garlic**, or **Rosemary** infused olive oil are delicious alternatives to the **extra virgin** olive oil, if you're looking for an even brighter flavor.

In a large frying pan over medium heat, warm the olive oil and then sauté the onion until tender, 5–8 minutes. Add a pinch of salt, mix to combine, then add the balsamic. Continue to sauté until the onion has absorbed all the liquid.

Add the tomatoes (with their juice) and chickpeas and allow the liquid to come to a boil. Stir the chickpeas, preventing them from sticking but still allowing the liquid to cook down until they are tender, 7–10 minutes.

Toss in the bell pepper and olives, mix gently, and remove from the heat. Sprinkle with parsley and serve.

At least twice a year when we owned our retail store, we used to host a night where all the staff created new dishes, using a fresh olive oil or balsamic vinegar. We all tasted the dishes and voted on flavor complexity, use of olive oil or balsamic, and several other fun categories. At the end of the night, the top three dishes were announced. This dish was a winner created by Nadia (the same amazing person who inspired the baked oatmeal on page 229). The herbaceous, sweet **Lemongrass Mint** white balsamic mixes delightfully with the bright citrus and the salty complexity of the soy sauce. **SERVES 2**

Asian Sesame Balsamic Salmon en Papillote

2 Tbsp **Lemongrass Mint** white balsamic
   vinegar
1 Tbsp orange juice
1 tsp honey
1 tsp soy sauce
1/2 tsp toasted sesame oil
1/2 tsp Chinese five-spice powder
2 carrots, sliced into matchsticks
1 medium zucchini, skin on, sliced into
   matchsticks
1 red bell pepper, sliced into matchsticks
2 (about 4 oz each) salmon fillets
Sea salt and ground black pepper
Cilantro (optional)

Use **Honey Ginger** white balsamic instead of the **Lemongrass Mint** for a slightly sweeter version of this recipe.

Use **Pomegranate** dark balsamic instead of the **Lemongrass Mint** white balsamic and omit the sesame oil for a rich, caramelized version of this recipe.

Preheat the oven to 425°F. Line a rimmed baking tray with two pieces of parchment paper. Each piece will need to be large enough to envelope a layer of veggies with a piece of salmon on top.

Combine the balsamic, orange juice, honey, soy sauce, sesame oil, and five-spice and set aside.

Divide the veggies evenly between the two sheets of parchment paper and drizzle each set with 2 tsp of sauce. Lay a piece of salmon on top of each set of veggies, season lightly with salt and pepper, and drizzle with the remaining sauce. Top with a few sprigs of cilantro, if using. Seal each packet by tightly folding the tops of the paper together and twisting the ends tightly. Bake for 8–10 minutes. Open the packets carefully when serving, because the steam will be significant.

Oregano

This is a savory vinegar, aromatic, tart, and extremely flavorful. It is, of course, wonderful in a Greek salad dressing, drizzled on fresh cucumbers, or as an ingredient in a marinade for chicken or fish. It pairs perfectly with the **Garlic** and **Tuscan Herb** infused olive oils. You'll find **Oregano** white balsamic vinegar in the following recipes (and in several recipe variations throughout the book):

This incredibly flexible recipe is a tasty weeknight staple for us. Don't hesitate to throw in whatever is in the fridge—spinach and kale are both great, for example, and leftover chicken is great if you want extra protein. The acidity in the vinegar balances out the starches and livens the flavor of the beans. It's also great for deglazing the pan and lifting out all the crispy bits, adding even more flavor and texture to the dish. **SERVES 2**

Black Beans & Rice

1 cup basmati rice

2 Tbsp **Garlic** infused olive oil

1 large onion, chopped

Sea salt

2 Tbsp **Oregano** white balsamic vinegar

1 (28 oz) can diced tomatoes

1 (19 oz) can black beans, rinsed and drained

1 tsp ground cumin

½ tsp ground turmeric

½ tsp smoked paprika

1 green or yellow bell pepper (or a combination), chopped

½ cup grated cheddar cheese

½ cup sour cream

2 Tbsp chopped cilantro

Lemongrass Mint white balsamic can be used in place of the **Oregano** for a softer approach, or try **Sicilian Lemon** or **Grapefruit** white balsamic for a refreshingly bright flavor.

Swap out the **Garlic** infused olive oil and use **Cilantro & Onion**, if you're a cilantro lover, or **Chipotle**, if you're looking to kick up the smoky spicy notes a notch.

In a saucepan, place the rice in 2½ cups water, bring to a boil over high heat, cover, turn down the heat to its lowest setting, and let the rice cook for 15 minutes to absorb the water. While the rice is cooking, prepare the black beans.

In a large frying pan over medium heat, warm the olive oil and then sauté the onion until tender, 5–8 minutes. Add a pinch of salt, mix to combine, then add the balsamic. Continue to sauté until the onion has absorbed all the liquid, stirring gently from time to time.

Add the tomatoes (with their juice) and beans and allow the liquid to come to a boil. Stir in the cumin, turmeric, and paprika. Keep stirring to prevent the beans from sticking, but allow the liquid to cook down, 7–10 minutes. Add the bell pepper and stir to combine.

Remove the rice from the heat and let sit, still covered, for 5 minutes. Fluff up the rice, place it in serving bowls, and top with the beans, a generous sprinkle of cheddar cheese, a dollop of sour cream, and a bit of cilantro.

The simple meat sauce in this dish is hearty and packed with flavor. Sautéing the onions and garlic with the **Oregano** white balsamic vinegar gives them a lovely and bright herbaceous flavor that will have your guests asking what your secret ingredient is! It reheats beautifully for lunches, and is the ideal option for feeding a crowd of neighborhood kids. Seriously, this pasta never fails to satisfy. **SERVES 4**

Herb Bolognese with Penne

2 Tbsp **Tuscan Herb** infused olive oil
1 white onion, chopped
3 garlic cloves, crushed
1 tsp sea salt
½ tsp cracked black pepper
¼ cup **Oregano** white balsamic vinegar
1 lb extra-lean ground beef
1 (28 oz) can crushed tomatoes
2 Tbps chopped fresh flat-leaf parsley, plus more for garnish
1 Tbsp chopped fresh basil
2 tsp fresh thyme leaves
1 lb penne pasta
½ cup grated Parmesan cheese

If the **Tuscan Herb** isn't handy, the **Basil**, **Rosemary**, or **Garlic** infused olive oil work well in this recipe.

In a large saucepan, heat the olive oil over medium-high heat. Sauté the onion and garlic for 2–3 minutes, until translucent and soft. Sprinkle with the salt and pepper and continue to cook, stirring, until very soft and starting to caramelize, another 3–4 minutes. Pour in the balsamic, stir well to combine, and scrape any bits off the bottom of the pan, deglazing it as the onion and garlic soak up all the vinegar.

Add the ground beef and, using a wooden spoon, break up the meat and let it brown evenly. When the beef is no longer pink inside, pour in the tomatoes and stir in the herbs, mixing well to combine. Turn down the heat to a simmer and allow the sauce to reduce while you prepare the pasta.

Bring a large saucepan of salted water to a boil and cook the penne until almost al dente. Drain it and return to the pot. Add the sauce and place the pot over medium heat. Stir well to combine and allow the sauce to finish cooking the pasta, about 2–3 minutes. Remove from the heat and serve immediately with a grating of Parmesan cheese and some parsley for garnish.

The sauce will keep in the fridge for up to 1 week in an airtight container. Once it's mixed with the pasta it will keep for up to 3 days.

Similar to tzatziki but with very different spices, this raita is the perfect dip to serve with spicy curries, or even roasted sweet potatoes. It's normally white, but I love to add a touch of color to mine by adding a pinch of turmeric. Serve alongside Chickpea Tikka Masala (page 149) and Easy Flatbread (page 22) in the form of naan for a simple hearty meal. **SERVES 2**

Yogurt Raita

1 English cucumber, peeled
2 ½ tsp sea salt, divided
1 garlic clove
¼ cup fresh cilantro leaves
1 ½ cups Greek yogurt
2 Tbsp **Cilantro & Onion** infused olive oil
2 Tbsp **Oregano** white balsamic vinegar
1 tsp ground cumin
1 tsp ground coriander
½ tsp ground turmeric
½ tsp ground cardamom
½ tsp cracked black pepper

Using a box grater or food processor, grate the cucumber. Place the cucumber in a fine mesh strainer and sprinkle with 2 tsp of the salt. Using your hands, mix to combine, and then let sit for 10 minutes to allow the salt to pull out the excess water. Press the cucumber into the strainer to extract as much water as possible. (You can pop a weight on top if you like.) Discard the water and set the cucumber aside.

Crush the garlic and mince finely and chop the cilantro leaves. Place the yogurt in a bowl and whisk in the olive oil, balsamic, all the ground spices, pepper, and remaining ½ tsp salt until the yogurt is smooth. Add the cucumber, garlic, and cilantro and stir to combine. Place in the fridge for about half an hour before you use it (although you can eat it straight away if your schedule is a bit out of whack).

This will keep in an airtight container in the fridge for up to 1 week.

Apple

Not quite apple cider vinegar, yet still tangy and bright, this **Apple** white balsamic will make a lovely addition to your balsamic collection, as it pairs well with both sweet and savory dishes and infused olive oils too! It's lovely on a fresh green salad mixed with **Herbes de Provence** infused olive oil, or drizzled over **Lemon** fused olive oil ice cream (see page 35). It's also tasty alongside pork or chicken, or added to chutneys and sauces. In fact, it enhances the flavor of whatever it's paired with, without overwhelming the other ingredients in the dish. You'll find **Apple** white balsamic vinegar in the following recipes (and in several recipe variations throughout the book):

I think we were all that child who couldn't stand liver. I know I was, but I have a fondness for it now, especially this adult version. The cream softens the chicken livers, the apple adds a sweetness to it, and the **Herbes de Provence** infused olive oil makes it rich and so flavorful. I serve this as an appetizer or as a lunch side to add some extra protein (and iron!) to a salad. Lovely for special occasions but simple enough for every day, this deserves to be enjoyed often. **SERVES 4**

Chicken Liver & Apple Pâté

1 small red onion

1 large tart apple (Granny Smith is perfect)

4 Tbsp **Herbes de Provence** infused olive oil, divided

½ tsp sea salt

2 Tbsp lemon juice

1 lb chicken livers

½ cup whipping (35%) cream

½ tsp ground black pepper

¼ cup **Apple** white balsamic vinegar

Peel and dice the onion, and peel, core, and roughly cube the apple. Place a large saucepan or frying pan over medium heat and add 2 Tbsp of the olive oil. Cook the onion in the oil, stirring to ensure the onion is softening evenly, about 2–3 minutes. Add the apple and continue to sauté for another minute or so, until the apple just starts to soften, and then sprinkle with salt and cook until the apple is golden on the outside but still holding its shape. Pour in the lemon juice and deglaze the pan, scraping up any bits that may have stuck to the bottom. Remove from the heat and set aside.

Pat dry the chicken livers. Carefully cut away and discard any veins, larger pieces of sinew, or dark spots.

Place the apple and onion mixture in a food processor or blender while you prep the rest of the recipe. Place the remaining 2 Tbsp of olive oil in the pan and return to medium-high heat. Let the oil warm for a minute or two, then add the livers to the pan and fry them, stirring to ensure they don't brown too much, until they're firm on the outside yet still pink and soft on the inside, about 5 minutes.

Pour in the cream and pepper and bring to almost a boil before you pour in the balsamic. Continue stirring as the pan juices begin to reduce, about 3 minutes. Check one of the larger pieces of liver to see if it is still pink inside. The livers are done when they are firm all the way through and no pink remains.

Add the livers and all the pan juices to the apple and onion mixture. Purée the warm mixture until it is completely smooth.

Pick out your serving dish of choice. I like to use a 1–2 cup wide mouthed jar, or a pretty shallow ceramic bowl so the pâté is 1–2 inches thick. Really, though, any container will do. The important thing is that the dish will allow you to get a knife in easily so you can spread lots of pâté on baguette.

Pour the pâté into the serving dish, scraping out any extra from the bowl. Cover with plastic wrap, pressing it onto the surface of the pâté. Chill for at least 6 hours, or up to overnight, to ensure the pâté is completely set.

This will keep in an airtight container in the fridge for up to 3 days.

Whenever I'm under the weather, this works as a pick-me-up, or a put-me-to-sleep, depending on what I need. The **Apple** white balsamic vinegar will kill any bacteria in your throat, the sweetness of the honey soothes, and the brandy fixes the rest. Enjoy often, even when you're not in bed with Netflix, feeling sorry for yourself. It's equally tasty when consumed in front of a warm fire with friends. **SERVES 1**

Apple Spiced Hot Toddy

2 tsp honey
1 Tbsp **Apple** white balsamic vinegar
1 shot brandy
1 cinnamon stick

If you're looking for a bit more spice, use **Honey Ginger** white balsamic instead of the **Apple**.

In a large mug, place the honey, balsamic, and brandy. Stir to combine, mixing in the honey. Top with almost boiling water and stir again to ensure the honey is fully melted. Add the cinnamon stick and allow to cool for a few moments before enjoying.

Oatmeal really is a standby for me. It's a favorite no matter the time of year. I love adding seeds and extra dried fruit to make it hearty, and in this version the **Apple** white balsamic vinegar brings out the flavor of the oats and omits the need for salt. Topped with Vanilla Yogurt Fruit Dip (page 300), it's a perfect start to my day. **SERVES 2**

Quick Apple Oatmeal

½ cup quick-cooking rolled oats
¼ cup pumpkin seeds
¼ cup raisins or dried cranberries
2 Tbsp **Apple** white balsamic vinegar
2 Tbsp flax meal
2 Tbsp sunflower seeds
1 tsp ground cinnamon
½ tsp ground nutmeg
Pinch of ground cloves

Mix all the ingredients in a small saucepan with 1 cup of water. Set it over medium-high heat and bring to a rolling boil, stirring constantly. When all the water is absorbed and the oatmeal is thick, divide it evenly between two bowls.

This will keep in an airtight container in the fridge for up to 2 days. Reheat by adding some water and stirring to loosen it up as you warm it in a saucepan on the stove.

COCKTAILS

Using balsamics in cocktails opens up a whole new world of possibilities. Whether you put a balsamic in a spritzer bottle and spritz the aroma over your drink right before enjoying it or add balsamic as an ingredient, these vinegars enhance every aspect of a cocktail.

Balsamic adds a cool and incredibly refreshing aspect to cocktails. The aromatics are very inviting and have a savory effect, which freshens sweeter drinks. If you add a little Coconut or Mango white balsamic to a piña colada, for example, the drink becomes refreshing and balanced rather than sickly sweet.

When you spritz a cocktail with balsamic, the aroma is the first thing you notice. When you pick up the cocktail, if you like the aroma, you feel excited about taking the first sip, creating expectation and evoking emotion even before the glass touches your lips.

Vinegars work best alongside citrus, which may come as a surprise to some people. Citrus is detected by the front and sides of your tongue, whereas vinegar is detected closer to the back. When you eat them in combination, you taste the citrus first and the vinegar then rounds out and finishes the experience. Using vinegar and citrus together not only creates a fuller experience, it also embellishes the flavors of the alcohol you're using. Even incredibly simple cocktails benefit from a dash of vinegar—it opens up a whole other world of flavor combinations and possibilities and adds an exciting depth and complexity.

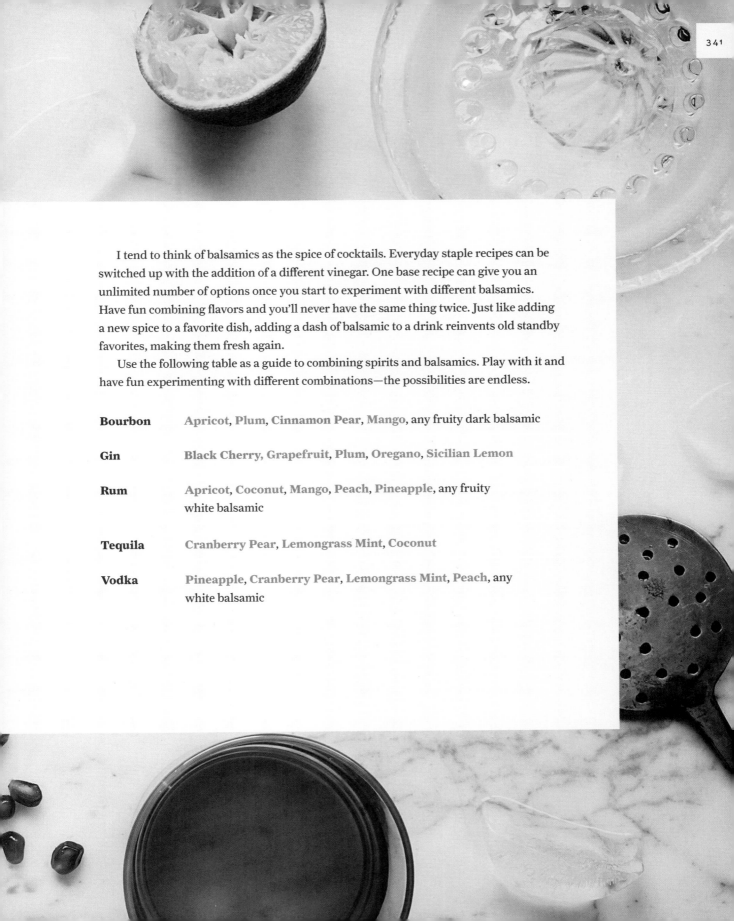

I tend to think of balsamics as the spice of cocktails. Everyday staple recipes can be switched up with the addition of a different vinegar. One base recipe can give you an unlimited number of options once you start to experiment with different balsamics. Have fun combining flavors and you'll never have the same thing twice. Just like adding a new spice to a favorite dish, adding a dash of balsamic to a drink reinvents old standby favorites, making them fresh again.

Use the following table as a guide to combining spirits and balsamics. Play with it and have fun experimenting with different combinations—the possibilities are endless.

Bourbon	Apricot, Plum, Cinnamon Pear, Mango, any fruity dark balsamic
Gin	Black Cherry, Grapefruit, Plum, Oregano, Sicilian Lemon
Rum	Apricot, Coconut, Mango, Peach, Pineapple, any fruity white balsamic
Tequila	Cranberry Pear, Lemongrass Mint, Coconut
Vodka	Pineapple, Cranberry Pear, Lemongrass Mint, Peach, any white balsamic

PERFECT PAIRINGS

Finding the right oil and vinegar combination can be overwhelming with so much selection in front of you. Everyone has different favorites and tastes, so creating the best combination is often dependent on what you want to pair with the oil and vinegar.

There are a few tricks that make flavors combine well. Mixing something acidic and something sweet (**Blood Orange** and **Honey Ginger** or **Lime** and **Coconut**, for example) with something herbaceous and something fruity is a bit more adventurous—and delicious! (For example, **Strawberry** and **Basil**, or **Herbes de Provence** and **Apple**, are great combinations).

Another trick is recognizing when foods go well together. I love lemon cheesecake with raspberry sauce, and knowing that these are tasty together, I experimented with raspberry balsamic and the lemon olive oil. And it was delicious!

The list below shows some of my favorite infused olive oil and vinegar combinations. They're perfect for salads, bread dipping, roasting vegetables, and meats.

OLIVE OIL + BALSAMIC VINEGAR

Any **extra virgin** olive oil + Traditional

Lime + Mango

Basil + Grapefruit

Basil + Peach

Basil + Strawberry

Basil + Wild Blueberry

Basil + Fig

Blood Orange + Chocolate

Blood Orange + Cinnamon Pear

Blood Orange + Cranberry Pear

Blood Orange + Espresso

Blood Orange + Rosé

Blood Orange + Plum

Blood Orange + Vanilla

Chipotle + Chocolate

Chipotle + Espresso

Chipotle + Mango

Lemon + Coconut

Lemon + Honey Ginger

Lemon + Peach

Lemon + Pomegranate

Lemon + Raspberry

Lemon + Maple

Lemon + Black Cherry

Garlic + Oregano

Garlic + Sicilian Lemon

Garlic + Neapolitan Herb

Harissa + Apricot

Harissa + Mango

Rosemary + Grapefruit

Rosemary + Sicilian Lemon

Lime + Blackberry Ginger

Lime + Plum

Lime + Coconut

Lime + Honey Ginger

Lime + Peach

Lime + Pineapple

Lime + Strawberry

Herbes de Provence + Sicilian Lemon

Herbes de Provence + Apple

Wild Dill + Pomegranate

Wild Dill + Sicilian Lemon

Tuscan Herb + Oregano

Tuscan Herb + Sicilian Lemon

Tuscan Herb + Traditional

Wild Mushroom & Sage + Honey Ginger

RESOURCES

The following resources are a mix of research-based information and more consumer-type information communicated via competition results.

CALIFORNIA OLIVE OIL COUNCIL: COOC.COM

This is the trade association for California olive oil producers, whose mission is "the consumption of certified California extra virgin olive oil through education, outreach and communications."

EVO INTERNATIONAL OLIVE OIL CONTEST: EVO-IOOC.COM

Every year the EVO puts out a buyer's guide for the highest-quality olive oils available throughout the world. This annual publication is a great resource for finding quality olive oil.

EXTRA VIRGIN OLIVE OIL WORLD RANKING: EVOOWORLDRANKING.ORG

This is an annual world ranking list of olive oils, producers, countries, and competitions, created with the intention of promoting awarded olive oils worldwide.

EXTRA VIRGIN ALLIANCE: EXTRAVIRGINALLIANCE.ORG

This is a trade organization that represents quality olive oil producers around the globe and recognizes the value of consumer confidence in olive oil.

INTERNATIONAL OLIVE COUNCIL: INTERNATIONALOLIVEOIL.ORG

The division of the UN that sets the standards for olive oil globally.

NEW YORK INTERNATIONAL OLIVE OIL COMPETITION: NYOLIVEOIL.COM

This competition takes place every May, with 1,000 samples generally being submitted for judging.

TRUTH IN OLIVE OIL: TRUTHINOLIVEOIL.COM

This very useful website is run by Tom Mueller, a freelance writer who has done an amazing amount of research into the world of olive oil. Not only does he provide lots of very helpful information, he also recommends lots of good places to source olive oil and lists many great websites to check out. He is the author of *Extra Virginity: The Sublime and Scandalous World of Olive Oil*.

UC DAVIS OLIVE CENTER: OLIVECENTER.UCDAVIS.EDU

This is the preeminent research center for olives in the USA. Housed at the University of California, Davis, it is an excellent source of information.

METRIC CONVERSIONS CHART

VOLUME		VOLUME		VOLUME	
⅛ tsp	0.5 mL	¾ cup	185 mL	7 cups	1.75 L
¼ tsp	1 mL	1 cup	250 mL	8 cups	2 L
½ tsp	2.5 mL	1¼ cups	310 mL	12 cups	3 L
¾ tsp	4 mL	1½ cups	375 mL	¼ fl oz	7.5 mL
1 tsp	5 mL	1¾ cups	435 mL	½ fl oz	15 mL
1½ tsp	7.5 mL	2 cups/1 pint	500 mL	¾ fl oz	22 mL
2 tsp	10 mL	2¼ cups	560 mL	1 fl oz	30 mL
1 Tbsp	15 mL	2½ cups	625 mL	1½ fl oz	45 mL
4 tsp	20 mL	3 cups	750 mL	2 fl oz	60 mL
2 Tbsp	30 mL	3½ cups	875 mL	3 fl oz	90 mL
3 Tbsp	45 mL	4 cups/1 quart	1 L	4 fl oz	125 mL
¼ cup/4 Tbsp	60 mL	4½ cups	1.125 L	5 fl oz	160 mL
5 Tbsp	75 mL	5 cups	1.25 L	6 fl oz	185 mL
⅓ cup	80 mL	5½ cups	1.375 L	8 fl oz	250 mL
½ cup	125 mL	6 cups	1.5 L	24 fl oz	750 mL
⅔ cup	160 mL	6½ cups	1.625 L		

WEIGHT		LENGTH		OVEN TEMPERATURE	
1 oz	30 g	⅛ inch	3 mm	40°F	5°C
2 oz	60 g	¼ inch	6 mm	120°F	49°C
3 oz	90 g	⅜ inch	9 mm	125°F	51°C
¼ lb / 4 oz	125 g	½ inch	1.25 cm	130°F	54°C
5 oz	150 g	¾ inch	2 cm	135°F	57°C
6 oz	175 g	1 inch	2.5 cm	140°F	60°C
½ lb / 8 oz	250 g	1 ½ inches	4 cm	145°F	63°C
9 oz	270 g	2 inches	5 cm	150°F	66°C
10 oz	300 g	3 inches	8 cm	155°F	68°C
¾ lb / 12 oz	375 g	4 inches	10 cm	160°F	71°C
14 oz	400 g	4 ½ inches	11 cm	165°F	74°C
1 lb	500 g	5 inches	12 cm	170°F	77°C
1 ½ lb	750 g	6 inches	15 cm	180°F	82°C
2 lb	1 kg	7 inches	18 cm	200°F	95°C
2 ½ lb	1.25 kg	8 inches	20 cm	225°F	107°C
3 lb	1.5 kg	8 ½ inches	22 cm	250°F	120°C
4 lb	1.8 kg	9 inches	23 cm	275°F	140°C
5 lb	2.3 kg	10 inches	25 cm	300°F	150°C
5 ½ lb	2.5 kg	11 inches	28 cm	325°F	160°C
6 lb	2.7 kg	12 inches	30 cm	350°F	180°C
				375°F	190°C
		CAN SIZES		400°F	200°C
		4 oz	114 mL	425°F	220°C
		14 oz	398 mL	450°F	230°C
		19 oz	540 mL	475°F	240°C
		28 oz	796 mL	500°F	260°C

ACKNOWLEDGMENTS

To all of the people who've helped me fall in love with food! My extreme food nerd-ism was born out of a love for delicious food and for the people it brings together. Thank you to my mom, who let me play with turkey gizzards and go on sweet potato gnocchi adventures. Thank you to Aunt Graziella for inspiring a love of olive oil in me. I still cannot believe I am teaching others how to play with all these amazing ingredients as a job. I am tremendously blessed!

Husband: Well, you're still here! Who knew that round two would be a reality when we dove into this project all those years ago. It feels like a lifetime and yesterday all at the same time. Your endless support and consistent encouragement means the world and I'm not sure how I would do it without you. From being the best dishwasher, grocery store and errand runner, to counting every brick that goes in the barbecue for me, and keeping Cedrik our pug away from the food on set within nose-sniffing reach, everything you do makes a huge difference and I so appreciate you. I love your un-boring life and love sharing this adventure with you. Thank you!

Photographer: Danielle, you are brilliant. Could we ever have guessed that we'd end up doing round two of this book, never mind the series and abundance of other projects? The first book was the beginning of a wonderful story, partnership, and friendship I will treasure always. This revised edition—every fresh, new, and incredibly beautiful page of it—is the continuation of that story, how we've grown, changed, and become even closer. Here's to the crazy shooting days, extra last minute images, unexpected cover shoots, late nights cleaning the kitchen, to James serenading us with his guitar. Thank you for opening up your home to me. Life with you is the best adventure. Thank you for pushing me and encouraging me; you make me a better person.

Publisher: Taryn! What a year! Or years! You are still the epitome of "beast-mode." From assembling the most badass team of creatives to smuggling treats across the border in order to share our love of olive oil, your passion and commitment inspire me! Your pomegranate ham-powered publishing team is incredible, and I can't thank them enough for working tirelessly to bring this book to life. You are a rock! Here's to many more delicious projects together.

INDEX

For more information, contact TouchWood Editions at www.touchwoodeditions.com.

LIBRARY AND ARCHIVES CANADA CATALOGUING IN PUBLICATION

Title: The olive oil & vinegar lover's cookbook / Emily Lycopolus ;
photography by D.L. Acken
Other titles: Olive oil and vinegar lover's cookbook
Names: Lycopolus, Emily, author.
Description: Revised & updated. | Includes index.
Identifiers: Canadiana (print) 20190081015 | Canadiana (ebook) 20190081023 |
ISBN 9781771513029 (hardcover) | ISBN 9781771513036 (PDF)
Subjects: LCSH: Cooking (Olive oil) | LCSH: Cooking (Vinegar) | LCSH: Olive oil. |
LCSH: Vinegar. | LCGFT: Cookbooks.
Classification: LCC TX819.O42 L93 2019 | DDC 641.6/463—dc23

Photography by DL Acken
Editing by Lesley Cameron
Cover design by Tree Abraham
Interior design by Tree Abraham and Colin Parks

The publisher gratefully acknowledges the financial support of the Government of Canada through the Canada
Book Fund (CBF) and the Province of British Columbia through the Book Publishing Tax Credit.

TouchWood Editions acknowledges that the land on which we live and work is within the
traditional territories of the Lkwungen (Esquimalt and Songhees), Malahat, Pacheedaht,
Scia'new, T'Sou-ke and W̲SÁNEC´ (Pauquachin, Tsartlip, Tsawout, Tseycum) peoples.

The information in this book is true and complete to the best of the author's knowledge. All
recommendations are made without guarantee on the part of the author or TouchWood Editions. The
author and publisher disclaim any liability in connection with the use of this information.

This book was produced using FSC®-certified, acid-free papers, processed chlorine free, and printed with soya-based inks.

PRINTED IN CHINA